THE FINANCIAL SERVICES ENVIRONMENT

3RD EDITION

David Brighouse
and
Janet Hontoir

Financial World Publishing
IFS House
4–9 Burgate Lane
Canterbury
Kent
CT1 2XJ
United Kingdom

T   01227 818687
F   01227 479641
E   editorial@ifslearning.com
W   www.ifslearning.com

Financial World Publications are published by The Chartered Institute of Bankers, a non-profit making registered educational charity.

The Chartered Institute of Bankers believes that the sources of information upon which the book is based are reliable and has made every effort to ensure the complete accuracy of the text. However, neither CIB, the author nor any contributor can accept any legal responsibility whatsoever for consequences that may arise from errors or omissions or any opinion or advice given.

Typeset by John Smith

Printed by IBT Global, London

© Chartered Institute of Bankers 2002

ISBN 0-85297-668-2

FINANCIAL
WORLD
Publishing
THE CHARTERED INSTITUTE OF BANKERS

CONTENTS

Contents

1

THE MONETARY SYSTEM

1.1 The Functions of Money

This book is designed to give a broad understanding of the financial services industry in the UK. The basic raw material of this industry is money, so it is essential to begin by defining what money is and what it is used for.

The existence of money is taken for granted in all advanced societies today – so much so that most people are unaware of the enormous contribution that the concept of money has made to the development of our present way of life.

The limitations of barter and the need for money

In the earliest civilizations, communities were self-sufficient and people laboured to provide goods and services for their own consumption only. This was eventually replaced by an exchange system, which allowed people to specialize to a certain extent. In such an economy, but before the concept of money was developed, transactions were carried out by **bartering**. Someone might offer one chicken in exchange for three bundles of wood; another person, having manufactured metal knives, might barter each knife for a specified number of loaves of bread or a supply of apples.

For such a system to work, there has to be a **coincidence of wants** (ie the person with chickens must need wood and the one with wood must wish to eat or keep chickens). In practice this rarely occurs except in the simplest of societies, and it is necessary to establish more complex transactions. Equally, many products being bartered are **indivisible**, eg if the chicken-owner wanted only one bundle of wood, he could not split his chicken into three parts. Again, there had to be **exchange rates** between every possible pair of products and, as the number of goods and services began to increase, this became very complex.

In a modern society, people still produce goods or provide services which they could in theory trade with others for the things they need. However, the complexity of life and the sheer size of some transactions make it impossible for people today to match what they have to offer against what others can supply to them. We need a third commodity which people will accept in exchange for any product, ie a common denominator against which the value of all products can be measured. This is money.

The functions of money

Money was invented by people to perform certain functions and so it can be defined in terms of these. The four traditional functions of money are:

(i)   a medium of exchange

(ii)   a store of value

(iii) a standard for deferred payments

(iv)   a unit of account

These are described below.

(i) A medium of exchange

This means that people will take and give money in **exchange** for goods and services because it is generally acceptable. We are all willing to give up goods and services in exchange for money because we know that other people will accept it from us in turn. Having a medium of exchange allows people to specialize in particular jobs, receive money in return and exchange it for a wide range of goods and services produced by other specialists; this leads to better services and more efficient production. Individuals do not have to buy and sell at the same time and in the same amounts.

In order to fulfil its function as a medium of exchange, money must have certain properties. It must be:

- **generally acceptable** to all parties in all transactions. This gives it exchange value, although it does not itself have to have any intrinsic value. For example, a £10 note will buy what society considers to be £10 worth of goods or services, even though the paper and other materials from which the note are made have very little value in themselves. The general acceptability of money depends on people's **confidence** in it. As we shall see below, money in a modern society comprises notes and coins and bank deposits. Notes and coins are generally acceptable because they are legal tender, ie they have backing from the government and the central bank. The deposits of commercial banks are generally acceptable because people have confidence in the banking system; it is thus vital for a modern financial system to be regulated in such a way that this confidence is preserved.

- **divisible** into small units, to enable transactions of all sizes to be carried out. With inflation over the years, smaller units of currency disappear as they become worthless, eg there is no half-penny coin in the UK. Bank deposits are given and received by means of cheques and credit transfers, which can be written for any amount.

- easily **recognizable** so that people accept it immediately. Legal tender notes and coins are familiar to everyone and their design must contain anti-forgery devices. The major banks and buildings societies are well-known institutions and people accept their deposits.

- **durable** so that it will not deteriorate over time. Coins have a very long life but notes are less durable and have to be withdrawn and replaced when they are worn out. Bank deposits do not exist in physical form but the banks must be recognized as being going concerns.

- **portable**, meaning that people can carry money around with them easily. Notes and coins are reasonably portable for small transactions but inconvenient for large ones; the latter are generally paid for via eminently portable cheque-books and credit cards and an increasing number of payments is made by direct bank transfers.

- **sufficient** but not too much in quantity. If there is not enough money in circulation, people cannot make all the transactions they want to. If there is too much of it, its value falls and we have inflation with its inherent problems (see later section).

Legal tender

Notes and coin are legal tender (with certain limits on the amounts offered in the case of some coins). Legal tender is a legally defined means of payment which cannot be refused by a creditor in satisfaction of a debt, ie if a purchaser wishes to pay a seller in notes or coin, the seller cannot refuse and insist on some other method of payment. However, in practice most people are willing to accept payment by a means which is not legal tender, eg by cheque, standing order or credit card, because they are confident that these instruments will deliver value.

(ii) A unit of account

This means that we can use money to **measure** and compare values and this function of money follows on from its use as a medium of exchange. If goods are exchanged for money, it follows that all goods will be priced in terms of money, which, therefore, automatically becomes a basis of reference for the relative values of other items. There is no need to have individual exchange rates between chickens and bundles of wood, bundles of wood and knives, knives and loaves of bread, or indeed loaves of bread and the provision of financial services. All the people who use the same currency speak the same 'money language' and know the real meaning of a money value by comparing it with another. Difficulties arise when, in the course of foreign trade, we have to convert one currency into another and it is the elimination of these difficulties which is one of the main arguments in favour of the UK's entry into the euro. (See Chapter 5).

(iii) A store of value

This means that we can **save** money because it enables us to separate transactions in time. Money received as payment for work done or for goods sold does not have to be spent right away but can be stored up in the knowledge that it can be exchanged for goods and services later when required, ie the use of money enables saving to be carried out. In order to fulfil this function, money must retain its exchange value or purchasing power; inflation has the effect of eroding the real value of money (see below).

(iv) A standard for deferred payment

This means that we can use money to borrow from each other because it allows us to exchange goods in one time period and to pay in a later one. This function enables people to grant loans, give credit and enter into contracts for future payment. If commodities were lent without money, each repayment would require a further coincidence of wants, and it is unlikely that the lender would require monthly quantities of a particular commodity in repayment.

These last two functions of money are two sides of the same coin. Saving is done by those whose income is greater than their expenditure and borrowing by those whose expenditure exceeds their income. For one group of people to be able to borrow, another must be willing to save. The existence of money thus makes it possible for saving to be channelled into investment, which is the basis of economic growth. It is only when a society is able to give up some current consumption in favour of investment that it gives itself the chance to produce more in total and to raise general living standards.

Money value and real value

Money represents real goods and services. These days it consists of notes and coins and bank deposits; these are assets that have no intrinsic value, ie they are not valuable of themselves and are seen to have value because people know that others will accept them in exchange for goods and services. We must distinguish between **money value** and **real value**. The money value of a product is simply the value expressed in terms of the money unit used by the society, eg we can say that a new computer system is worth £1,000 because this is the money price the system costs to buy. But the real value of a product to someone is its value in terms of other products, eg the number of weekly food bills which make up the price of the computer or the amount of time someone has to work in order to earn the £1,000 to buy it. Real value makes us compare the values of various products with each other and it recognizes that money value is simply a way of putting all values into the same money 'language'. We shall see later that money values change when inflation happens but real values do not necessarily change.

Money is the raw material of financial institutions, and the services provided by banks and other financial institutions are based on the above four functions of money.

● They create the majority of the money supply (see later section).

● They provide payments mechanisms, eg the cheque clearing system or the computerized BACS system.

- They offer a wide range of current and savings accounts where people can store their money until they want to spend it.

- They offer a wide range of credit facilities, including credit cards, overdrafts and loans.

What constitutes money?

In other words, what do we actually use as money? In theory money can be anything which people are generally willing to accept and in the past it has taken the form of seashells, gold and even cigarettes. Nowadays it consists of a limited range of items, which are seen as assets by those who hold them and as liabilities by those who issue them. In order to be able to perform all the functions of money, these assets must be liquid.

Liquidity

Liquidity is the ease and speed with which an asset can be converted into cash, and thus into real goods and services, without significant loss of capital value or of interest. We can represent assets along a liquidity spectrum (see diagram below), which goes from notes and coins at one end (totally liquid) to immovable property (land and buildings) at the other (almost totally illiquid). Notes and coins are legal tender and must therefore be accepted by one party from another in exchange for a product or in settlement of a debt (there are some limits on the number of coins someone is legally bound to accept). So if a person pays for something by cash, he or she can take possession of the goods immediately and does not lose any value since cash in hand earns no interest and there is no penalty in converting it into another asset. At the other end of the spectrum, land cannot be quickly turned into cash and thus into other assets. There is a lengthy legal procedure associated with property transactions and a purchaser often has to spend time arranging a loan to finance the deal; a landowner might be able to find someone to bring him a suitcase full of cash one hour after putting his or her land on the market, but he would have to reduce his or her price so much for this to happen that the loss of capital value suffered would prevent the asset from being classed as liquid.

Between the two extreme ends of our liquidity spectrum, there is a wide range of assets of varying amounts of liquidity. A few are included in our diagram for the purposes of illustration but there are many other types of assets which could be included at different stages along the line.

Figure 1.1
Liquidity Spectrum

Liquid					Illiquid
Cash	Current account	Deposit account	Treasury bills	Shares	Land

At what point on the liquidity spectrum can an asset be liquid enough to be classed as money? Cash is wholly liquid and is obviously money; whereas land, even though it may be a good store of value, is patently not immediately convertible into other assets and cannot be used as a medium of exchange, neither can it be the standard by which the values of all other goods and services are measured. But what about the assets in between?

The answer depends on the purpose for which the definition of money is to be used. In the UK and in other countries, there are several different definitions of money, each of which includes different groups of these assets and which relates to a different purpose.

1.2 Measures and Components of the Money Supply

The money supply is a fundamental economic identity which is closely linked to other variables like inflation and interest rates. The government needs to have a definition of what constitutes money so that it can determine and control the money supply and the rate at which it is increasing.

Money can be seen as an economic commodity with a demand, a supply and a price. We shall begin by looking at its supply and then we shall briefly consider the demand for it. Finally we shall look in some detail at its price – interest rates.

In the UK, and in many other countries, a distinction is made between broad and narrow definitions of money.

- **Narrow definition of money**: This is money that is held as a medium of exchange and it includes only the most liquid asset in the spectrum, ie cash. This represents immediate purchasing power.

- **Broad definition of money**: This represents both immediate and potential purchasing power and includes not only the narrow money we described above but also money held as a store of value. We include in this definition assets like bank accounts and certificates of deposit (see Chapter 2) which can be turned into cash reasonably quickly without losing too much value.

Some assets seem to be money but do not really fulfil the functions of money directly. For example, a cheque is not usually held on to as a store of value; nor is it necessarily always acceptable, particularly without a cheque card. Cheques are accepted only because they can be paid into an account to result in an increased balance. They are, therefore, not money but a means of transferring money, because they represent a claim to money that is held in the form of a bank account. It is the balance in the account itself that is money.

Other assets fulfil certain of the functions of money but only to a limited extent. For example a deposit account, while fulfilling most of the functions, may be subject to a period of notice for withdrawal, so it may not quickly be exchanged for goods, except with a loss of interest. The longer the period of notice and the more interest lost, the more illiquid the asset. However, bank deposit accounts are regarded as being liquid enough to be included in broad definitions of money since most can be turned into cash fairly quickly.

The UK monetary aggregates

The Bank of England, which is the central bank of the UK and which we shall discuss in more detail in Chapter 3, publishes two main measures of the total UK money supply – M0 and M4, which are known as the monetary aggregates.

M0

M0 consists of:

(i)   notes and coin in circulation outside the Bank of England (ie notes and coin held by the general public plus banks' till money)

(ii) bankers' non-statutory operational deposits at the Bank of England (operational deposits are described in Chapter 2).

M0 is the narrower aggregate and contains no interest-bearing elements. In November 2001, it stood at just under £35 billion and represented less than 4% of the total money supply (see M4 below).

M0 consists of legal tender currency only (see below) and is a liability of the Bank of England; all legal tender banknotes are issued by the Bank and are backed up by government securities. M0 includes money which is used for medium of exchange purposes as people hold notes and coin only for the purposes of spending and not of saving since it does not earn interest and is not safe to hold. Some economists argue that since it is, in theory, not affected by interest changes, it should give an accurate indication of the growth of the money supply.

M4

M4 consists of the following:

(i)   Notes and coin held by the private sector

(ii)   Private sector sterling non-interest bearing sight bank deposits, ie current accounts.

(iii) Private sector sterling interest-bearing sight and time bank deposits

(iv)   Private sector holdings of sterling certificates of deposit (see Chapter 2)

(v)   Private sector holdings of building society shares and deposits and sterling certificates of deposit

(vi)   Building society holdings of sterling bank deposits, bank certificates of deposit and notes and coin.

M4 can be analysed either:

- in terms of its **components**, ie cash and deposits (these are the assets held by those who own money)

- or in terms of its **counterparts**, ie banks' and building societies' lending to the private sector and their transactions with the public sector and with overseas residents. In other words, the money supply components are the liabilities of banks and building societies.

M4 is the broader aggregate and includes money held for savings purposes as well as money held for spending. It, therefore, fulfils the two main functions of money, ie medium of exchange and store of value. In November 2001, M4 stood at £943 billion, more than 96% of which was not legal tender currency but was represented by the liabilities of banks and building societies.

1.3 The Creation of Money

As we saw above, most of the spending money in the UK economy is held in the form of bank deposits, and cash forms only a very small part of the total. Banknotes are issued by the Bank of England according to people's demand for them and coin is produced by the Royal Mint. But the majority of the money supply consists of the liabilities of banks and building societies and so these institutions play a major part in the creation of money through a process known as **credit creation** (or **deposit expansion**). The process is best explained by means of an example. Bear in mind while reading it that we are talking about the whole banking system and not just one bank.

Credit creation

A bank has to keep a certain proportion of its funds in liquid form to meet daily requirements such as cash withdrawals. People's confidence in the banking system would be dented if they could not withdraw cash when they wanted it. However, banks find that the amount of liquid funds required in practice is quite small in relation to the total amounts deposited since deposit-account (and even current-account) customers leave some of their money at the bank in the form of short-term savings. On a daily basis banks find that only a small proportion of their total deposits is being withdrawn and so they can lend out most of it to people who want to borrow money. Banks make their profits by charging a higher interest rate to their borrowers than they pay to their depositors.

The percentage of deposited funds that a bank considers sufficient to cover customers' cash withdrawals is known as the **reserve asset ratio**. In order to show how much credit is created by a deposit at a bank, we will assume in this simplified example that banks are using a reserve asset ratio of 10%.

Now consider the following theoretical chain of events which is set in motion by Andrew depositing £10,000 in his current account at Southern Bank:

● Because the reserve asset ratio is 10%, Southern Bank lends £9,000 of Andrew's deposit to Barbara by crediting her current account with £9,000. At this point the money supply has increased by £9,000 since, although the bank has put it into Barbara's account, it has not taken the money away from Andrew.

● Barbara uses the money to buy a car from Charles and she writes out a cheque on her account for £9,000 and gives it to Charles, who deposits it in his account with Northern Bank. The money supply does not change at this point as money has simply been transferred from Barbara to Charles.

● Northern Bank now has an extra deposit of £9,000 and it can use this to make a loan as long as it complies with the reserve asset ratio of 10%. So it lends £8,100 (ie 90% of £9,000) to Diana by crediting her account with this amount. The money supply now increases by £8,100 because Diana's account has been credited with this amount without anyone's account being debited.

● Diana uses her money to book a wonderful holiday for her and her family. She gives the travel agency a cheque for £8,100 which they pay into their account at Western Bank; this bank now gains an extra deposit which it can use as the basis for a fresh loan of £7,290.

● And so on …

If the process is continued to a very large number of transactions and taken on to its logical conclusion, the total additional lending activity generated by the initial £10,000 deposit is theoretically £90,000 (try it on your calculator!).

What is happening here is that deposits allow a bank to make loans but those loans become new deposits when the money is spent and put back in a bank account. Because most individuals and all businesses have bank accounts, most money spent comes back into the banking system. The credit creation process happens across the banking system as a whole.

Limitations to credit creation

In practice there are certain limitations to a bank's ability to create money:

● Not all loan funds turn up again as deposits, and some may be retained as cash or may be transferred overseas.

● If the demand for loans is low, banks' ability to create money is reduced.

● Some money flows out of the mainstream system; the two main examples of this are money used in payment of tax, which goes to the government, and money used to pay for imports, which goes abroad. (However the government spends money and domestic firms earn money by exporting goods and services abroad, so this money does come back in again).

- Governments may impose restrictions on banks' ability to create credit. We shall consider these in a later section.

The bank multiplier concept

The process described above leads to the concept of the bank multiplier, which is a numerical factor calculated as:

Bank multiplier = 1/(Reserve asset ratio)

In the above example, the bank multiplier = 1/10% = 10. In other words, the theoretical total lending activity generated by the £10,000 deposit, including the initial deposit itself, is 10 times the initial deposit, ie £100,000.

So banks create credit because they are able to credit one customer's account without debiting anyone else's. Why does this work? Nobody else can do this seemingly magic trick so why can banks? The answer is that people have confidence in the banking system and are happy to let them do it. We all accept that our bank deposits have value because we are fully confident that we can turn them into cash whenever we want to. The fact is that the amount of bank deposits is many times the supply of cash; if everyone went to their banks at the same time to turn their current and deposit accounts into cash, all the banks would fail because they simply would not have it. But people do not behave in this way when the economy is stable and when there is general confidence both in the money supply and in the banks that create it. It is for this reason that the monetary authorities of all countries are so concerned to create and maintain this confidence and to regulate their banks so they have enough liquidity and capital (we shall study this in more depth in Chapter 3).

1.4 The Demand for Money

To know what factors affect the demand for money in the economy, we need to know why people want to hold the assets which we regard as money and not any other assets which might earn them a better return. John Maynard Keynes, who was one of Britain's most famous economists, analysed the reasons why people want to hold money. He identified three specific motives:

- **Transactions motive:** This is the requirement to have money for daily, weekly and monthly purchases and payments. The average amount held depends on the value of the transactions people want to make and on the degree of synchronization of payments and receipts. For example, people who are paid weekly will hold smaller average transaction balances than those whose income is received monthly but will make more frequent payments. People develop expenditure patterns which change only slowly. A person's transactions demand rises as his or her income rises or as prices increase.

- **Precautionary motive**: This is the need that people have to hold money balances against uncertain events. These might be impulse purchases, eg in response to a sudden bargain, or emergencies, eg if a car suddenly breaks down and has to be repaired. People on higher incomes generally hold more money for this reason than those on low incomes, since the latter do not have much left over after making their normal transactions.

Both the transactions and precautionary motives are reasons for holding narrow money, ie money balances which will act as a medium of exchange. However, these motives are less important as far as the M4 aggregate is concerned, because this includes interest-bearing time deposits and is mostly money acting as a store of value. The broader the monetary aggregate, the less significant are the transactions and precautionary motives for holding money as a medium of exchange and the more significant is money as a store of value.

- **Speculative motive**: This arises because people dislike risk. They will hold cash (or capital-secure deposits) during a period when they believe that it will hold its value better than more speculative assets such as ordinary shares. This demand is, therefore, likely to be high at times when stock markets are expected to fall, which will often occur if interest rates are low but expected to rise. There is an inverse relationship between the speculative demand for money and the rate of interest.

If we add the three motives together, we arrive at the total demand for money. This is called **liquidity preference**. We can make the following conclusions about the overall demand for money:

(i)   the demand for money rises as the rate of interest falls (this is the liquidity preference theory);

(ii)   at each rate of interest, the demand for money increases in a period of economic growth as more people find jobs and real incomes increase;

(iii)   with the rapid innovation in methods of payment, the demand for cash balances has declined in comparison with the demand for interest-bearing deposit accounts. This is because people can make their transactions using credit cards and direct debits instead of cash. This trend will probably continue and we may one day be a cashless society. Mondex is an electronic cash system which will allow holders to download cash value from their bank accounts to their cards and use these to purchase goods, either at shops or via the Internet. Eventually all sellers of all goods and services will have the technology to allow their customers to use this 'electronic purse' and physical cash may be used much less in the future.

1.5 Inflation

Since money exists in a society to represent goods and services, it follows that there should be an optimum amount of money which is just enough to enable everyone to make all the transactions they want but is not too much either. But as an economy grows, so does its money supply and if this growth gets out of hand, the economy suffers from inflation.

Inflation can be defined as a situation where the rate of growth of the money supply is higher than the rate of growth of the production of real goods and services. In other words, there is 'too much money chasing too few goods'. An economy which is suffering from inflation shows several symptoms:

- the prices of goods and services are rising

- the money incomes of people are rising

- the money supply is rising

As this process happens, the value and purchasing power of money is falling so that the amount of goods and services which can be bought with £1 is less now than it was 10 years ago.

The problems associated with inflation

Inflation affects individuals, companies and nations in various undesirable ways:

- It affects the distribution of incomes because people with strong wage-earning capability can push their earnings ahead of price rises and gain over those on relatively fixed incomes, such as pensioners and workers who do not have the negotiating power to ensure that their money wages always keep up with inflation.

- If the inflation rate in the UK is higher than inflation rates in other countries, then UK goods and services become less competitive in both the domestic and export markets. Other things being equal, exports fall, imports rise and the balance of payments is adversely affected.

- Inflation affects the way in which money performs its functions:

   (i) As a unit of account: money is used to measure value but this very value is changed by inflation. This means that it becomes a less efficient measuring rod. As money prices change, people become unsure of what exactly £1 is worth and, in a time of very rapid inflation, this uncertainty can lead people to abandon the currency altogether. But even gradual inflation causes some uncertainty because prices change over time and it creates problems for accountants when valuing assets such as stocks.

   (ii) As a store of value and as a standard of deferred payments: it is useful to look at these two functions together since they are the mirror image of each other for these purposes. Inflation affects saving and borrowing and discriminates between savers and borrowers, depending on the rate of interest. To follow this argument, you must understand the concept of the **real interest rate**. This is the nominal interest rate (ie the percentage figure quoted on a savings account or on a loan) minus the rate of inflation. In other words, the real interest rate is what is left of the nominal rate of interest when the rate of inflation has been deducted.

If nominal interest rates are higher than the rate of inflation, ie if real interest rates are positive, then savers gain because they are receiving an interest rate which more than compensates them for inflation; borrowers lose because they are paying more than the rate of inflation for their loans. However, if nominal interest rates are lower than the rate of inflation, ie if real interest rates are negative, then savers lose as the interest rate they are being paid is not enough to make up for general price rises and the purchasing power of their savings is falling; they will thus be discouraged from saving. In this situation borrowers gain as the interest they are paying does not reach the inflation rate and the real value of their outstanding loan is going down. Anyone who saves by keeping a suitcase of cash under their bed is obviously losing a lot of real value in a time of inflation because the real value of their treasure is falling and they are receiving no interest at all.

(iii) As a medium of exchange: when inflation is fairly low and under control, money continues to perform its medium of exchange function in the normal way. However, in a time of very high and persistent inflation (known as hyperinflation) when prices are rising continually and quickly, people lose confidence in the money supply and turn to real goods and services, ie they revert to barter. In such a situation, the government of the country must restore confidence in the currency, probably by scrapping the old one and issuing a new one.

● Inflation is also connected with other economic variables, notably the rate of employment and of economic growth. It is generally believed nowadays that a high inflation rate leads to economic instability and destroys the confidence of investors. It can thus be associated with high unemployment and low economic growth. It is argued that investment will take place only in an economy where individuals and companies feel secure and confident about the future and are willing to take the risk of expanding their businesses. When an economy has a stable price level, individual price signals can be read more clearly and decisions on consumption, saving, borrowing, investment and production can be taken more rationally.

Measuring inflation

As we shall see below, governments take responsibility for controlling the rate of inflation and so it necessary to have an official measure of the rate at which prices are rising. If a packet of biscuits which cost £1.00 a year ago now costs £1.05, then the annual rate of inflation for that particular product is clearly 5%. It would not be appropriate, however, to use the price of biscuits – or of any other individual item – to gauge the value of money when the economy is composed of an enormous range of goods and services.

The Retail Price Index

The most commonly-quoted measure of inflation in the UK is the **Retail Price Index** (RPI), which is calculated each month based on a 'basket' of goods and services representative of the average consumption pattern of a typical family. Items are grouped into categories, eg food, housing, clothes, motoring etc, and each item is then given a weighting according to its relative significance in people's spending. Price changes are recorded for all items and the overall result shows price trends since the previous month; an annualized rate is also published. There are three versions of the RPI:

- The **headline rate** (RPI), which includes all items of expenditure.

- The **underlying rate** (RPIX), which excludes mortgage interest payments and which is the rate targeted by the government. Since interest rates are not only an item of expenditure but also the tool by which inflation is controlled, it is more logical to exclude interest from the measurement of the inflation rate. If inflation is too high, interest rates are increased to dampen down spending but the first effect is to increase the cost of living as existing borrowers face higher mortgage payments. To eliminate this effect, mortgage payments are therefore taken out of the RPI.

- The **core rate** (RPIY) which excludes both mortgage interest payments, indirect taxes and the council tax. The effect of an increase in VAT, for example, is to increase the cost of some of the items included in the RPI and so this effect is also taken out.

There are several other measures of inflation:

- The **Producer Price Index (PPI)** measures change in the prices of finished goods when they leave the factory, and this is a good indicator of the RPI.

- The **Wholesale Price Index** is based both on the prices of raw materials that form the input for products and on the wholesale prices charged by manufacturers.

- The **national average earnings index** reflects the changes in the level of earned income in the UK and generally increases more quickly than the RPI.

- **Unit Labour Costs** show the labour cost per unit of output of goods and services.

- The **Harmonized Index of Consumer Prices (HICP)** is a standardized way of comparing changes in the costs of living between member states of the European Union and it is this measure of inflation which is the target of the European Central Bank.

Recent inflation experience in the UK

We have already seen why inflation is a problem and over the last few decades it has been a major priority of British (and other) governments to minimize the rate of inflation in the economy. In 1990-91, the RPIX in the UK stood at 8.1% but has fallen steadily since then to its present annualized rate of 1.8% (November 2001). At this date, the RPI (including mortgage interest payments) stood at 0.9% – lower than the RPIX as mortgage payments had fallen and yet were not reflected in the RPIX. Measured using the HICP, UK inflation was 0.8% whereas the same index showed 1.8% for the 15 countries of the European Union. (See Chapter 5 for a discussion of the consequences of a low inflation rate.)

The causes of inflation

There are various theories of why inflation happens:

● The **demand-pull** school believes that inflation is caused by excess demand in the economy, normally as a result of the amount of money available in the economy exceeding the supply of goods or of government expenditure exceeding taxation. When people have a lot of money to spend, they force up the prices of goods and services.

● The **cost-push** school attributes inflation to an increase in the costs incurred by businesses. This may result from increases in the cost of raw materials or equipment (for example the huge increase in the price of oil in the early 1970s), from wage rises in excess of productivity, or from a fall in the value of the local currency leading to higher raw material costs if supplied from abroad.

● The **monetarist** school blames inflation on an increase in the money supply not backed up by an increase in the production of real goods and services. They blame the monetary authorities for allowing banks to create too much credit.

Whatever the cause of inflation, it results in a wage-price spiral. An increase in prices causes workers to seek increases in their wages to ensure that they do not suffer a fall in their real incomes; and an increase in wages puts up firms' costs and forces them to increase their prices. At the same time, the money supply is increasing. So all three theories contribute valuable insights as to what starts the inflationary process off and what causes it to continue. These insights give clues as to how governments can design policies to bring down inflation.

1.6 Interest Rates

Interest is the **price of money**, ie it is the cost of borrowing money and the reward for lending it. Financial institutions pay interest to their savers and charge it to their borrowers, making a profit on the difference between these rates. Interest is intended to compensate a lender for:

- the loss of liquidity suffered by the lender

- the risk that the borrower will not repay the loan

- the rate of inflation which eats up the value of the loan

Notice that part of the interest rate charge by a lender is to compensate for inflation; the other elements of interest make up the **real interest rate**, ie the price paid for the service received.

Interest is both an income and an expense to both individuals and firms.

Individuals

- Many households borrow money for different reasons and over different periods. For example they might have taken out a mortgage loan to finance the purchase of their house and a personal loan with which to buy their car and they may use a credit card when they go shopping. They pay interest on the amount borrowed.

- Many private individuals have surplus income over and above their expenditure or they make themselves save for a 'rainy day' or for their retirement. They therefore choose a suitable savings scheme and the interest earned becomes part of their income.

Firms

- Most businesses need to borrow money from time to time, for instance to purchase new machinery which will contribute to future profits or to finance a cash shortage. The interest rate paid on this borrowing becomes an expense for the business which reduces its profits and which means that the business must have enough liquid funds to keep up the servicing of its debt. When assessing whether to borrow to finance expansion, a firm must compare the expected interest rate over the life of the debt with the expected return from the life of the investment.

- Companies which have surplus liquid funds (cash-rich firms) can save these by lending them out to others who wish to borrow and can earn an income by so doing.

Financial institutions offer many different products to satisfy the saving and borrowing demand of both firms and households. Each of these products carries a different interest rate and the reasons why some interest rates are higher than others at the same time are given below.

The interest-rate structure

When we talk about the 'rate of interest' in force at any particular time, we are actually referring to a bundle of rates which apply to the many different financial products available. When the general interest rate level changes as a result of government policy, all these individual rates move up or down together in the same direction. Within the general level, therefore, we need to find out what factors determine the interest rate on any particular financial product. We shall study each factor in isolation but remember that in each case we have to make the assumption that 'other things are equal'. Individual rates are affected by all of these factors to a greater or a lesser degree.

- **Risk**: Other things being equal, the greater the risk the higher the interest rate. As far as savings are concerned, higher-risk investment products offer a potentially higher rate of return; simple deposit accounts offer the lowest rates of interest because there is a negligible risk of losing the capital invested. On the borrowing side, higher risk loans cost more, eg a bank charges more for loans for speculative business ventures than it does on a secured mortgage loan for private house purchase. Credit card interest rates are notoriously high but are justified by the high risks faced by the lender, eg the risk of default, of fraudulent use and of being jointly liable for having to pay out if a supplier defaults.

- **Term** (ie length of time the money is borrowed or lent for): the normal rule is that, other things being equal, the longer the term, the higher the rate of interest. A saver tying up his money for five years requires a higher rate than if the investment were for only one year. This is because liquidity is lost for longer and because uncertainty increases with time, ie there is a higher risk of default in the long-term and future inflation rates are also unknown.

  There can be an exception to this general rule when interest rates are expected to fall in the near future. Banks 'buy in' funds at a fixed rate for onward lending to customers and obviously want to purchase these funds at the lowest possible rate. If they think that interest rates are about to fall, they do not want to lock themselves into a long-term agreement now at a higher rate but will choose instead to purchase their funds on a short-term basis. They can then repay this borrowing and make longer-term contracts after the interest rate has fallen. This means that their demand for short-term funds is high. The behaviour of the lending institutions is the exact opposite and the supply of short-term funds is low. The interest rate on short-term lending is thus temporarily higher than on long-term lending. The analysis of the term structure of interest rates is known as yield curve analysis and is beyond the scope of this book.

- **Amount**: Other things being equal, the larger the sum borrowed by a customer or lent by a bank, the lower the interest rate. This is because of the economy of scale involved, ie it is administratively cheaper for a bank to handle several large loans than many small ones. Conversely, we can see that some banks and buildings societies offer slightly higher interest rates on accounts with larger balances to encourage people to save more.

- **Profit margin**: Whatever the risk, term or amount associated with a loan, financial intermediaries charge a higher interest rate to their borrowers than they pay to their lenders. The difference is their profit margin.

The general level of interest rates

As we have seen, there are many individual interest rates, some higher and others lower depending on the type of borrowing or lending. But over time the whole of the rate structure can rise or fall so that all interest rates become higher or lower, even though each still retains its place in the structure as a whole. What determines whether the general level of interest rates is low or high? Why might it rise or fall? A purely economic approach would connect the supply of loanable funds with the demand for them and arrive at a price, which is the interest rate. As we have already seen, the money supply is created by banks in response to people's demand for borrowing and this can be affected by government policy regarding credit creation. The demand for money is subdivided into three motives and a change in any of these will affect this demand. In recent times, for instance, transaction demand has been affected by the wider acceptability of credit and debit cards, which reduce the need to hold cash balances. Similarly, precautionary demand can be affected by people's expectations about their future incomes. During the early 1990s the savings ratio increased as people put money aside to repay accumulated debts; they also saw that the real value of the state pension was falling and felt it necessary to save for their retirement. However, the savings ratio has fallen significantly since 1995 with a consumer boom which has meant that people are willing to borrow to purchase goods and services which improve their quality of life in the present.

Although the conditions of demand and supply in the market for loanable funds tell us a lot about the underlying state of the market and of the economy as a whole, changes in the general level of interest rates is determined by the policies of the monetary authorities, ie the government and the central bank. These policies are designed to achieve certain economic objectives.

1.7 Government Macroeconomic Objectives

At this point it is useful to consider the long-term objectives which the economic policies of most governments try to achieve. (These are known as 'macroeconomic' objectives because they concern economic aggregates, ie totals which give us a picture of the economy as a whole, as opposed to 'microeconomic' objectives which concern individual firms or consumers.)

- **Price stability**, ie a low and controlled rate of inflation. However, this does not mean that zero inflation is desirable and there is a body of economic opinion which believes that moderate inflation can stimulate investment, which is good for the economy. The current official target for inflation in the UK is an RPIX of 2.5%; the Governor of the Bank of England is obliged to write an open letter to the Chancellor of the Exchequer if inflation deviates more than 1% on either side of the 2.5% target. The underlying rate at the time of writing is 1.8%, with the headline rate at 0.8%, so the government is currently achieving its target.

- **Low unemployment**, ie to expand the economy so there is more demand for labour, land and capital. Although full employment is virtually impossible to achieve, unemployment has fallen from more than 3 million in the 1980s to just over 1.5 million people in September 2001, around 5% of the workforce.

- **Balance of payments equilibrium**, ie more or less the same amount of foreign currencies earned and spent by the economy should be neither a deficit nor a surplus over the medium term. In other words, there should be a balance between the country's imports and exports and between its purchase and sale of foreign currencies. The UK has for some years been experiencing a deficit on its balance of payments current account, with a deficit on manufacturing and on money transfers partly compensated for by a surplus on services and on income on investments. The capital account shows a small surplus.

  The exchange rate of the country's currency is linked to the balance of payments and most governments aim to keep the price of its currency stable at a level that is not so high that exports will be discouraged but not too low so as to increase inflation. The exchange rate of sterling against the US dollar fell after being high for the second half of the 1990s up to 2000. It is also high against the euro.

- **Satisfactory economic growth,** meaning that the output of the economy is growing in real terms over time and that standards of living are getting higher. The UK economy, like that of other industrialized countries, grew quite fast in the years up to 2000, but this has fallen off with the onset of recession which has affected the US and the European economies. GDP growth in the UK was 2.1% in the 3rd quarter of 2001; GDP stands for gross domestic product, which is a measure of the value of the goods and services produced within the country within a specified period of time.

In practice it has proved impossible to achieve all these objectives simultaneously, as the history of the British economy shows. If a government tries to reduce the rate of unemployment by means of expansionary measures such as lower interest rates and lower taxation, demand is boosted and inflation begins to rise. At the same time people buy more imports and the balance of payments suffers, although the economy will probably grow.

The four objectives given above tend to fall into two pairs: policies to reduce unemployment will also boost growth and measures to reduce inflation will also help to improve the balance of payments. Governments generally have to 'trade off' objectives against each other, eg they want price stability but they know that the price of getting rid of inflation altogether would be very high unemployment, so they accept a low inflation rate so as not to push the economy into recession.

Economic policy in the UK from the beginning of the 1960s until fairly recently was of the 'stop-go' variety, whereby governments accelerated and decelerated the economy in turn, leading to a situation where periods of fast growth, high employment and high inflation were followed by a slowing-down into high unemployment and lower inflation.

The current approach in both the UK and Europe is of a growth via price stability.

We should note that the economic problems facing an individual nation like the UK are the product not only of the circumstances prevailing within that country and of the policies followed by its government but also of global economic trends and of the policies followed by the governments of other countries, particularly of the rich developed nations. A recession in the USA, for example, will spread to the rest of the world.

Objectives, targets and instruments

The overall long-term **objective** aimed at by the Labour government in the UK at the beginning of the 21st century is to keep inflation steady at a low rate in the hope that price stability will lead to a long period of sustained economic growth. It aims to keep aggregate demand in line with the productive capacity of the economy.

In order to achieve this objective, the government has set an official **direct target**, which is to keep inflation (as measured by the RPIX) at an average annual rate of 2.5% with a maximum divergence either side of 1%, ie inflation should always be at an annual rate of between 1.5% and 3.5%. It believes that, if this target can be achieved, inflation will be low and fairly constant and price stability will have been achieved. People's economic decisions will be taken in the expectation that prices will not change much in the future.

The government may set itself **intermediate targets** the achievement of which will help to attain the direct target. The main intermediate target is to control the growth of the money supply because it is believed that a fast-growing money supply is one of the main factors that leads to inflation. Since money supply growth is caused by credit creation, the monetary authorities must control the amount of lending being done by banks and building societies. This is not an end in itself but a means of achieving the direct target, ie a lower inflation rate. Actually the Bank of England does not set any official intermediate target for money supply growth but it does monitor the growth rates of the two monetary aggregates – M0 and M4.

To achieve both the intermediate and direct targets, the monetary authorities have at their disposal a range of **instruments**. The main instrument of monetary policy used to keep inflation in check in the UK is the rate of interest, which is manipulated by the Bank of England according to economic circumstances.

Types of policy

There are two major types of policy used by modern governments in their attempts to achieve their long-term economic objectives:

● Monetary policy, which acts on the money supply and on interest rates

● Fiscal policy, which acts on public sector spending, revenue and borrowing or saving

Both types of policy try to influence the level of aggregate demand in the economy and therefore the level of output, unemployment and prices. Most governments use a combination of the two.

1.8 Monetary Policy

Monetary policy describes the way in which governments attempt to regulate the economy by controlling the growth of the money supply. Its overall aims are the same as those of fiscal policy but the difference lies in the means used to attain the objectives. There is also a close connection between monetary and fiscal policy.

Several decades ago, monetary policy generally took second place to fiscal policy because governments believed that fiscal policy was the best way of making large adjustments to demand, whereas monetary policy was felt to be suitable only for fine tuning.

Since 1979, however, mainly due to the monetarist policies of successive Conservative governments, monetary policy has become the most important means of controlling the economy. The present Labour government has continued to use it although it has made some changes in the targets aimed at and in the methods used.

Monetary policy is based on the ideas of the monetarist school, and particularly those of Professor Milton Friedman of Chicago University. Monetary economists believe that inflation is a monetary phenomenon and that it is caused by an independent increase in the money supply. We know that the money supply consists of notes and coin and bank deposits and that notes and coin make up only a small percentage of the total. We can conclude that most of the growth in the money supply is caused by an increase in credit creation by banks. Logically therefore, if a government wants to control the growth of the money supply, it must control the amount of credit creation carried out by banks.

Be careful not to say that governments try to 'decrease the money supply'; if the total money supply were actually to fall, this would be very serious because people would not have enough money with which to make their purchases and the economy would suffer a liquidity crisis. A government implementing monetary policy realizes that the money supply will continue to grow but it aims to decrease the rate of growth. To understand this, think of a car speeding at 70 mph. The aim is to cut speed to, say, 50 mph by decelerating but not to suddenly change into reverse gear and attempt to go backwards.

Monetary policy is a general market policy, affecting the whole economy, and cannot therefore be used to boost a certain area or region, or to attempt to redistribute wealth.

There are various instruments which the government has at its disposal when trying to slow down monetary growth. Current monetary policy is carried out by manipulating interest rates, but you should also be aware of the other instruments which have been used in the past. Let us look briefly at these first.

- **Reserve asset ratios** which would require banks to keep a certain percentage of their liabilities in the form of specified liquid assets.

- **Direct controls on bank lending** whereby banks are allowed to lend only up to a certain maximum amount.

- The Bank of England could require the banks to lodge **special deposits** with itself, of a specified percentage of the banks' liabilities. These deposits would not count towards the banks' reserves and are therefore a very effective way of taking liquidity out of the system. The Bank has made no call for special deposits since 1979. (Note that the requirement on the banks and building societies to place 0.15% of their liabilities with the Bank on a non-interest bearing basis is not a monetary measure but is intended to provide an income for the Bank).

- **Restricting consumer credit** by laying down a minimum deposit for people purchasing goods on hire purchase or by setting a maximum repayment period for consumer credit. Another method is to encourage lending for particular purposes while discouraging it for others; for example a directive might be issued to influence banks towards lending for the expansion of export business, or away from lending for property speculation.

Reserve asset ratios and special deposits attempt to limit the credit created by banks by restricting the supply of loanable funds, ie borrowers may want to take out loans but banks cannot lend to them.

Although all of these measures been used in the past, none is in force in the UK at present (2002). It is not possible to enforce them in today's deregulated and highly competitive global markets as, if one group of banks is unable to make the loans that people want, other banks can easily enter the market to fill the gap.

The only instrument of monetary policy currently in use is the manipulation of interest rates. As we shall see in more detail below, interest rates act on the demand for loanable funds; by making it more expensive for people to repay, they ensure that both individuals and firms will decide either not to borrow or at least to borrow less.

They also affect banks' willingness to lend to customers. Other things being equal, a higher interest rate means higher interest payments and marginal borrowers may be refused loans.

Monetary policy since 1997

The Monetary Policy Committee (MPC) of the Bank of England decides on the rate of interest at which the Bank of England will deal with the short-term money markets; this is known as the 'repo' rate (see below) and it is this official rate that determines all the other interest rates in the system charged to borrowers and paid to lenders. Changes in interest rates cause changes in asset prices, aggregate demand, output and employment, ie they affect the whole economy.

Factors affecting the mpc's interest rate decisions

The Monetary Policy Committee of the Bank of England was established by the Bank of England Act, 1998. It was given the operational responsibility for setting interest rates with the overall aim of achieving an inflation target (set by the government and confirmed in each Budget Statement) and thus to work towards price stability and economic growth. The current inflation target is 2.5% and the MPC must inform the government if inflation fails to meet this target by more than 1% either way.

The MPC meets every month to decide whether or not to change interest rates and, if so, in what direction and by how much. It announces its decision immediately after the meeting and publishes the minutes of the meeting two weeks later. The government (ie the Treasury) retains the right to give instructions to the Bank of England regarding its monetary policy in 'extreme economic circumstances'; otherwise the Bank acts independently of the government.

The following are the factors that the MPC takes into account when making its decision on interest rates every month.

●   If inflation is higher than its target, interest rates are raised to make borrowing more expensive and thus to control the amount of credit created by banks. This dampens down consumer demand and puts the brake on price increases. We would expect higher inflation to cause a rise in interest rates in any case because, when savers see the value of their investments being eroded by price increases, financial institutions have to pay higher rates of interest to attract new savings and to retain existing funds. When high inflation is increasing the prices of goods and services, people may decide to borrow in order to buy now before prices go up. This increases the demand for money, so the interest rate – the price of money – goes up.

●   Conversely, if inflation is very low and the government wants to expand the economy, interest rates are lowered, borrowing becomes cheaper and banks are able to lend more. Overall demand increases as people spend more (a lot of consumer spending depends on people's ability to borrow) and economic activity increases.

●   Interest rates can be changed in order to influence the exchange rate of the currency. There is a close relationship between interest rates and exchange rates. Companies and governments with surpluses place this money in interest-bearing assets which are denominated in various currencies. If the general interest rate level in the UK is higher than in other countries, sterling balances will attract higher interest rates and so these investors will move their funds from other currencies into sterling. The demand for sterling thus increases and the demand for other currencies falls, thus boosting the price of sterling. If the UK government feels that sterling is under pressure and wants to support its price so that imports can be purchased more cheaply, it can raise interest rates. Conversely, a fall in interest rates will, other things being equal, cause the value of sterling to fall and this will make UK exports more competitive in foreign markets.

- A movement in UK interest rates to influence the value of sterling might be the result of a change in the interest rates of other major trading nations, notably the USA. A rise in dollar interest rates may mean that sterling interest rates will have to rise to prevent an outflow of funds.

- If the MPC sees that inflation is on target and that the economy is growing at a satisfactory rate, it will probably make no change in the interest rate.

The process by which interest rates change

The official repo rate changes only following a decision by the MPC. But how does a change in this rate filter through to the rest of the system? The answer is via **open market operations**; the Bank of England charges this rate to the banks when they become short of funds and need to borrow. And if they do not become short of cash independently, the Bank can create a situation where they will become short. In this way, whatever rate the Bank decides to charge is enforced on the banking system as a whole. Here is the process in a little more detail.

One of the main functions of the Bank of England is to be banker to the UK banking system. Daily transactions between the commercial banks are settled through accounts held with the Bank on the understanding that each bank must hold a positive balance on that account. If, during a working day, one bank has a deficit and another has a surplus after these transactions are cleared, then the deficit bank will borrow from surplus banks via the interbank market. But sometimes the banking system as a whole finds itself short of funds; this can be due to large amounts of money flowing from the private sector to the government, as happens for example every January/February when self-employed people pay their taxes. In this case the Bank of England, through its daily operations in the money market, supplies the necessary funds at a rate which it sets. This now takes place by the banks selling gilt repos to the Bank. A repo is a sale and repurchase agreement whereby the bank sells gilts to the Bank of England on the understanding that it will repurchase these gilts at a predetermined price and date. It is a sort of cash loan with the gilts used as security. (To understand this, think of someone pawning a watch to raise money and then redeeming the watch from the pawnbroker when he has enough money.) The assets involved are gilts and sterling Treasury bills, UK government foreign-currency debt, eligible bank and local authority bills and certain sterling bonds. The repo rate is the annualized rate of interest implied by the difference between the sale and repurchase price.

A situation whereby there are large outflows from the private sector to the public sector does not happen every day but the Bank of England can create shortages for the banks via the operation of government accounts, including money market operations, ensuring that banks begin each day with a prospective shortage of funds. The Bank of England lends these funds to banks, building societies and securities dealers (known as the Bank's counterparties) who deal in the short-term money market (see Chapter 2). These are assets for the Bank of England and they mature continually; on every business day, some of these are due for repayment by the counterparties. But they do not always have the funds to repay and so they are forced to raise additional funds from the Bank in order to repay the older obligations. The Bank thus has the opportunity to lend to them at a rate of its choosing, ie the repo rate decided by the MPC.

The mechanism by which interest rate changes are transmitted to the rest of the economy

The power of the Bank of England to influence interest rates throughout the whole economy lies in the fact that there is a mechanism that transmits changes in the official repo rate to all the other interest rates in the economy. The links in the chain of causation are as follows. We shall assume that the MPC has just changed the official repo rate; as an example we have considered an increase in the rate but the argument can be turned around for a decrease.

1. This increase is immediately transmitted to **other short-term sterling wholesale money market rates**, eg repo contracts of maturities other than two weeks or interbank deposits.

2. Since the marginal cost of funds to banks is the repo rate, banks now adjust their **base rates** (their standard lending rates). This change affects the various **short-term interest rates** which banks charge their borrowers for variable-rate loans, eg overdrafts. (They may also change their rates on **standard variable-rate** mortgages, although this is not automatic and may not happen immediately.)

3. Since banks want to preserve their profit margins, they also change the rates they pay to their **depositors**. Actually banks can and do change these profit margins, depending on competitive conditions, but this is not usually a response to changes in the official interest rate.

4. The next link in the chain is **long-term interest rates** but these do not always change in the same direction as the policy change. Long-term rates are determined to a large extent by expectations regarding future short-term rates. If an increase in the official rate is accompanied by expectations in the markets that rates will rise again, then long-term rates will probably also rise; but if the markets believe that inflationary pressures are under control and expect interest rates to fall again, long-term rates may well fall.

5. **Asset prices** are also affected by interest-rate changes. The price of fixed-interest bonds is inversely related to the percentage interest rate paid on them (see Chapter 2) so a rise in interest rates causes bond prices to fall.

6. A rise in interest rates generally results in a fall in the prices of assets such as equities. The market price of a security is the sum of the expected cash flows from that security discounted to present value. Thus if interest rates rise, cash flows are being discounted by a higher percentage and so the price of the security falls (see Chapter 2) .

7. The **exchange rate** of sterling is also affected by changes in the sterling interest rate. Other things being equal, a rise in interest rates results in a rise in the price of sterling in terms of other currencies on the foreign exchange markets; this is because sterling is now relatively more attractive to international investors who move their short-term balances to the currencies that pay the highest rates.

8. A rise in the exchange rate of sterling affects the **prices of imports and exports**. Imports become less expensive to buy for UK residents and this is a deflationary pressure; exports however become less competitive in foreign markets and UK firms may sell less abroad. These trends depend on the price elasticity of demand for exports and imports, ie on the degree to which people respond to the price changes. There will be an overall effect on the balance of payments although this cannot easily be predicted since many factors are at work here.

9. A change in the official interest rate influences expectations about the level of economic activity and confidence about the economy in general and may affect the **future level of employment, earnings, sales and profits**. However, expectations are hard to predict and may go in various directions. For example, if people see a rise in the official interest rate as a sign that a boom is on the way and that the Bank of England is trying to avoid it, they may believe that the boom will happen despite the interest rate rise and may expect lower unemployment. In such a case many companies would increase investment plans in the belief that they will be able to sell their products more easily. Conversely, people may see a rise in the official interest rate as a move into economic contraction and they may be less likely to borrow money for investment purposes.

10. **Spending decisions** are affected by the changes we have discussed above. We shall consider this in a separate section because it is vital for you to know the effects of interest rate changes on various sectors.

1.9 The Effects of Interest Rate Changes

Changes in interest rates have various effects on various groups of people. In this analysis we need to distinguish between:

● savers and borrowers

● existing savers and borrowers and potential savers and borrowers

● those on variable-rate schemes and those on fixed-rate schemes

● individuals and firms

It is important to be able to discuss the effects of interest rate changes on any combination of the above, eg on personal savers on variable interest rate schemes or on corporate borrowers paying a fixed interest rate. We shall structure the analysis by dividing bank customers into two groups: individuals and firms. Under each heading we shall discuss both savers and borrowers, both existing and potential, under both variable and fixed-rate schemes.

Individuals

Interest rate changes cause changes in the following identities.

(a) The disposable incomes of existing savers and borrowers

The overall effect on any particular person depends on whether he or she is a net borrower or a net saver. Savers' interest incomes vary in the same direction as interest rate changes and the effect on their expenditure depends on the percentage of their income accounted for by interest.

Existing borrowers on a variable interest rate scheme feel the effects of interest-rate changes in their weekly or monthly expenditure; around 80% of personal debt consists of loans secured on houses and most people have floating-rate mortgages which are influenced by interest-rate changes. A family paying off such a mortgage benefits from a lower monthly payment when interest rates fall and has to pay more when they rise. These changes in disposable income affect the level of their consumption of other items and the extent to which they can afford additional borrowing to finance hire purchase schemes or personal loans. Again, the rate of inflation must be taken into account when assessing whether they are better or worse off in real terms. However, when a loan has been taken out to finance the purchase of an asset like a house, we also have to look at what is happening to the value of the asset. During 2000/2001, interest rates fell 7 times (from 6% in February 2000 to 4% in November 2001) and so did people's mortgage payments, while at the same time the average price of houses rose. Borrowers were, therefore, paying less per month to finance an asset which was increasing in value. Of course, a mortgage loan is a very long-term one and trends like this can be cancelled out by opposite movements sometime in the future. (See Chapter 5 for the effects on morgage borrowers of low inflation.)

Existing borrowers on a fixed-rate scheme do not see any change in their monthly payments whether interest rates rise or fall. How they feel about this depends on which way interest rates are moving; if rates are rising, they are gaining but if they are falling they will want to convert to a variable scheme as soon as possible (most fixed-rate mortgage schemes have a lock-in period of several years which can be broken only on the payment of a penalty).

(b) Decisions of potential savers and borrowers

The effect of an interest rate change on potential savers is not always clear. It is possible that a fall in interest rates will cause people to look around for higher-income accounts (although these will almost certainly be less liquid and possibly more risky). Conversely, an increase in interest rates might attract more savings into bank and building society accounts. However it is important to remember that, although the rate of interest is an important factor in determining savings, it is less important than income. The amount that people are able to save depends on their incomes and the extent to which they have surplus funds left over when they have made their regular expenditures. So we cannot look at interest rates in isolation and must also take into account factors like earnings, employment rates, attitudes to savings etc. As people's incomes increase, they tend to save more; however the explosion in consumer expenditure which has taken place in all developed countries means that people spend increasingly large amounts on durables like cars, computers etc.

Potential borrowers look carefully at interest-rate changes to see if they can afford to borrow under the new rates. People borrow to finance the purchase of houses, cars and other consumption. Their reaction to a change in interest rates depends on their ability to meet the interest payments and on the extent to which they want to buy the goods. For example, the amount a couple can spend on a house depends on their joint income, ie on their ability to repay. An increase in interest rates increases the monthly payments and may decrease the amount they are willing and able to borrow. Someone borrowing money over a long period should always take into account whether he or she can afford their repayments if interest rates rise. The demand for the goods being bought is also important. Many families borrow a lot of money at Christmas time to finance their children's presents and it is doubtful whether they would borrow less if interest rates increased. If the product being financed is only of a low value, a small change in interest rates will not make a lot of difference to the repayments in any case.

Actually the real effect on savers and borrowers depends on whether the real interest rate is positive or negative, as discussed in an earlier section of this chapter. For example, if interest rates decrease in a situation where real interest rates are positive, the money value of the interest they receive falls but the real value of this is still keeping them ahead of inflation. If inflation has also fallen at the same time and to the same extent as the interest rate fall, these savers are more or less in the same position as before. However many individuals fail to take inflation into account when considering how they are affected by an interest-rate change. Suppose a savings account is paying 3% at a time when inflation is 2%. Many savers would feel that earning £3 on every £100 saved is very low and they may not remember that they need only 2% to keep them in line with price increases.

(c) Asset prices and people's financial wealth.

An increase in interest rates tends to decrease the values of bonds and securities, as we saw above. House prices are also affected and this is significant because houses are a major component of personal wealth and, for many people, the biggest asset they own. An increase in interest rates will discourage demand for mortgage loans by new borrowers or for people seeking to buy a bigger house; this is because increased interest payments means they cannot now afford a bigger loan. Other things being equal, house prices fall, thus causing the market value of properties to depreciate. This not only depresses people's 'feelgood' factor but also leaves them with less equity in their houses which they can offer as security against a further loan, and this also dampens consumer expenditure.

(d) Expectations

Expectations about future employment and income. If people see an increase in interest rates as a sign that the Bank of England is trying to contract the economy, they may feel that their jobs are now less secure and will be less willing to take on a long-term borrowing commitment.

(e) Exchange rates

A rise in interest rates will, other things being equal, cause the exchange rate of sterling to rise. Sterling will now buy more foreign currency and imports will become cheaper in terms of sterling, possibly motivating consumers to switch to imports from domestically produced goods, eg the demand for foreign holidays may rise if they become less expensive.

Firms

The effects of interest-rate changes on firms depend on the nature and size of the firm and its sources of finance. In general interest-rate changes cause changes in the following.

(a) **The overhead costs** of firms with existing loans, depending on the amount and type of borrowing they have undertaken. A rise in interest rates means an increase in debt servicing costs and thus lower profits and the cost of holding stocks also rises; and it makes further borrowing less likely as firms require a higher rate of return from a potential investment to cover the interest rate on the loan. An increase in interest payments puts pressure on the company's cash resources while at the same time reducing its profitability. The probable decrease in consumer spending accompanying the interest rate rise will mean that firms expect a lower demand and see expansion as less attractive; this will have a negative effect on employment.

(b) **The income** of cash-rich firms which save surplus funds in instruments such as certificates of deposit. A rise in interest rates results in a rise in interest income and means a higher cash-flow; it may affect the type of financial assets the firm decides to hold. A firm may respond in various ways to this, eg it may decide to proceed with investment plans or alternatively it may pay higher dividends to shareholders. As far as potential saving is concerned, a change in interest rates may make such savings more or less attractive but they are more likely to be affected by factors such as corporate profitability, expansion plans and the firm's general policy on what to do with its reserves.

(c) **The cost of long-term capital**, ie the cost of raising new equity or loans. The interest rates on long-term bonds are affected by changes in the official interest rate only indirectly and the effects on the cost of equity is hard to predict. Large corporates have access to international capital markets and, to the extent that they can raise funds in foreign currencies, they remain unaffected by a change in domestic interest rates. Companies borrow to finance investment, eg the purchase of new technology, expansion into a new market or research into a new product. Future borrowing decisions are determined by comparing the rate of interest charged by the bank with the rate of return the company expects to receive from the investment. Where a loan carries a variable interest rate, the firm is uncertain as to what future interest will be, and the longer the term of the loan, the greater this uncertainty. It is probably true to say that investment decisions are determined more by companies' future expectations of their markets and of economic conditions than by changes in interest rates alone, although the level of interest rates is certainly a factor contributing to economic conditions.

(d) **Asset prices**, which changes the value of the security which firms can offer to back up their debt.

(e) **Exchange rates**, which affects the competitiveness of firms both at home and abroad. A rise in interest rates, other things being equal, causes a rise in the exchange rate of sterling and UK firms become less competitive in both the domestic and the export markets. However, they could import raw materials more cheaply and lower their costs.

(f) **Expectations** of future economic performance in terms of inflation and growth. These affect firms' investment decisions and thus employment.

We can also briefly look at the effects of interest rate changes on banks and on the government.

Banks

When the Monetary Policy Committee of the Bank of England announces an interest rate change, all major financial intermediaries follow this change by adjusting the rates they pay to their savers and those they charge to their borrowers. Actually no law or regulation forces them to do so, but competition and the nature of the market means that they generally do. Their profit margin may remain unchanged, eg if interest rates rise by 1% and a bank pays an extra 1% to all its savers and charges an extra 1% to all its borrowers, its profit margin remains the same although the actual profit it makes will depend on how customers react to the change.

Other things being equal, a very high interest rate will attract more savings but dampen down the demand for loans so that banks will have plenty of funds to lend but not enough people wanting to borrow. Conversely a very low interest rate will encourage people to borrow but not to save so that banks will find it difficult to supply the demand for loans. Even where a bank lends money on fixed interest rates, there will be no effect on its profits since such lending is matched by fixed-rate deposits. However banks will gain from an increase in interest rates to the extent that they raise funds from current-account holders to whom they do not pay interest. This is known as the **endowment effect**. Actually this effect has reduced in recent years as an increasing number of current accounts now pay a rate of interest; and we should not forget that there is an implied rate of interest on current accounts to the extent that banks now operate these accounts without making charges.

Another factor to consider is the effect of an interest rate change on borrowers' ability or otherwise to repay their loans. When interest rates rise, the rate of defaults grows as both individuals and companies find it increasingly difficult to make their payments; in such a case banks have to increase their provisions for doubtful debts, and this decreases their profitability.

The government

Although it is the government that instigates interest rate changes, it is also affected by them. As we shall see below, the public sector does not always raise enough money from tax revenues to cover its expenditure and it has to borrow money from the private sector. When interest rates are high, its interest-rate payments increase and there is an increasing burden on the Exchequer. Conversely and perhaps confusingly, when the public sector needs to borrow more, interest rates may have to increase to attract people into buying public sector debt.

1.10 Fiscal Policy

Fiscal policy (which is sometimes called budgetary policy) involves influencing the money supply and the overall level of economic activity, including consumption and investment, by manipulating the finances of the public sector (which comprises the central government, local authorities and public corporations).

The public sector has a responsibility to provide certain services that are of national or communal importance, such as education, healthcare and transport. To pay for these services, the government must raise funds from the private sector, ie from individuals and firms, in the form of direct and indirect taxes.

Because the public sector is responsible for taking a large amount of money from the private sector and for making large amounts of expenditure on its behalf, any changes in either side of the account and thus in the balance, have a significant effect on the economy as a whole. Keynsian economic theory describes public expenditure as an injection into the circular flow of income; when the government spends money it demands goods and services and creates employment. Conversely, taxation is seen as a withdrawal from the flow that leaves people with less money to spend and that creates unemployment. There are three general outcomes:

●   A balanced budget, the effect on the economy being neutral (but see below) as the amount taken away in taxation is put back into public spending.

- A budget surplus where the amount of money taken away is more than that put back; the effect is contradictory in terms of employment and deflationary in terms of the money supply. A government with a budget surplus can save the difference to spend later, spend it on capital investment or repay earlier by borrowing or buying back gilts; this reduces the size of the National Debt.

- A budget deficit where the amount of money put back is more than that taken out (the difference being the amount borrowed); the overall effect is expansionary in terms of employment and also inflationary in terms of the money supply.

Public sector borrowing

A government that has a deficit must borrow to finance it. This borrowing is expressed in two identities:

- **Public Sector Net Borrowing (PSNB)** which is the sum of current public spending (including depreciation) and net public investment, less total public revenues;

- **Public Sector Net Cash Requirement (PSNCR)** (formerly known as the Public Sector Borrowing Requirement or the PSBR). This is the PSNB plus financing requirements arising from financial transactions (eg net asset sales, lending to the private sector and abroad and accruals adjustments). The PSNCR is a cash measure of the public sector's short-term net financing requirement. When there is a budget deficit and the public sector has to borrow, this borrowing adds to the total of outstanding debt which the public sector owes to the private sector and which has accrued over many years of borrowing. This total is known as Net Debt and, when expressed as a percentage of Gross Domestic Product (GDP), is a key economic indicator. Public sector borrowing is achieved by the issue of government stocks (gilt-edged securities or gilts), by the issue of Treasury Bills, which are short-term gilts and through a variety of National Savings products. The nature of these financial instruments is described in Chapter 4. They are purchased by private sector individuals and firms, including banks.

Fiscal measures

The relationship between the three sides of the public sector Budget (revenue, expenditure and balance) and changes in this relationship have important effects on the economy. These are summed up in the phrase **overall fiscal impact**. This impact is made up of changes in:

- that part of the Public Sector Net Borrowing which results from cyclical movements in the economy through the operation of **automatic stabilizers**. In a boom, for example, companies make bigger profits, individuals earn higher incomes and spending increases so government receipts of both direct and indirect taxes increase; at the same time unemployment decreases and government expenditure on benefits falls. The automatic effect on the Budget is that the PSNB falls.

- that part of the PSNB resulting from changes in the **fiscal stance**. This can change as a result of either discretionary Budget measures (eg a decision to increase tax rates will, other things being equal, decrease the PSNB) or of non-discretionary factors (eg an increase in the price of oil will bring in more revenue from tax receipts on North Sea oil and, other things being equal, will decrease the PSNB).

The key indicator for assessing the overall fiscal impact is the change in Public Sector Net Borrowing (PSNB). An increase in the PSNB is expansionary because it adds to aggregate demand; a decrease in the PSNB is contradictory because it subtracts from aggregate demand.

A government that wants to bring down the rate of inflation can, apart from implementing the monetary measure of increasing interest rates, readjust its own accounts by increasing tax revenues and cutting public spending. If it already has a deficit, it must cut this; and if it has a surplus, it must increase it.

If the government sees that inflation is low and it wants to expand the economy, it will do the opposite, ie decrease tax receipts and increase public expenditure, thereby increasing the deficit or decreasing the surplus.

At the beginning of the 21st century, the central economic goal of the UK government is to achieve high and sustainable levels of growth and employment. Fiscal policy is directed towards maintaining sound public finances over the medium term, based on strict rules, and towards supporting monetary policy where possible over the economic cycle. The government has specified two key fiscal rules:

- **the golden rule:** over the economic cycle, the government will borrow only to invest and not to fund current spending; and

- **the sustainable investment rule:** public sector net debt as a proportion of gross domestic product will be held over the economic cycle at a stable and prudent level.

A reduction in net public sector debt to below 40% of GDP over the economic cycle is seen as being desirable.

The government outlines its fiscal policy in the annual Budget statement by the Chancellor of the Exchequer, normally in March. The statement includes revenue plans (including taxation of individuals and companies) and the government's planned expenditure, including the projected size of the PSNB if any. At least three months prior to the Budget, the government publishes a Pre-Budget Report that allows it to consult the public on specific policy initiatives.

Monetary policy via changes in the general level of interest rates acts on the economy as a whole. Although fiscal policy too can have an overall macro-economic effect on the level of activity in the economy, it also has micro-economic effects and can be targeted to particular areas of the economy. For example, tax incentives can be given to manufacturing industries to boost employment in what is a declining sector; or government grants can be given to firms which move to relatively under-developed geographical areas.

The link between fiscal policy and monetary policy

In practice, fiscal policy and monetary policy are not applied in isolation, but are closely linked. To explain this, we shall take a situation where a government has a deficit and is borrowing to finance it. The process of borrowing from the private sector affects the money supply and so any change in the fiscal situation has a monetary effect. There are various methods of borrowing which the government may employ, and each will affect the money supply in different ways:

- Borrowing from the non-bank private sector through the sales of gilt-edged securities or National Savings has little effect on the money supply. At first sight this may not seem to be the case, because the amount borrowed has been removed from the purchaser's account, thereby reducing the banks' deposits and so reducing the money supply. However, it has to be remembered that the government has borrowed this money in order to spend it, and the money will find its way back into the money supply when it is paid into the account of the recipient of the government spending.

  This form of borrowing can, however, increase interest rates, as attractive rates must be offered in order to persuade the public to choose government securities.

  Borrowing from the non-bank private sector is known as **funding**. If the whole of the public sector deficit is financed in this way, we say it is **fully funded**, and there is no net increase in the money supply.

- The government can also borrow from the bank and building society sector through the issue of Treasury bills and other government securities. When banks lend money to a customer, they create credit (as we have seen) and there is no difference when the government is the customer. The effect of this method – known as **under-funding** – is therefore to increase the money supply because the banks do not take the money they lend from anybody's account and yet, when the government spends it, it finds its way into a lot of bank accounts.

- The government may also borrow from overseas. If the borrowing is in the form of foreign currency, the money supply will not change, because the sterling deposits of the banking sector will be unaltered. If, on the other hand, this borrowing involves selling government securities to overseas customers who pay in sterling, the money supply will increase because these are new funds to the system which find their way into bank deposits. The net effect is to increase the money supply, and this is again known as under-funding.

All the methods of financing the PSNCR have drawbacks associated with them, either by having an inflationary effect on the money supply, by putting upward pressure on interest rates or by leading to balance of payments problems. A large PSNCR can make it difficult for governments to achieve the monetary policy targets they have set for themselves or to which they have agreed as part of broader financial agreements.

The fiscal situation in 2002

The UK government's accounts are currently showing a small surplus, ie total revenues exceed total expenditure. This can be accounted for partly by the government's policy of controlling public spending and partly by the economic boom, which has boosted government tax revenues and reduced the total spent on unemployment benefit. In 2000, government debt stood at £395 billion and this represents around 45% of gross domestic product.

This surplus could soon turn into a deficit if recession causes economic activity to fall significantly; added to which, the Labour government has committed itself to increased spending up to the next election.

2

THE MAJOR FINANCIAL INSTITUTIONS

2.1 The Functions of Financial Intermediaries

In any economy we find surplus and deficit sectors. The surplus sector comprises those people and firms that are cash-rich, ie they own more liquid funds than they wish to spend currently. They want to lend out their surplus funds to earn money. The deficit sector comprises those who own less liquid funds than they wish to spend and they are prepared to pay money to anyone who will lend to them.

In this context, a financial intermediary is an institution which borrows money from the surplus sector of the economy and lends it to the deficit sector. It pays a lower rate of interest to the person with the surplus and charges a higher rate of interest to the person with the deficit, its profit margin being the difference between the two interest rates. It provides a service to both sectors.

But why do these sectors need the services of a financial intermediary? Why can they not just find each other and cut out the middleman's profit? Actually, there are many cases where this does happen and it is known as disintermediation, eg when a company raises funds from the general public by issuing shares; we shall consider disintermediation later. But otherwise there are several reasons why both individuals and companies need the services of the intermediaries and these are the benefits which the intermediaries provide to their customers.

- **Geographic location:** Firstly, there is the physical problem that individual lenders and borrowers would have to locate each other and would probably be restricted to their own area or circle of contacts. A lender in London is unlikely to know of the existence of a likely borrower in Cumbria. Intermediaries overcome these search and location problems through the provision of a national branch network, and more recently by the introduction of telephone banking.

- **Aggregation:** Even if a potential borrower could locate a potential lender, the latter might not have enough money available to satisfy his requirements. The majority of retail deposits are relatively small, averaging under £1,000, while loans are typically larger, with many mortgages being for £30,000 and above. But intermediaries can overcome this size mismatch by aggregating small deposits, and, if necessary, by accessing the wholesale money markets for funding (see later).

- **Maturity transformation**: Even supposing that our borrower could find a lender who had the amount he or she wanted, there is now another problem: the borrower may need the funds for a longer period of time than the lender is prepared to part with them. The majority of deposits are very short-term (eg instant access accounts), whereas most loans are required for longer periods (personal loans are often for 2 or 3 years, companies often borrow for 5 or more years and typical mortgages are for 20 or 25 years). Intermediaries are able to overcome this maturity mismatch by offering a wide range of deposit accounts to a wide range of depositors, thus helping to ensure that not all the depositors' funds are withdrawn at the same time. They can thus combine short-term liabilities with longer-term assets, ie they can give their depositors access to their funds while at the same time promising their borrowers that they do not have to repay for some time. They can do this because experience shows them that not all depositors want their money out immediately. They can calculate statistically the amount of money they must have in liquid form at any one time and can lend the rest out for varying periods; this is similar to the reasoning behind credit creation which we looked at in Chapter 1. In addition, intermediaries have access to wholesale money markets such as the interbank market, where they can raise short-term finance should they encounter a shortage.

- **Risk transformation:** Finally, let us assume that our borrower can find a lender who has enough money and who does not need it back until after the borrower wants to repay it. There is still something stopping the transaction from the lender's point of view and that is the large amount of risk he or she will be facing. Individual depositors are generally reluctant to lend all their savings to another individual or company, principally because of the risk of default or fraud. But intermediaries enable lenders to spread this risk over a wide variety of borrowers so that, if a few fail to repay, the intermediary can absorb the loss (banks do in fact have to write off a certain amount of bad debts each year). Intermediaries also have the experience and the skills needed to improve credit management – for instance they often use credit scoring systems for personal loans, and financial covenants for corporate loans so they can eliminate high-risk borrowers and lend only to those who are more likely to repay.

Accepting deposits from lenders and making loans to borrowers comprises a large part of the work of banks. But they also offer other financial services, as we shall see shortly.

2.2 The Classification of Financial Markets

Buyers and sellers of financial services come together in financial markets. In this chapter we shall study the institutions that operate in these markets and consider the services they provide. Financial institutions deal not only with non-financial customers, eg individuals and companies, but they also deal with each other.

We can classify financial markets, according to the type of services or products being bought and sold, under the following headings:

- Retail and wholesale business

- Personal and corporate sectors

- Short-term, medium-term and long-term lending and borrowing

- Secured and unsecured lending and borrowing

- Sterling and foreign currency business

Let us look briefly at each of these distinctions.

Retail and wholesale business

The main distinction between retail and wholesale transactions is one of size, wholesale transactions being generally much larger than retail ones (a figure of £100,000 is often quoted as the point where retail transactions become wholesale). Because of this, the end-users of retail services are normally individuals and small businesses whereas wholesale services are provided to large companies, the government and to other financial institutions.

Retail banking is primarily concerned with the more common services provided to personal and corporate customers, such as deposits, loans and payment systems. It is largely the province of the High Street banks and the building societies, delivering their products through extensive branch networks.

These institutions are in effect acting as intermediaries between people who wish to borrow money and people who have money they are prepared to deposit. The price of borrowing, and the reward for investing is, of course, interest.

With the widespread replacement of cheques by the use of credit and debit cards, the traditional suppliers of retail banking are experiencing increasing competition from major stores, such as Marks and Spencer, which are offering their own credit cards and other financial services.

Wholesale banking refers to the process of raising money through the wholesale money markets rather than by attracting deposits from the general public. This can be done through a centralized operation, and usually involves large transactions in excess of £1 million.

This is the method normally used by finance houses, but the main retail banks are also heavily involved in wholesale banking in order to top up deposits from their branch network as necessary. For example, if a bank has the opportunity to make a substantial profitable loan but does not have adequate deposits, it can raise the money very quickly on the interbank market. This is a very large market encompassing over 400 banking institutions, which serves to recycle surplus cash held by banks, either directly between banks or more usually through the services of specialist money brokers.

The rate of interest charged in the interbank market is the London interbank offer rate (LIBOR). It acts as a reference rate for the majority of corporate lending, for which the rate is quoted as LIBOR plus a specified margin. LIBOR rates are fixed daily, and vary in maturity from overnight up to one year.

Another major element of wholesale banking is the sterling certificate of deposit (CD) market. A CD is a receipt given for the deposit of funds with a bank, and is payable to the bearer. CDs are normally for periods of between three months and five years, and for amounts of between £50,000 and £500,000. Although they are for a fixed term, they are issued in bearer form and can therefore be considered a liquid asset because there is an active secondary market.

Building societies are also permitted to raise funds on the wholesale markets, up to 50% of their liabilities.

The distinction between retail and wholesale in financial services is much less obvious than it used to be, with many institutions operating in both areas.

The words 'retail' and 'wholesale' are not part of the day-to-day terminology in other financial areas such as life assurance, pensions and unit trusts, but the concepts are present in the background:

● Some organizations are clearly based at the wholesale end of the market, notably the product providers such as life assurance companies and unit trust managers.

● Other organizations and individuals, such as insurance brokers and financial advisers, are purely retailers of the products and services offered by the providers.

Here again, however, there is some blurring of the boundaries, with many providers employing their own salesforce to sell direct to the public. Similarly, some financial advisers are tied to one company, selling only the products of that company.

A recent trend has seen the development of direct organizations, selling their life assurance, investment or mortgage products direct to the public through telephone call centres and the Internet, thereby effectively combining wholesale and retail activities.

Personal and corporate sectors

Intermediaries lend to people as individuals and to organizations, mainly the corporate sector, although they also lend to not-for-profit organizations and even to governments. The distinction between the personal and corporate sectors mirrors that between the retail and wholesale sectors to some extent since clearly individuals borrow and lend smaller amounts on the whole than do companies. However we are also interested in the type of products demanded by each sector, eg individuals need deposit accounts and personal loans to finance consumer expenditure while companies need a way of depositing larger amounts and business loans to finance expansion into new products and markets. There is a very wide range of products available to meet the needs of each sector and we shall look at personal sector products in more detail in Chapter 4.

Short-term, medium-term and long-term lending and borrowing

Under this heading we classify markets by the length of time for which money is borrowed and lent. Different terms constitute different financial products and the market for each has its own special characteristics. For example, the shortest period over which money is lent is the overnight borrowing and lending which banks do with each other in the interbank market; a bank with a deficit at the end of the trading day must borrow from a bank with a surplus in order to start the next day in funds. At the other end of the scale, we have the mortgage loan market whereby house purchasers borrow money from banks and building societies for terms up to 25 years. Between these two extremes, we can find money being borrowed and lent for many different time periods. We saw in Chapter 1 how interest rates differ depending on the time period of a loan.

Secured and unsecured lending and borrowing

Financial intermediaries lend money both on a secured and on an unsecured basis. Security is an asset or assets which the borrower puts forward to guarantee the loan and it is safer for an intermediary to lend on this basis than simply on the supposed creditworthiness of the borrower. A good example of a secured loan is a house purchase loan secured by a mortgage on the property being bought; if the borrower defaults, the intermediary can take possession of the property and sell it to repay the debt. However, there is also a market for unsecured loans, eg credit card loans do not require the borrower to provide any security, although the high rate of interest charged reflects the comparatively high rate of default. Intermediaries also lend money to each other in both secured and unsecured markets, eg a repo is a sale and repurchase agreement whereby a loan is secured by the underlying asset (look back to Chapter 1 on the market in gilt repos).

Sterling and foreign currency business

UK intermediaries deal in many currencies. Most of their business with their domestic customers is in sterling, although they do provide a wide range of foreign exchange services to their importing and exporting customers. However, they also offer accounts and loans in foreign currencies, particularly the US dollar and now the euro. They do a large amount of business in the foreign currency markets and in securities denominated in all currencies.

So if we want to describe a particular financial product, we can do so under the above headings. For example, a mortgage loan is a retail, personal sector, long-term, secured sterling loan; and an overdraft to a large company is a wholesale, corporate sector, short-term, sterling loan which may be secured or unsecured depending on the creditworthiness of the company.

In the next sections of this chapter we go on to describe the financial intermediaries which deal in the above markets and products. Some years ago we could also have classified the intermediaries according to the products they dealt in, eg we could have said that commercial banks served the retail sector and that merchant banks served the corporate sector. But this is no longer the case. All the major banks deal in virtually every market you can think of and are thus subclassified into divisions, according to the above analysis.

2.3 Banks

According to the Banking Acts of 1979 and 1987, a bank is an institution that provides a wide range of banking services or a specialized service and which has a high reputation in the financial community. It must be authorized as a deposit-taker and must have a minimum capital of £5 million. More specifically, the Acts go on to give a list of services which banks are expected to provide to their customers. These are:

● Current and deposit account facilities

● Loan and overdraft facilities

● Finance for foreign trade

● Financial advice

● Investment management

● Facilities for the purchase and sale of securities

(See Chapter 3).

The big well-known UK banks offer all of these services and more and they operate in virtually all sectors and markets. Most of these banks are household names, eg Barclays, Royal Bank of Scotland (incorporating the Nat West), HSBC and Lloyds TSB and some former building societies, eg Halifax (now known as HBOS since its merger with the Bank of Scotland) and Abbey National. The commercial banks used to be classified as retail banks because their original role was to provide money transmission, deposit and personal loan and overdraft services to the personal sector and to small businesses. Other types of non-banking financial institutions existed to serve other markets, eg investment banks, merchant banks, stockbrokers, finance companies, building societies etc. The commercial banks began to acquire these companies so they could enter new markets and the distinction between banks and non-banks became more blurred. For example, merchant banks used to exist to accept bills of exchange, to advise companies on the issuing of new share or loan capital and to manage investments. Nowadays these functions are carried out by the banks themselves in their corporate and investment departments. For example, Barclays owns Mercantile Credit, a consumer finance house, Barclays Life, a life assurance company and the Woolwich Building Society as well as subsidiaries offering stock-exchange services and independent financial advice.

The number of banks authorized by the Financial Services Authority in 2000/2001 was 664 compared with 629 a year previously; the corresponding figures for authorized investment firms were 7,612 and 7,329. Although there have been mergers and take-overs in the banking sector, several new banks have appeared on the scene as a result of the de-mutualization of certain large building societies, such as Abbey National and the Halifax, which have become public limited companies operating as retail banks (see later section).

The trade body for banks in the UK is the British Bankers Association (see Section 2.15).

Banks are public limited companies which are owned by their shareholders. Their main aim is to make a profit and they do this by borrowing money at a lower rate of interest and lending it out at a higher rate, the difference being their profit margin. The UK banks offer a very wide range of deposit and lending services to a large number of market segments and they also offer many other financial services for which they charge a fee. Many of these services are listed below, classified under the headings of retail and wholesale services.

Retail services

Banks offer a wide range of retail services to both the personal and the small business sectors. We can classify these services under the following headings:

- Money transmission services, eg the provision of cash, cheque clearing, direct debits and standing orders, credit and electronic transfers and credit card services. The branch network allows customers to visit the banks to make their transactions and see their personal or business manager but various other methods of delivery are now also provided. These include Automatic Teller Machines for cash dispensing and telephone banking and online banking for account management and payment of bills.

- Acceptance of deposits in current accounts and a wide range of deposit savings accounts which offer varying interest rates and required periods of notice for various amounts of savings.

- Arranging loans, eg overdrafts on current accounts, personal loans, credit cards, small business loans.

- Granting of mortgages for house purchase.

- Money managing services for personal customers, eg budget accounts.

- Business banking services for small businesses, eg advice before starting up, help with drawing up a business plan, continuing help and advice including the financing of working capital and purchase of fixed assets.

- Investments and ISAs.

- Stockbroking.

- Pensions.

- Life assurance and general insurance.

- The provision of foreign exchange.

- Personal services including making a will and setting up a trust fund.

  (For more details of some of these personal services, see Chapter 4)

Wholesale services

These are the financial dealings carried out by the banks in the wholesale markets with governments, supranational organizations, corporates, banks, insurance companies and other institutional investors. Some years ago these functions were carried out by separate types of banks, in particular merchant banks, but nowadays the major commercial banks provide these services within a complex organizational structure via specialist departments and subsidiary companies. Here is a list of the main services offered by banks to its wholesale customers.

1. Raising finance

(a) For working capital purposes, to help firms to avoid cash-flow problems, including:

- Overdraft facilities

- Factoring of invoices (where the bank buys the firm's debtors for a discounted amount and then collects the money owing)

- Export finance

- Trade finance, including forfaiting (a type of factoring involving discounting bills of exchange) and acceptance credits

(b) Loans and longer-term finance including:

- Variable-rate, fixed-rate and capped-rate loans

- Commercial mortgages

- Professional practice finance loans for people like solicitors and dentists to buy into or improve their practice

- Environmental loan facilities for businesses investing in environmentally beneficial projects

(c) Asset finance to allow companies to spread the cost of asset acquisition over a period:

- Leasing of equipment and vehicles under various schemes

- An asset acquisition account, whereby a business can purchase and finance equipment up to an agreed credit limit without discussing each one separately with the bank

- Computing funding management and support services

- Keyman protection insurance to safeguard the business against the death or prolonged illness of a key employee

- Keyasset protection insurance to safeguard the business against losses resulting from accidental damage or breakdown of important assets

(d) Private equity finance: financing businesses which are not public limited companies. These can be established businesses, high-growth technology businesses requiring venture capital or smaller companies which are finding it difficult to raise finance.

(e) Corporate finance: Banks assist companies to raise finance, for instance by organizing share issues. In this capacity they may act as underwriters and/or brokers. They also act as advisers to companies in relation to take-overs and acquisitions. These are merchant banking functions.

(f) Structured finance:

- Project and export finance, ie preparing feasibility studies and arranging and underwriting major transactions

- Finance to enable a company's management to stage a buyout, to convert public limited companies to private limited companies or to fund mergers and acquisitions

- Property finance, including sale and leaseback

(g) Government schemes, ie providing finance to businesses using the backing of schemes such as:

- The small firms loan guarantee scheme

- The small firms training loan

- The environmental loan facility

2. Investing funds for businesses with surplus cash to invest:

(a)   instant access: a range of accounts with varying interest rates

(b)   term deposits: a range of products for different fixed periods of time

(c)   notice accounts combining varying periods of notice

(d)   foreign currency current and deposit accounts with varying interest rates and terms

(e)   treasury management, ie giving advice to companies on how to optimize the use of their liquid funds

(f)   fund management of investments, particularly equities, and the provision of financial advice. The major clients are pension funds and life assurance companies.

3. Payments and cash management

(a)   Online cash management

(b)   Making and collecting payments by means of:

- Cash
- Cheques
- Direct debits and credits via BACS
- Payroll
- Using and accepting credit and debit cards
- Making and receiving international payments in foreign currencies using cash cheques and electronic payments
- Corporate credit cards
- International bank accounts

4. Operations in financial markets

(a)   foreign exchange in both the spot and forward markets where dealers make arrangements to buy and sell other currencies now (the spot market) or at some future date (forward).

(b)   currency options, where dealers have the right but not the obligation to buy and sell currencies at some future date, and currency swaps where two parties agree to exchange equivalent borrowed sums of two different currencies.

(c)   money market operations, where large amounts of money are borrowed and lent on a short-term basis.

(d)   commercial paper, where unsecured notes issued by companies are purchased directors by investors. This is an example of disintermediation.

(e)   interest rate derivatives, including interest rate swaps where two parties borrow money independently and exchange the associated interest payments.

(f)   government bonds and gilts where banks and other corporates lend money to the government by purchasing its debt.

(g)   dealings in financial futures in stocks, interest rates and currencies, which are standard two-way contracts for future delivery of the underlying asset.

(h)   research and information on all these markets.

Banks and other financial intermediaries are active in all these specialist markets. For example, forward agreements for foreign currency transactions enable importers and exporters to reduce the risk and uncertainty of future financial transactions by buying or selling foreign currencies at some time in the future at an exchange rate arranged at the time of purchase or sale.

It is beyond the scope of this book to go into further detail.

5. International services

(a)   international cash-flow management, including the making and receiving of payments in foreign currencies

(b)   finance of international trade via letters of credit, collections and guarantees

(c)   financing exports via forfaiting (described in a previous section) and debt purchase

(d)   financing imports via overdrafts and loans

(e)   insurance of foreign trade, eg cargo and goods in transit and credit and political risk

(f)   import and export intelligence including country profiles, documentation details, trade terminology and a guide to organizations that provide support and export information

The clearing process

Clearing refers to the process of the settling between banks, on a daily basis, of the transfers of money outstanding as a result of the use of cheques by customers. In spite of the development of more automated methods of fund transfer, such as direct debits and automated teller machines (ATMs), cheques still account for a substantial number of transactions, with millions of cheques passing through the clearing system each day.

Not all retail banks are clearing banks. Clearing banks are those that have established their own clearing systems in conjunction with other clearing banks. Other banks, and some building societies, which require payment systems to be set up but do not have their own clearing service have to establish an agency arrangement with one of the clearing banks.

Broadly speaking the clearing process is as follows:

- Banks constantly receive payments from other banks as their customers deposit cheques (and also by automated means such as direct debit).

- The same banks are also being asked to pay money by other banks, for the same reasons.

- The net effect of these two types of transactions is that each bank, at the end of each day's trading, is liable to pay a small balance – or is due receive a small balance – from each other bank.

APACS

APACS (the Association for Payment Clearing Services) was set up in 1985 as a non-statutory association of major banks and building societies and is the umbrella body at the centre of the UK payments industry. It is a forum where banks and building societies can discuss non-competitive issues relating to money transmission. Its main job is to manage the major UK payment clearing systems and to maintain their operational efficiency and financial integrity via three operational clearing companies:

- the Cheque and Credit Clearing Company which oversees the paper clearing

- BACS which operates the bulk electronic clearing

- CHAPS Clearing Company which provides electronic same-day clearings in sterling and euro

These organizations are described below. Institutions that wish to be members of one or more organization must demonstrate that they meet certain criteria, which include:

- They must be subject to appropriate supervision, which in future will be by the Financial Services Authority (see Chapter 3).

- They must have a specified minimum volume of transactions.

- They must maintain settlement account facilities at the Bank of England.

Institutions can be members of one part of the clearing system without having to be a member of another. Membership of any one part carries with it membership of APACS. There are currently 31 members of APACS, including all the main UK clearing banks and several foreign banks.

The Cheque and Credit Clearing Company

This organization operates the two bulk paper clearings in London, namely cheques and paper credit clearing. Cheque and paper credit clearings operate on a three-day processing cycle as follows.

Day One: A cheque is paid into a branch of a member bank or an agency of a member and is processed by the collecting bank that evening. At the clearing centre of the collecting bank, the information on the cheque is passed electronically through a secure data exchange network to the appropriate paying bank clearing centre.

Day Two: The cheque is delivered to an Exchange Centre where members of the cheque clearing hand over all the cheques drawn on the other banks and collect all the cheques drawn on themselves.

Day Three: Cheques presented for payment are reviewed by bank staff, who decide whether to pay or return them. The members settle the net values of the totals of the cheques exchanged between them via their accounts at the Bank of England.

Many banks are currently investigating the possibility of moving to a two-day clearing cycle, particularly as customers complain of the long time it takes to clear a cheque as they do not have full access to cheques they have paid into their accounts until these cheques have been cleared.

To allow for the possible dishonouring of cheques, banks may not actually permit customers to withdraw funds until a further period of a few days has elapsed, although some banks now permit customers to draw against uncleared funds.

The clearing process is carried out on a daily basis by the clearers (ie those institutions who are members. Membership consists largely, but not exclusively, of the main retail banks).

Other organizations that wish to offer financial services involving payment systems must open an agency arrangement with one of the clearers, under which payments drawn on – or credited to – their accounts can be handled by the clearing system. The same basic principle applies, in that the non-clearing institution operates an account with the clearer, and payment is achieved by debiting or crediting that account.

Nearly twelve million cheques and credits are cleared each working day. Cheque volumes reached a peak in 1990 but have fallen off since then as personal customers are increasingly using credit and debit cards and direct debits to make payments. Cheques remain popular in the business sector for paying suppliers, although an increasing number of companies now pay their employees via BACS (see below). Overall cheque volumes are expected to continue to fall from a level of 2.8 billion in 1999 to about 1.7 billion by 2009. 75% of cheques issued are for £100 or less.

BACS

The Bankers Automated Clearing Services Ltd (BACS) is owned by the major banks and building societies. It provides the Electronic Funds Transfer (EFT) of direct debits, direct credits, standing orders, information advices and the management of interbank network services. More than 40,000 companies are currently registered users of the BACS service and an even larger number have indirect access via banks. Over 46 million transactions are processed on a peak day. It is much cheaper for companies to make their payments and collections via BACS and they save up to 85% when compared with cash and cheques. BACS manages the Interbank Data Exchange service on behalf of the Cheque and Credit Clearing Company Ltd.

Like the cheque clearing system, settlement takes place over a three-day cycle.

Settlement takes place through the settlement accounts held by BACS members at the Bank of England. In addition to the full members, the system deals with transactions initiated by a very large number of sponsored service providers which use the members' clearing facilities through a form of agency arrangement.

CHAPS

CHAPS (the Clearing House Automated Payment System) is an electronic transfer system for sending same-day value payments from bank to bank. It operates in partnership with the Bank of England in providing the payment and settlement service. It offers its member an efficient, risk-free, reliable same-day payment mechanism because every CHAPS payment is unconditional, irrevocable and guaranteed. Since January 1999, CHAPS has operated two separate clearings, CHAPS Sterling and CHAPS Euro; 21 member banks participate in these clearings.

CHAPS is one of the largest real-time gross settlement systems in the world, processing an average of more than 80,000 payments a day with a daily average value of £150 billion.

Overseas banks

Banks from all around the world operate in the UK, particularly in London, the most significant being American and Japanese banks. They take the majority of their deposits in foreign currencies.

Overseas banks have not yet made a large impact in high-street retail banking in the UK, except for HSBC through their purchase of Midland. Several overseas banks are, however, members of APACS, including the Bank of Tokyo-Mitsubishi and the Deutsche Bank.

Banks authorized in other EU states can operate in the UK without having to be authorized here, under the terms of the EU Second Banking Directive. Further details of this are included in Chapter 3.

2.4 The Balance Sheet of a Bank

By studying the balance sheet of a bank, we can gather information about the types of assets the bank owns and the liabilities it owes, about the relationship between the two sections and the relative sizes of the individual items. We can use this information to draw conclusions about the bank's profitability and liquidity.

A hypothetical example of the balance sheet of a typical bank is shown in Figure 2.1. It indicates the items normally to be found in a bank balance sheet and these are identified by the descriptions actually used by the large commercial banks in their balance sheets. Although the figures quoted are imaginary, they are intended to show the likely relative sizes of the various assets and liabilities.

Figure 2.1: A Sample Bank Balance Sheet

	£000m
Assets	
Cash and balances at central banks[1]	1.5
Items in course of collection from other banks[2]	1.3
Treasury bills and other eligible bills[3]	1.7
Loans and advances to banks[4]	16.7
Loans and advances to customers[4]	84.2
Debt securities[5]	28.3
Equity shares[5]	1.2
Interests in associated undertakings and joint ventures[5]	0.6
Intangible fixed assets[6]	6.1
Tangible fixed assets[7]	3.7
Prepayments and accrued income[8]	2.2
Total assets	**147.5**
Liabilities	
Deposits by banks[9]	18.6
Customer accounts [10]	84.5
Debt securities in issue[11]	9.4
Items in course of transmission to other banks[2]	0.6
Accruals and deferred income[10]	3.8
Provisions [12]	6.6
Loan capital[13]	6.9
Minority interests[14]	0.4
Called-up share capital[15]	2.3
Share premium account[16]	12.6
Reserves[17]	1.8
Total liabilities and shareholders' funds	**147.5**

Explanatory notes

Assets

[1] Cash and balances at central banks: This is:

(a) notes and coin in the tills at the branches. Although a certain amount of cash is required to meet withdrawals by depositors, banks hold as little as possible because it is expensive to store, involves security risks and earns no interest. The amount required depends on the types of business conducted: clearing banks with a high volume of current accounts, for instance, would need to hold more cash than other types of banks.

(b) Balances at central banks. Banks which are part of the clearing process are required to maintain two accounts with the Bank of England:

- Operational deposits which are used for drawing cash and for settlement of clearing and which are non-interest-earning.

- Non-operational deposits which are based on a specified proportion (0.3% in April 2001) of the bank's eligible liabilities, ie its sterling deposits from non-bank customers. These deposits cannot be withdrawn and are used by the Bank of England for its market operations. These deposits are also non-interest-earning.

[2] Items in course of collection from other banks. Notice that there is a corresponding liability entitled 'Items in course of collection due to other banks'. These are outstanding cheques drawn in favour of or on the bank by its customers; at any point in time such outstanding items will always exist.

[3] Treasury bills and other eligible bills: there are three types of bills:

(a) **Eligible bank bills:** These are bills that are eligible for re-discount by the Bank of England in the discount market. They are the highest quality commercial bills because they have been accepted by an eligible bank, thus guaranteeing their payment. They are usually for 91 days duration.

(b) **Treasury bills:** These are promissory notes issued to cover the government's short-term borrowing. They are usually for 91 days duration and are issued by weekly tender from the Bank of England, usually to banks and discount houses. They are liquid instruments and can be traded in the discount market.

(c) **Local authority bills:** Similar to Treasury bills, these are a method used by local authorities to raise short-term finance.

[4] Banks lend money to other banks and to corporate and personal customers. Here are some of them:

- Loans to the London discount market are a form of secured lending at call to the discount houses to enable them to operate their bill dealings.

- Loans to other UK monetary sectors include funds held with other banks through the interbank system on a short-term unsecured basis.

- Some certificates of deposit are acquired by banks as an investment.

- Other loans may be made to local authorities or to markets overseas.

- Sterling advances to corporate and personal customers. Durations range from very short-term, eg overdrafts, to very long-term, eg mortgages. Advances may be both secured or unsecured.

- Lending is concentrated mainly in the UK private sector, but banks also make substantial loans to overseas borrowers.

5 Banks make investments in securities and shares in the government and in other companies; some are debentures (debt) and some are shares (equities).

6 Intangible fixed assets refers to the bank's goodwill, ie the amount by which its total assets exceed its physical and financial assets because of its good reputation.

7 Tangible fixed assets are premises, furniture, computer hardware etc.

8 Prepayments are expenses which the bank has made in advance and accrued income is money owing to the bank from interest etc which customers still have not paid but which relate to the financial year. The equivalent of this asset is the accruals item in the liabilities section; these are amounts which the bank owes on account of business done during the year but which it has not yet paid.

Liabilities

9 Deposits by banks are amounts deposited at the bank by other banking institutions through the interbank market.

10 Customer accounts refers to the money deposited at the bank by the UK private sector. These include sight deposits (current accounts) and time deposits of various fixed lengths or notice periods. Certificates of deposit (CDs) are receipts given for the deposit of funds with a bank for a fixed period of between three months and five years. They are negotiable instruments, payable to the bearer and are for amounts of more than £50,000. There is an active secondary market in CDs, which has led to them becoming a common means of interbank adjustment of liquidity.

Since the abolition of exchange controls in 1979, UK residents have been able to hold foreign currency accounts, but the majority of currency deposits are held by overseas residents. Funds are deposited by private investors, companies and financial institutions.

11 Debt securities in issue are securities issued by the bank that have been purchased by other counterparties, eg short-term paper.

[12] Provisions refers to provisions for bad debts and for liabilities which the bank may have to pay.

[13] Loan capital, ie debt borrowed by the bank from debenture-holders.

[14] Minority interests represent the proportion of a company's profit and loss attributable to outside shareholders in subsidiary companies which are not wholly owned.

[15] Called-up share capital is the share capital subscribed by the bank's owners.

[16] The share premium account is the amount paid by shareholders for their shares over and above the nominal value of the shares. It is held as a reserve on behalf of the shareholders.

[17] These are other types of reserves held for the shareholders, including the balance of the profit and loss account.

As with all businesses constituted as limited companies, banks have capital and reserves which represent shareholders' funds. The amount of share capital is small in relation to the total liabilities, but public confidence in the financial stability of banks enables them to operate using other people's money. If the ratio of capital to deposits falls below the level that the bank and its regulator consider acceptable, new share capital is raised by way of a rights issue. Capital enables banks to cover losses without affecting depositors' funds, to finance purchases, and to avoid the systemic risk (where the collapse of one bank leads, through a high level of interbank claims, to the collapse of other banks). In addition, banks need to comply with the internationally-agreed capital adequacy requirements known as the Basle Agreement. These are mentioned in Chapter 3.

Tier 1 capital consists of paid-up ordinary shares, non-repayable share premium account, general reserves, retained earnings, non-cumulative irredeemable preference shares and minority interests in subsidiaries. Banks must hold a minimum of 4% of risk-weighted assets as Tier 1 capital.

Tier 2 or supplementary capital consists of general provisions for doubtful debts, asset revaluation reserves, cumulative irredeemable preference shares, mandatory convertible notes and similar capital instruments, perpetual subordinated debt and redeemable preference shares and term subordinated debt.

Tiers 1 and 2 together must be no less than 8% of risk-weighted assets. Tier 1 capital must always exceed Tier 2.

A subordinated loan is one which ranks behind other debts if a company is wound up and would be paid a higher interest rate than one which comes higher up in the list of creditors. Banks can use subordinated loans to boost their potential borrowing base.

Profitability and liquidity

Banks make their profits on the difference between the interest rates they charge to their borrowers and the interest rates they pay to their depositors. In addition, they charge fees and commission for various services. Of the bank's assets, advances provides the best rate of return and so banks generally have a large proportion of their assets in this form. However longer-term advances tie up money for long periods and these assets are not liquid; in addition, it is the asset with the greatest risk of default. Banks, therefore, must balance the need to make profits against the need to control risk and to maintain sufficient liquidity.

Like all other businesses, banks have to maintain a balance between profitability and liquidity. The more profitable an asset, the less liquid it is. If a bank aims to maximize its profits at the expense of keeping enough liquidity, it will eventually fail through lack of liquid funds to pay its short-term debts. A bank failure would have very drastic consequences on the economy as a whole since banks create the money we use. If a major bank were to default, there would be a huge crisis of confidence in the financial system as a whole. Banks must ensure that they have adequate liquidity positions not only for their own survival but also because the regulatory body, the Financial Services Authority, requires them to do so.

Equally, the more liquid an asset, the less profitable it is. This means that if a bank were to keep too many assets in liquid form, just to be on the safe side, its profitability would suffer and its shareholders would complain and eventually its survival would be threatened.

As we go down the asset side of the bank's balance sheet, liquidity becomes less. Cash and balances at the central bank is the most liquid and fixed assets, at the other end, is the most illiquid. But profitability increases as we go from top to bottom, showing this inverse relationship between profitability and liquidity.

2.5 Finance Houses

Finance houses are also known as finance companies. They are non-bank financial institutions that provide a source of consumer and commercial finance. They are organizations which provide both smaller-scale lending on consumer goods and large corporate loan packages. They fund their operation mainly through the wholesale finance market rather than by attracting deposits from the general public.

Finance houses fall into three categories:

(a) Subsidiaries of banks, eg HSBC Equipment Finance (UK) Ltd and Lloyds TSB Leasing Ltd.

(b) Independent companies, eg the Funding Corporation and On-Line Finance Ltd.

(c) Manufacturer-owned finance operations, eg Toyota Financial Services (UK) plc and Xerox Finance Ltd.

The main types of service offered by finance houses are included in the following list. These services are not, of course, exclusive to finance houses and many of them are also commonly offered by retail banks, building societies and other organizations.

(a) **Unsecured loans:** These are usually fixed-rate loans for terms of one to five years, which can be used for any purpose – holidays, buying a car or consolidation of other borrowing. The service is often provided through agency packages with sales outlets such as car showrooms. Finance houses are often prepared to consider greater risks than retail banks, and this fact is reflected in higher rates of interest. Acceptability of customers for unsecured loans is generally based on a credit-scoring system.

(b) **Secured loans:** Finance houses also provide secured loans for home improvements and other purposes. Although low-risk mortgage customers can usually obtain a further advance from their original lender, others (for instance those with unsatisfactory payment records) may not be accepted for additional finance. In that case a finance house may be prepared to lend against the security of a second charge on the property. The rate of interest will be higher than the standard mortgage rate.

(c) **Hire purchase:** This is the process of buying items by instalments, most commonly used for buying cars and household goods. The goods belong to the lending institution until they are fully paid for, and can be legally repossessed in the event of default.

(d) **Leasing:** This is a method of acquiring a physical asset for a fixed period, and is commonly used by businesses for acquiring company vehicles and expensive items of equipment such as photocopiers. The lending organization retains ownership of the item, receives payments over a specified period (say three years) and then takes back the item, selling it to recoup outstanding costs (sometimes to the person who has been leasing it).

(e) **Factoring:** Some finance houses provide factoring services to businesses. They manage the company's invoices and debtors, and collect (and retain) the money owed to the company. In exchange for this, they advance to the company a proportion (eg 80%) of the value of the debts to be collected. They aim to make a profit from the discount at which the debts are purchased, but this must also take into account the delay in collecting the debts, and of course the risk that some debts may be difficult or even impossible to collect.

Finance houses often try to attract business from specific groups of the population, whom they perceive to be acceptable risks, by circulating advertising material with renewal notices from, for instance, motoring organizations or charitable bodies.

The Finance and Leasing Association is the trade body of finance companies (see Section 2.15).

2.6 Building Societies and other Mutual Institutions

Mutuality

Mutuality is a long-established concept in the world of financial institutions. A mutual institution is one that is not constituted as a company and, therefore, does not have shareholders to whom the profits are distributed.

The most common types of mutual organizations are building societies and friendly societies, all of which are mutual by definition, and life assurance companies, of which only a small proportion are mutual. Some mutual life companies can be recognized by the use of the word 'mutual' in their name.

A mutual organization is in effect owned by its members, who can determine how the organization is managed, through general meetings similar to those attended by shareholders of a company. In the case of a building society, the members comprise its depositors and borrowers; for a life company, they are the with-profit policyholders.

Since the Building Societies Act 1986, building societies have been able to de-mutualize – in other words to convert to a bank (with their status changed to that of a public limited company). Such a change, of course, requires the approval of the members, but this approval has in practice generally been readily given, not least because of the windfall of free shares to which the members have been entitled following conversion to a company.

The trend to conversion was led by Abbey National, followed throughout the 1990s by a number of the larger societies, including Halifax, Woolwich and Northern Rock. Their purpose in converting has been to provide access to the wider range of business opportunities available to banks, as a result of the consequent freedom from the restrictions of the Building Societies Act 1986 (see Chapter 3).

Developments in building society legislation, however, have significantly broadened the societies' spheres of activity, and several prominent societies, notably the Nationwide, have resisted the pressure to convert, believing that there are more benefits to be gained by remaining mutual. The main argument in favour of mutuality is that societies' profits are not distributed to shareholders and they can therefore offer higher deposit rates and lower loan rates. This view of the advantage of retaining mutual status is shared, according to a 1997 survey, by the majority of financial journalists.

The possibility of a windfall on conversion has led to a spate of carpetbagging; this refers to the practice of opening an account at a society which is believed to be going to convert, purely in order to obtain the allocation of shares. Societies considering conversion have, in response, sought to protect the interests of their long-term members by placing restrictions on the opening of new accounts.

In recent years, some mutual life assurance companies, including Norwich Union, have also elected to de-mutualize.

Building societies

Building societies first appeared in the eighteenth century as cooperatives formed to help their members to obtain housing. The earliest societies were closed societies which took in savings from their members and used these funds to build houses which were occupied by – and eventually owned by – those same members. Finally, when all the members owned a home, the society would be terminated.

These terminating organizations were gradually replaced during the nineteenth century by others, similar to the modern building societies, which accepted savings and used those savings to create mortgage finance on an ongoing basis. Since they did not plan to terminate like their predecessors, they became known as permanent building societies, a phrase which is still found in the names of some societies today.

The building society movement grew rapidly throughout the twentieth century, as the proportion of households owning their own homes grew from only 10% in 1900 to around 70% by the end of the century. Over the same period, the number of societies fell from more than 2,000 to fewer than a hundred, mainly as a result of mergers.

The remaining societies, however, developed extensive networks of high-street branches and agencies, thus retaining a presence not only in cities and larger towns, but also in most smaller towns and even some villages. This, coupled with their mutual nature, has encouraged societies to promote themselves as offering a more personal service than some other financial organizations.

Until quite recently, building societies continued to dominate the markets in retail savings and residential mortgages. This is less true today, with the banks and other organizations taking a larger share, particularly of the mortgage market. This trend was accentuated by the conversion of the Halifax, which is the largest mortgage lender in the UK. There are 65 building societies in the UK with total assets of over £170 billion. About 15 million adults have building society savings accounts and over 2.5 million adults are buying their own homes with the help of building society loans.

Over the same period – roughly since the early 1980s – the scope of building societies' business activities has widened considerably. Although it remains a legal requirement for building societies that their main activity should be the provision of mortgage loans on owner-occupied residential property, funded by deposits from their members, they have also been able to diversify into other activities which were previously the province of the banks and other financial institutions. As a result of the more flexible regime ushered in by the Building Societies Act 1986, which permitted societies to broaden the scope of their business, they now offer a comprehensive range of retail financial services and products in addition to their traditional savings and mortgage arrangements. These include:

- Cheque accounts and money transmission;

- Unsecured loans, leasing and hire purchase;

- Investment services, including unit trusts and pension management;

- Life insurance and general insurance;

- Trustee and executor services;

- Estate agency, valuations and conveyancing.

Development of the building societies' activities has gone hand in hand with development of the regulatory regime to which they are subject. This regime is described in more detail in Chapter 3. The products themselves are covered in Chapter 4.

The momentous changes felt in the personal financial services market in the 1980s and 1990s led to an element of uncertainty about the future of the building society movement. Recently, however, the situation has looked more stable, and the survival of building societies as a major contributor to the market seems to be more assured.

The trade body for building societies is the Building Societies Association (see Section 2.15).

2.7 The Balance Sheet of a Building Society

A typical building society balance sheet follows broadly the same general principles as for a bank, but reflects two major differences:

(i) because it is a mutual institution there are no shareholders' funds;

(ii) in accordance with the requirements of the Building Societies Act 1986, the bulk of the assets are advances secured on residential property, and the bulk of the liabilities are retail deposits. A hypothetical example of a building society balance sheet is shown in Figure 2.2.

Figure 2.2: A Sample Building Society Balance Sheet

	£000m
Assets	
Liquid Assets	
Cash in hand and balances with the Bank of England[1]	0.3
Loans and advances to credit institutions[2]	1.9
Debt securities[3]	8.8
Loans and advances to customers	
Loans fully secured on residential property[4]	36.7
Other loans[5]	4.8
Investments	
Equity shares[6]	3.6
Investments in subsidiary undertakings[7]	5.5
Tangible fixed assets[8]	0.5
Prepayments and accrued income[9]	0.6
Total assets	**62.7**
Liabilities	
Shares[10]	42.0
Amounts owed to credit institutions[11]	1.8
Amounts owed to other customers[12]	5.8
Debt securities in issue[13]	8.1
Accruals and deferred income[14]	1.2
Provisions for liabilities and charges[15]	0.1
Subordinated liabilities[16]	0.2
Subscribed capital[17]	0.1
Reserves[18]	3.4
Total liabilities	**62.7**

Explanatory notes

[1] Notes and coin held in tills and at the Bank of England.

[2] Some of this figure is repayable on demand and the remainder represents loans and advances for various periods from less than 3 months up to 5 years.

[3] These are securities issued by public bodies and corporate borrowers. They consist of certificates of deposit and bonds.

[4] Mortgage loans secured on customers' land and buildings. These are Class 1 advances (first charges on residential property) with a smaller proportion of advances secured on other land. Regulation requires that this item should be at least 75% of commercial assets, ie assets not including liquidity and investments.

[5] Unsecured loans, eg personal loans and overdrafts.

[6] Owned by the building society in public limited companies.

[7] Investments in subsidiary undertakings, eg life assurance companies, unit trust companies etc which are wholly or partly owned by the building society.

[8] Land and buildings, plant and machinery, equipment, fixtures and fittings and vehicles.

[9] Expenses prepaid by the building society for the coming year and accruals owing to the building society for the current year or previous years.

[10] Shares held by individuals and by other depositors. The term is rather confusing because it does not refer to shareholders' equity but is used to refer to qualifying savings accounts.

[11] Accrued interest and amounts borrowed from other financial intermediaries.

[12] Amounts owed to depositors with varying types of accounts.

[13] Certificates of deposit, fixed and floating-rate notes and other debt securities.

[14] Interest on subordinated liabilities and on subscribed capital.

[15] Including deferred taxation.

[16] Unsecured notes issued for varying maturities.

[17] Permanent interest-bearing shares which are deferred shares of the building society and which rank behind the claims of all subordinated noteholders, depositors, creditors and investing members of the society.

[18] This could be a revaluation reserve or general reserves put aside out of past surpluses.

Just like banks, building societies must have enough liquid funds to be able always to satisfy their customers' demands for cash. As long as they have a cushion of liquid assets of varying maturities, they can lend out the majority of their deposits in loans to their borrowing customers.

However, unlike banks, it is not the aim of building societies to make a profit since they are not-for-profit institutions. Any excess of income over expenditure is known as a surplus; there are no shareholders to distribute this to but it is used to build up reserves and it may enable the society to pay a higher rate of interest to its depositors.

The relationship between liquidity and the ability to make a surplus is very similar to that between liquidity and profitability. The more liquid an asset, the less income it will provide and vice versa. The building society must find a balance between the two.

2.8 Gilt-Edged Securities and National Savings

The UK government, like those in other countries, is responsible for spending large amounts of money on areas which are for the common good or in the national interest. These include social security, the provision of the health and education services, transport and general infrastructure, the maintenance of law and order and the armed forces.

The government's main source of income to finance this expenditure is from taxation, including income tax, capital gains tax, value added tax, inheritance tax and national insurance contributions. These taxes are described in more detail in Chapter 4.

When the government's spending exceeds its income, it borrows money to finance the difference or the Public Sector Net Cash Requirement (PSNCR) (see the section on fiscal policy in Chapter 1). The government has two main methods of borrowing:

- selling gilt-edged securities (bonds) mainly in the wholesale market, eg to pension funds and investment companies. These securities include short-term Treasury Bills and gilts, which are longer-term securities of varying maturities. At any given time, there is a wide spread of redemption dates (ie the dates when the government will repay the loans) of anything up to 30 years in the future, as well as a range of interest rates (known as coupon rates). Further details of gilts from the point of view of the investor are given in Chapter 4.

- selling savings and investment products to the retail market through National Savings.

The total outstanding amount of money borrowed by the government is called the National Debt. The cost of paying the annual interest on this debt is a significant part of total government expenditure. National Savings helps to keep this cost down by providing and managing funds at a cost which is lower than that of providing the same amount of funding through selling gilts. The cost saving in 2000-2001 was estimated to be £117 million.

National Savings

The National Savings movement has a long history. It began in 1861 as the Post Office Savings Bank with the joint aims of providing a secure environment for the savings of working people, and of developing a fund which the Treasury could use to finance various projects. During World War I, when full employment was threatening to lead to inflation, Lloyd George introduced Savings Certificates to divert surplus income to the war effort.

In 1969, the Post Office Savings Department became a separate government department and was renamed the Department for National Savings. In 1996, it became a government department and an Executive Agency of the Chancellor of the Exchequer.

With the Debt Management Office, National Savings is one of the Treasury's two agents for financing the national debt. Each year, National Savings agrees with the appropriate

Treasury minister (currently the Economic Secretary) how much it will raise and at what cost – interest and management costs. This has to be broadly in line with the costs of raising money through gilts, but National Savings is also acutely aware of the intense market in which it must compete for savings.

National Savings is one of the largest savings organizations in the UK and offers a wide range of savings and investment products to personal savers and investors. The money placed with it is used by the Treasury to help to manage the national debt cost effectively and to contribute towards the government's financing needs. When customers invest in National Savings, they are lending money to the government, which pays them interest in return. All its savings and investment products are government securities, which are the most secure cash deposits available in the UK.

Its aim is to help to reduce the cost to the taxpayer of government borrowing. Its strategic objective is to provide retail funds for the government which are cost effective in relation to funds raised on the wholesale market. Over £60 billion of funds are invested with the organization and annual cash-flows exceed £20 billion. It accounts for 10% of the cash-based deposit market and finances nearly 18% of the national debt.

National Savings is undergoing a radical overhaul based on partnership. In April 1999 it entered into a partnership with Siemens Business Services (SBS) to cover operational service delivery. This has meant faster service, extended opening hours for telephone sales, faster access to money and new ways to invest. It has a new computerized banking system, purpose-built call centres, faster and more secure systems and a customer-centres database. In April 2001 the organization published a Customer Code which sets out the standards of good practice customers can expect.

National Savings also has a long-standing relationship with the Post Office, now part of Consignia plc. The aim is to improve the effectiveness of the Post Office and financial intermediaries as sales channels as well as further developing its own direct channels.

The main objectives of National Savings are to deliver good service to its customers, to change and adapt for the future and to implement strategies to secure its business in the long-term. It operates in a very competitive market and it has to offer customers a good range of products which suit their needs and offer them security, benefits and returns.

Details of individual National Savings products are included in Chapter 4.

2.9 Lloyd's of London

Insurance as a major financial industry had its beginnings in the development of international trade, and was initially designed to cover ships and their cargoes. Perhaps the most famous name in insurance is Lloyd's, but, paradoxically, its founder Edward Lloyd was not himself involved in insurance!

Lloyd himself provided the premises – a coffee shop in Tower Street, by the Thames in the City of London. He also provided shipping news and other facilities which attracted ships' captains and merchants to his premises. There they were able to meet wealthy individuals who would take a share of the risks involved in insuring vessels and cargo.

These wealthy individuals would sign their names under each other at the bottom of the insurance contract, together with the amount of risk they would accept – this was the origin of the word underwriter.

The exact date when Lloyd's began is not known, but it was certainly operating in 1688. By 1774, Lloyd's had elected a committee and moved to new premises at the Royal Exchange. A hundred years later, the Society of Lloyd's was incorporated by the Lloyd's Act 1871, and by 1900 it had become an international market for insurance risks of every kind. In 1909, its first motor policy was issued, and in 1911 it moved into aviation insurance.

1986 saw a move to its present building, 1 Lime Street, following which Lloyd's went through a turbulent period, with unprecedented losses of nearly £8 billion between 1988 and 1992. These losses were due in part to very substantial claims resulting from the harmful effects of asbestos, which coincided with a period of global recession.

This traumatic time for Lloyd's led to a reconstruction and renewal plan, which was implemented in 1996. As part of the reconstruction, it is now possible for corporate bodies to become members of Lloyd's as well as private individuals.

Today Lloyd's is a unique insurance institution, providing a marketplace where those seeking insurance can have risks underwritten by syndicates. These syndicates are funded by Lloyd's **names**, who are effectively the owners of the business. They take any profits that are made, but they also carry unlimited liability, which means that if their syndicate makes a loss they may have to sell their own private assets in order to make the necessary payments.

Lloyd's remains very heavily involved in marine and aviation insurance, but also covers a wide range of general insurance policies, including unusual and celebrity items. Lloyd's carries out a Global Risk Survey to give it the best information regarding the state of worldwide risk; since the attack on the USA on 11 September 2001, this Survey has been suspended because it considered that any analysis of results gathered before that date would now be meaningless. The survey will be restarted in 2002.

2.10 Insurance Companies

Insurance falls broadly into two categories:

- Insurance against the effects of the loss of – or damage to – property is known as general insurance. It includes motor insurance, home and contents insurance, cover for businesses, holidays, and many other risks. In fact, any insurance that does not fall within the definition of life assurance (see below) is termed **general insurance**.

● General insurance does not fall directly within the current remit of the Financial Services Authority (see Chapter 3). Consequently these notes do not deal with general insurance, which is a very large subject in its own right.

Both general insurance and life assurance are available from insurance companies in the UK. Most companies specialize in one or the other, although some of the larger groups deal in both, in which case they are known as composite insurers. A typical example of a **composite** insurer is the CGNU group, trading under the Norwich Union name.

Life assurance

Forms of life assurance have been known at least since Roman times, when soldiers contributed part of their wages to a fund used to compensate the families of those who were killed fighting for the empire, and rich citizens could save with burial clubs designed to enable them to have a suitably impressive funeral.

Life assurance in the UK began as an adjunct to marine insurance, with the lives of seafaring men being insured for a limited period – perhaps for the duration of a voyage, or for a period of one year. Initially the same premium rate was charged in each case, whatever the age of the person being insured, but – not surprisingly – people over about age 40 were refused cover because they were considered to have too high a risk of dying.

In the late eighteenth century, one prospective customer was so incensed at being turned down on account of his age that he determined to develop a scientific basis on which people of any age could be offered life assurance at an appropriate premium. He was James Dodson, a mathematician, and his first step was to produce a set of **mortality tables** (tables of death rates) using data collected during an exhaustive study of gravestones throughout the UK.

Dodson might therefore be said to have been the first actuary – actuaries are insurance mathematicians who set the premium rates for life and other insurance policies – and he certainly was the father of modern scientific life assurance. Applying his new-found skills, he was instrumental in establishing a life assurance company (Equitable Life) that offered cover on a fair or equitable basis.

From that time, scientific life assurance has been based on estimates of the future levels of three main factors that affect the premiums to be charged and the subsequent profitability of the business. These are:

● **Mortality rates:** these determine when, and how many, claims will be paid out.

● **Investment returns:** the company can invest its funds to await the time when they will be paid out.

- **Expenses:** there are costs of running the business, including staff salaries, premises, marketing expenses, etc.

Because precise estimates of those factors were difficult to obtain in the early days, they tended to be overestimated, and as a result surpluses arose in the companies' funds. Those surpluses were used (and still are used when they arise) in three different ways:

- **Distribution to the shareholders:** If the company is a proprietary company, its Articles of Association will specify the proportion of the surplus that can be distributed to shareholders. This is often 10%, with the remaining 90% going to with-profit policyholders (see below). For mutual companies, the whole of the distributable surplus goes to the with-profit policyholders.

- **Transfer to reserves:** Most companies consider it prudent to transfer some surplus to reserves, which can be drawn on in years when claims are higher than expected or investment returns fall. This procedure enables them to smooth out their bonus rates (see below) over good and bad years.

- **Declaration of bonuses:** In early years, bonuses arose simply from inaccurate estimates of mortality, investment returns and expenses, but they proved so popular that the process was formalized by the introduction of a new type of policy on which an additional premium is paid, entitling the policyholder to receive a share of any surplus made. This type of policy, known as with-profits, is still popular today, although many customers have in recent years shown a preference for unit-linked policies, on which the policy returns are much more closely linked to the performance of particular sectors of the stock market.

Modern life assurance products tend to fall into two categories, with the more sophisticated products combining elements of the two types:

- **Protection products:** These provide protection for individuals or businesses against the adverse financial effects of death or illness. Examples are term assurance, designed to pay a lump sum on death within a specified term, and permanent health insurance, which replaces income in the event of the insured being unable to work due to sickness or accident.

- **Savings products:** These are mainly forms of endowment assurance, which are regular savings schemes that pay out a lump sum at the end of a certain term. They usually also provide an element of protection in the form of a payment if death occurs before the end of the term.

More details of life assurance products are given in Chapter 4.

The trade association for insurance companies is the Association of British Insurers (see Section 2.15).

2.11 Friendly Societies

Friendly societies first came into being as small insurance 'clubs' in the eighteenth century, collecting premiums and paying out small benefits for sickness or funeral expenses. They generally served a local community or a particular occupation, and because of the service that they provided for mainly working-class people they were granted exemption from tax on their funds. Today they still operate in effect as small (and in some cases not so small) life assurance companies, and continue to take advantage of the fact that their funds – within certain limits – are tax-free. Policies with monthly premiums of up to £25, or annual premiums up to £270, can be part of the tax-free fund. Each member of a family, including young children, can have one policy with premiums up to the specified limits.

People increasingly doubt the ability of the Welfare State to provide for everyone's needs and friendly societies are coming back into their own by promoting the idea of self-help. Some societies specialize in healthcare and provide permanent health insurance and critical illness schemes (see Chapter 4 for more details of these products).

Many friendly societies today offer larger policies, and other types of financial services. These, however, cannot be held in the tax-free fund, and are taxed in the same way as those offered by life assurance companies.

The trade body is the Association of Friendly Societies (see Section 2.15). Three examples of friendly societies are the Homeowners Friendly Society Limited, Harrogate, the Bus Employees' Friendly Society, Reigate, and the Royal Liver Assurance Limited, Liverpool.

2.12 Pension Funds

Medical advances and improvements in living conditions in the UK – particularly since the 1950s – have led to greater average life expectancies. This, coupled with the trend to earlier retirement, means that it is not unusual for men and women to live for thirty years or more after they stop work. It is therefore vitally important that people make adequate provision, while they are still earning, for maintaining their standard of living after their earnings cease.

There are three broad sources of pension provision in the UK:

● state schemes

● occupational schemes

● private plans.

State schemes

The government first introduced state pension provision in 1908, with a pension of 5 shillings (25 pence) a week to people over the age of 70 whose income was less than 8 shillings (40 pence) a week. The National Insurance Act 1946 provided for pensions to be payable to employed people on retirement at age 65 (men) or 60 (women). These ages still apply today, but by the year 2020 state retirement age will have been equalized at 65 for both men and women.

This flat-rate pension, now known as the **basic state pension**, was not related to an employee's earnings. It was later extended to include self-employed people and others who have made sufficient National Insurance contributions – which basically means that they have contributed for 90% of their working life (with benefits being scaled down pro rata for lower contribution levels).

The National Insurance Act 1959 first introduced a second tier of state pensions, in which benefits were earnings-related. This was known as the graduated pension scheme, and operated from 1961 to 1975. It was replaced, as a result of the Social Security Pensions Act 1975, by the **state earning-related pension scheme** (SERPS), which came into operation in 1978.

Basic state pension

The basic state pension always was – and still is today – designed to provide little more than a subsistence-level standard of living. It is set at approximately 25% of the national average earnings level. The current (2001/2002) pension for a single person is only £72.50 per week, while that for a married couple (where the wife has not made her own National Insurance contributions) is £115.90 per week. Couples who have both fully contributed can each receive the full single person's rate.

The pension is administered on a pay-as-you-go basis, with current National Insurance contributions from the working population being immediately paid out as current pensions to those entitled to receive them. It is readily apparent that with the number of pensioners increasing and the numbers in employment decreasing, there is little scope for increasing state pensions by anything more than the rate of inflation.

SERPS

The objective of the state earnings-related pension scheme was originally to boost pension provision from 25% of national average earnings (ie the basic pension) to a level around 50%. Like the basic pension, it is funded on a pay-as-you-go basis, a system that is coming under increasing cost pressures. This has resulted in a scaling-down of prospective benefits, which are determined by a complex formula, and there is every likelihood of further reductions in the future.

The government has announced plans to replace SERPS with effect from 2002, with a new scheme, the **Second State Pension** (or S2P). Though initially on an earnings-related basis, it will change to a full flat-rate basis after about five years.

Unlike the basic pension, SERPS is available only to employed persons who are paying Class 1 National Insurance contributions. Self-employed people cannot be members of SERPS. In fact, employed people are obliged to be in SERPS unless they contract out, or are contracted out by their employer on the basis of membership of the employer's pension scheme. Contracting out is permitted only if the employer, or the individual, provides acceptable alternative pension provision. If an employer runs a contracted-out pension scheme, the employer, and employees who are members, pay a reduced level of National Insurance contributions. If an employee contracts out individually, full contributions are still paid but a rebate is given in the form of a transfer to his or her alternative pension arrangement.

Occupational schemes

Employers often establish pension schemes for some or all of their employees. A good scheme is generally viewed by management as a means of attracting and retaining quality staff. It is, however, no longer permitted for employers to make membership of their scheme a condition of employment, and employees can make their own private arrangements if they wish.

Employers, on the other hand, do not generally contribute to private arrangements, whereas they often contribute substantial amounts to their own schemes. As a broad guide, it is therefore generally recommended that employees should join, or remain in, their employer's scheme if one is available.

From 2001 onwards, employers with 5 or more employees, who do not provide an occupational pension scheme, must make a **Stakeholder Pension** scheme available to their employees. (See Chapter 4).

Revelations that people had been wrongly advised to leave their employer's scheme, and take out personal pensions, lie at the heart of the pensions mis-selling scandal which surfaced during the 1990s.

Most occupational schemes, unlike the state schemes, are not run on a pay-as-you-go basis. They are run on a **funded** or **advance funding** basis, which means that contributions are invested and build up into a fund from which it is expected that future pensions will be paid whether or not contributions are still being received at that time. This is necessary because it cannot be known for certain whether any particular employer will continue in business, so the future flow of contributions cannot be guaranteed.

The only exception to this is found in the Civil Service pension schemes, which are on a pay-as-you-go basis. The reason why it is considered acceptable in that case is that the government is the one employer of whom it can be safely assumed that it will continue to operate.

Within the concept of advance funding, there is a further distinction that needs to be understood:

- **Final salary schemes:** These are schemes in which the pension benefits payable are based on a proportion of the final remuneration, the actual proportion being related to the length of an individual's membership of the pension scheme. It is the employer's responsibility to ensure that sufficient contributions are made to meet the promised benefits.

- **Money purchase schemes:** In this case there is no fixed pension benefit. Agreed contribution levels are paid by employers (and possibly employees) into a fund that is invested to produce lump sums which will be available at employees' retirement dates. The level of pension that is received depends on:

  - The amounts contributed by employer and employee.

  - The success of the investment of the contributions.

  - The rate of return available when using the final lump sum to purchase a pension for life (the annuity rate).

  Money purchase schemes have gained popularity with employers in recent years, because they encompass a fixed commitment, whereas the benefit payable from a final salary scheme can depend on factors beyond an employer's control, such as inflation.

Because the government is keen to encourage people not to rely on state pensions, there are a number of tax incentives for occupational pension schemes (and similar incentives also apply to private pension provisions). These include:

- Tax relief on an employee's contributions at his or her highest rate of tax;

- Corporation tax relief on an employer's contribution;

- Exemption from capital gains tax on scheme investments;

- A tax-free lump sum can generally be taken on retirement.

In view of the tax benefits offered, it is not surprising that the government imposes restrictions on how much money can put into, and taken out of, pension schemes. These rules are administered by the Pensions Schemes Office of the Inland Revenue (PSO), which is the organization responsible for the approval of occupational schemes for tax relief purposes. The rules are complex, but the following examples will give an idea of their nature:

Contributions

- Employers must contribute to the scheme (at least 10% of the total of contributions). There is no direct maximum limit on employers' contributions, but they may be restricted as the result of other rules.

- Employee contributions are not a required element of pension scheme design, and schemes where only the employer contributes are known as non-contributory. There is, however, a maximum level of employee contribution, which is 15% of remuneration, up to a remuneration limit known as the **earnings cap**. This cap was set at £95,400 in 2001/2002, and is normally increased annually in line with inflation.

Benefits

- Maximum allowable pension is 2/3 of final remuneration, with eligible remuneration again limited by the earnings cap. The definition of final remuneration is flexible enough to allow for variable earnings.

- Maximum allowable tax-free lump sum on retirement is 150% of final gross remuneration, subject to the earnings cap.

- Maximum total dependants' pensions in the event of death before retirement is 2/3 of the pension that would have been payable if the employee had retired on the date of death.

- Maximum **death-in-service** life cover is four times gross remuneration at date of death, plus return of the employee's contributions.

Private pension plans

Employees who are not members of an occupational pension scheme (either because the employer does not provide one, or because they choose not to join, or are ineligible to join) have no provision for retirement other than the basic state pension and SERPS, unless they make their own arrangements. The situation is worse for self-employed people, who would have only the basic state pension.

For individuals in these categories, there is the facility to contribute to their own pension arrangements through personal pension plans (PPPs) and stakeholder pensions. PPPs were introduced by the Finance Act 1986, and have been available since July 1988 as a means by which individuals can contribute in a tax-efficient way to their own retirement funding. Stakeholder pensions became available from April 2001. Personal pension plans and stakeholder pensions are offered by most insurance companies as well as many banks, building societies, friendly societies and unit trust managers.

Details of both these plans are included in Chapter 4.

Additional voluntary contributions (AVCs)

It has been estimated that less than 1% of all occupational pension scheme members will obtain the maximum permitted benefits. There are various reasons for this, the most common being:

- Their employer's scheme provides benefits that are less than the maximum allowed (for example, if pensions are not based on full gross remuneration).

- Changes of employer have reduced their overall entitlement.

Occupational scheme members whose prospective benefits are below the permitted maximum are entitled to make further personal contributions to an arrangement designed to make up the shortfall, and (within specified limits) to have those contributions dealt with in the same tax-efficient manner as other approved pension arrangements.

Such contributions are known as additional voluntary contributions (AVCs), and since April 1988 it has been obligatory for company pension schemes to provide facilities for employees to pay AVCs to the scheme. These may be money purchase contributions building up to a fund with which to buy extra pension at retirement, or they may be used to purchase additional years' entitlement under a final salary arrangement.

There are, of course, limitations on how much additional contribution an employee can make:

- The contributions must not be such that they lead to the individual's overall pension benefits exceeding the maximum permitted levels.

- The individual's total contributions (ie AVCs plus employee contributions to the basic scheme) must not exceed 15% of gross remuneration, with an overall maximum of 15% of the earnings cap (£95,400 in 2001/2002).

Free-standing additional voluntary contributions (FSAVCs)

The Finance Act 1987 enabled employees to purchase benefits in addition to those from their occupational scheme without participating in the employer's AVC scheme. This is achieved by means of a free-standing additional voluntary contribution scheme (FSAVC) supplied by a separate pension provider. FSAVCs are available from a range of financial institutions, including insurance companies, banks and building societies.

This facility appeals to employees who prefer to keep their financial arrangements as far as possible private from their employers, and to those who would like to have more direct control over the way in which their pension contributions are invested. All FSAVCs are money purchase arrangements, and individuals can choose which fund or funds to use from the range offered by the pension provider.

As with employers' in-house AVCs, an employee's total contributions (FSAVC plus main scheme) must not exceed 15% of his or her net relevant earnings, subject again to the earnings cap. As an additional guard against over-funding, where an individual's gross contributions to an FSAVC scheme exceed £2,400 pa, the FSAVC provider must check – in conjunction with the employer – that overall benefits will not exceed permitted limits. This is known as a headroom check.

2.13 Estate Agencies

The majority of vendors (sellers) of residential property in England and Wales appoint an estate agent to act for them in relation to the sale. In Scotland, solicitors have traditionally carried out this role, and many solicitors south of the border have also now expanded into estate agency.

An estate agent acts, in legal terms, as the agent of the vendor and not the purchaser, although he may choose to advise both parties on matters where a conflict of interest does not arise.

An estate agent's basic task is to bring the property to the market either by private treaty or by auction. Private treaty refers to the more common practice in which a vendor seeks offers from prospective purchasers and chooses what he considers to be the most attractive offer: this is often the highest offer, but may not be so due to other factors such as a purchaser's need to sell his or her own property.

An estate agent's work on behalf of a client normally includes the following stages:

- Assessing the property's market value, and agreeing an asking price with the vendor. Some estate agents are also qualified surveyors (for example F.R.I.C.S.).

- Preparing publicity material, and advertising the property. Following the Property Misdescriptions Act 1991, estate agents must take great care not to mislead potential purchasers, because selling agents are now liable for fanciful sale particulars that are subsequently found to be exaggerated or untrue.

- Accompanying prospective purchasers to view the property (in some cases).

- Receiving offers and keeping the vendor informed as to the current state of interest in the property. As a consequence he or she may also advise the vendor regarding an appropriate price to accept.

- Receiving offers and negotiating with prospective purchasers.

- Liaising with the vendor's solicitors to progress the formal sale of the property.

Estate agents are usually paid on a commission basis, expressed as a percentage of the sale price (typically 1.5% – 3%). Some estate agents charge a flat fee. Solicitors with an estate agency arm may charge a combined rate for selling the property and carrying out the conveyancing and other legal work involved. Many estate agents also offer other property-related services such as letting and property management, and survey and valuation services.

Although estate agents are, of course, working for the vendor, it is clearly in their interest to provide the purchaser with any assistance that might facilitate the sale! It is, therefore, not unusual for them to be involved in arranging mortgages and insurance policies related to the sale – which also provide additional income in the form of commission. Another way of looking at the same situation is to observe that every house sale carries with it the potential for the sale of mortgage finance, life assurance, investments, general insurance, and a range of other ancillary services. For that reason, a number of large financial services groups invested heavily in the late 1980s in estate agencies, and re-branded them under their own names. Unfortunately this turned out to be a disastrous move for many of them, because it was followed almost immediately by a severe and prolonged slump in the housing market, leaving them with an expensive asset generating very little income.

The trade body for estate agents is the National Association of Estate Agents.

2.14 Stockbroking and Share-dealing Services

Stocks and shares are the major means by which joint-stock companies and public bodies in the UK raise capital. Companies can issue both types of security, whereas publicly owned bodies can issue stocks but not shares:

- Stock represents a fixed quantity of a company's issued capital or of a public authority's borrowings. Stockholders normally receive interest from the company or body, until the capital is repaid on a specified date; they are creditors and not owners of the bodies they lend to.

- Shares represent the equal parts into which a company's issued capital is divided, and shareholders receive dividends, which are their entitlement (in proportion to the size of their shareholding) from the company's distributable profits. Unlike stock, shares are a permanent source of funding, ie they do not normally have a redemption date. A company's ordinary shareholders are in fact the owners of the company, and are entitled to influence the way in which the company is run by voting at company meetings.

Details of shares, and other stock market investment, from the investor's point of view, are given in Chapter 4.

The London Stock Exchange

The London Stock Exchange is the main marketplace in the UK where stocks and shares are bought and sold. It comprises both a primary and a secondary market.

A **primary market** is one through which organizations can raise new capital by offering newly created stocks or shares for sale to the public and to financial institutions.

- The government is the largest issuer on the Stock Exchange, and issues its securities in the form of gilt-edged stocks.

- New companies can raise capital for their planned operations by means of a **flotation** on the Stock Exchange.

- Existing companies that are already quoted on the Stock Exchange can raise additional cash by means of a **rights issue**, which gives every existing shareholder the right to buy new shares in the company. Companies can also raise long-term funding by the issue, for example, of loan stock.

- Some previously state-owned businesses, such as British Telecom, have been privatized by means of an offer of shares.

A **secondary market** is a place for buying and selling existing securities.

- It is necessary because shareholders who wish to cash in their investments cannot sell their shares back to the company which issued them; the money is simply not available, having been used in the development of the business. Similarly, stocks are normally repaid only at a specified date – or some may, like shares, be irredeemable. The only way in which investors can cash in their investments is, therefore, to sell them to other investors.

- This facility is an essential element in the overall picture of public and commercial financing for, in the absence of an accessible and active secondary market, it would be very difficult to raise finance on the primary market. It is not an exaggeration to say that the success of the primary market depends upon the existence of an active secondary market.

The Stock Exchange was established in London in 1773 to provide a market for buying and selling securities. Two-and-a-quarter centuries on, it still provides a very similar market, though on a much larger – and international – scale, and with a much wider range of securities catered for.

The London Stock Exchange is one of a number of exchanges worldwide, other well-known ones being in the USA, Japan, Germany and Hong Kong. Because of the nature of world time zones, the London markets have opening times that overlap the same trading days in New York and Tokyo, and the rapid advance of electronic communications has effectively enabled continuous 24-hour trading to become a reality.

In addition to its role as a marketplace, the Stock Exchange also performs a number of other functions which help to smooth the financial activities of commerce and government. These include:

- **Investor protection:** The Stock Exchange indirectly ensures a limited level of protection for investors, in that the presence of a company's shares on the Stock Exchange's official list implies that the company is believed to be reputable. If there is any doubt about the conduct of a company, permission to deal in that company's shares may be withdrawn.

- **A measure of economic progress and prospects:** The Stock Exchange publishes prices of stocks and shares, enabling investors to keep track of the value of their investments. Certain groups of these published prices are combined together to give a general indication of the level of the market and the direction in which it is moving.

The FTSE

Stock Exchange indicators act as a sort of barometer of economic and commercial progress. The official indices which track the Exchange's bond and equity markets are managed by FTSE; this was established in 1995 and is jointly owned by London Stock Exchange plc and by the Financial Times Limited. The UK series of indicators is designed to measure the performance of the major capital and industry segments of the UK market. It comprises 12 separate indices, the best-known of which are:

- **The FT-SE 100 Share Index:** Perhaps better known (for obvious reasons) as the Footsie, this index – as its name suggests – is based on prices of the 100 largest companies by value. It was introduced in 1984 to provide a more broadly-based indicator and is calculated on a real-time basis throughout the day.

  The list of 100 companies changes from time to time, and attainment of a place on the list is an achievement that all major companies strive for and to retain.

- **The FSE 250** which is a real-time benchmark for medium-sized UK companies, consisting of the 250 next largest companies after those in the FTSE 100.

- **The FTSE 350** is a combination of the FTSE 100 and the FTSE 250 indices.

- **The FTSE All-Share Index** which is the principal benchmark for UK portfolio performance and which covers the three segments (large, medium and small) of the UK series. It is also calculated in real-time.

Share indices can also be used as a means of assessing the relative performances of investment fund managers. In recent times there has been much debate about the merits of active fund management as against passive management (where the fund manager simply invests in a tracker fund, which tries to match the composition of a particular index).

Organization of the Stock Exchange

The Stock Exchange is not a public body; it is a private organization, owned by its members. They own the shares which provided the capital to establish the organization, purchase the site, develop the buildings, install the systems, etc.

Prior to 1986, there were two classes of Stock Exchange members, and members were required to be either one or the other:

- **Stockbrokers:** When individuals and institutions wanted to buy or sell shares they approached a stockbroker, who would act as their agent and arrange the deal for them, charging a commission for the service. A fixed scale of minimum commissions was imposed by the Stock Exchange.

● **Jobbers:** The actual trading in securities was carried out by jobbers, who bought and sold on their own account, making a profit out of the difference between buying and selling prices. They were not allowed to deal directly with the public.

The catalyst for change in the UK stock exchange was the so-called May Day Revolution in the USA in 1975, when stockbrokers' commissions were de-regulated. The need for the UK stock market to follow suit was immediately recognized, and the Restrictive Trade Practices (Service) Order 1976 was introduced. It was, however, a further ten years before any dramatic change took place.

In 1979 the Office of Fair Trading ruled that the Stock Exchange's requirement for its members to use a fixed scale of commission was not in the best interests of the public. Gradually the Stock Exchange bowed to government pressure, and in 1983 it agreed to phase out fixed commission rates. This led in 1986 to what was known as the **Big Bang,** in effect a huge updating and upgrading of the structure, procedures and systems used for trading securities.

The main features of the Big Bang were:

● Fixed commissions were abolished, leading to greater competition between dealers in securities and the likelihood of a better deal for investors. In fact the general level of commission rates is now about half what it was prior to the Big Bang.

● There are now three categories of Stock Exchange member:

(a) **Agency brokers:** They act as the client's agent and arrange deals by taking an order and contacting a market maker (see below) to complete it – very much as stockbrokers did in pre-Big Bang days. Agency brokers are free to negotiate commission rates with their individual clients, according to the volume of business expected and other marketing-related factors.

Clients often use agency dealers rather than going direct to market makers, because the broker is able to obtain quotes from a number of market makers and choose the best deal for the client. In fact brokers are obliged, under the best execution rule introduced by the Financial Services Act 1986, to obtain the best price available for the client.

(b) **Market makers:** They hold stocks in their own name and make profits by correctly anticipating market price movements and buying and selling shares accordingly. Some market makers specialize in a particular type of share, for example, pharmaceuticals.

They are obliged to make a **continuous market** in the shares in which they have chosen to deal (in other words if asked to sell a certain share which they do not hold, they must still execute the order. If the market maker is short of the shares, he or she may borrow shares from an inter-dealer broker).

(c) **Broker-dealers:** They can carry out all the instructions given by a client, acting as agency brokers and market makers. To ensure that this does not work against the client's interest (for instance if a broker dealer held stock that a client was seeking, and sold it without ascertaining whether other market makers were offering it cheaper), the broker-dealer must check prices on SEAQ (see below) and may only use his or her own stock at better than the best price being offered.

At the same time as the Big Bang, a new computerized information system was introduced, known as SEAQ (Stock Exchange Automated Quotations). Market makers feed into the system the prices at which they will deal in particular stocks and shares, and brokers can access the SEAQ screens to see who is offering the best price for the shares they are seeking to buy or sell. SEAQ enables the prices of securities to become available worldwide simultaneously.

Market makers have to report deals to SEAQ, and these are also displayed on the screens.

The floor of the Stock Exchange – the area where all trading used to be done in person – is no longer used. Instead, business is done by telephone, based on the information available on the computer screens. It was felt that electronic trading should be accompanied by a paperless settlement system. The system that was developed – Transfer and Automated Registration of Uncertified Stock (Taurus) – was intended to reduce the need for handling share certificates on the Stock Exchange. Taurus acted as a clearing house by making book changes in ownership of securities and then confirming these to traders. Taurus, however, was not a success and was abandoned in 1993, following which a new system known as CREST was developed.

CREST is managed by a company set up for the purpose (CRESTCo). It is (in CRESTCo's own words) 'an electronic settlement system for corporate securities in the UK and Ireland, which enables participants to hold securities in uncertificated form and transfer them in real time with effective delivery versus payment'.

This means that market makers can buy and sell shares through a system of pooled nominee accounts. This has obvious advantages from a trading viewpoint, but does distance a client somewhat from his or her portfolio – although shareholders can choose to have share certificates rather than be involved in the CREST system. CREST settles around 200,000 transactions daily in up to 16,500 different securities, with a daily value of £200 billion.

Chinese walls

Following the Big Bang, other financial institutions were permitted for the first time to become owners of, or hold an interest in, stockbroking and dealing firms, and many have since done so.

This situation gives considerable scope for conflicts of interest to arise within member firms, particularly in integrated firms where bankers, brokers and market makers may form parts of the same firm. A conflict of interest could arise in a take-over situation, for instance, where the banking arm of a firm would be privy to confidential price-sensitive information that would be of great interest to market makers!

To avoid such conflicts, the concept of Chinese walls was introduced. This means that, in firms where such a conflict could arise, an established arrangement must be in place whereby information known to persons in one part of the business cannot become available to persons in another part. This means that staff and management should be different, and normally the departments or firms are in different locations. Such arrangements are designed to prevent **insider dealing**. This is the use of confidential inside knowledge to profit from the buying or selling of shares before the business world is fully aware of the situation, and is a criminal offence.

New issues and listings

When a company wishes to come to the market for the first time, it normally approaches a bank to advise it on how best to carry out the process. The bank also sets in motion all the necessary administration.

The process generally begins with an accountants' report on the affairs of the company. This is a confidential report for the company, but forms the basis of the prospectus when it is issued. Following a satisfactory report, particulars for the listing are prepared and filed with the Stock Exchange Quotations Department for approval. The general and financial information that must be disclosed in listing particulars is lengthy and complex, and is designed to enable a prospective investor to make a reasonable assessment of the company's activities, financial standing and prospects.

If the issue is to go ahead, the company must agree to the continuing obligations that bind it to keep the rules of the Stock Exchange. At least two market makers must have agreed to make a market in the shares, and the application must be supported by a sponsoring stockbroker.

The main methods by which an official listing may be obtained are as follows:

- **Offer for sale:** This is the most common method. The securities are purchased from existing shareholders by an issuing house, which in turn offers them to the public at a slightly higher price. Potential investors submit applications for shares: some offers are oversubscribed, in which case a form of allotment of shares is chosen, and some money is returned to some or all investors.

  If an offer is undersubscribed, the issuing house will have arranged for underwriters to purchase any shares for which applications have not been received. Underwriters – who are often banks but could be other investment institutions – are paid a commission of around 1.5% of the value of the shares they underwrite, whether or not they do purchase any shares.

- **Offer for sale by tender:** Similar to the above, but investors are required to submit tenders stating the price at which they would take the shares and how many they would want. If the share issue is oversubscribed, priority is given to those investors who tendered the highest price. This method was used by the government for the second BP privatization issue.

- **Placing:** The issuing house sells the shares privately to a range of its own clients and other investors. This method has the attraction of being administratively much simpler, and therefore less expensive.

- **Introduction:** This method may be permitted for a company that is not listed but already has a wide spread of shareholders – and wishes merely to obtain the facility for shares to be traded on the Stock Exchange, rather than to raise fresh capital.

AIM

In addition to the main Stock Exchange, there is a market on which the shares of certain smaller firms can be traded. This is the Alternative Investments Market (AIM), which came into operation in 1996, replacing the Unlisted Securities Market (USM).

Membership of AIM provides a valuable way of raising capital for young companies or for those too small to obtain a full listing. It can also raise the profile of the company, and provide a useful stepping stone from which it could later apply for a full Stock Exchange listing, perhaps by means of an introduction (see above).

A number of football clubs are listed on AIM, and a few – for example Manchester United plc – have a full Stock Exchange listing.

2.15 Financial Services Subsidiaries of Retail Organizations

The deregulation of the financial services market, from the mid-1980s onwards, brought with it the opportunity for organizations not previously active in that market to diversify into it.

A number of large retail groups have set up subsidiary organizations to offer financial products. Their initial aim was to provide facilities that would increase the retail sales of their normal product ranges, but organizations soon realised that financial services could generate profits in their own right.

For example, Marks and Spencer began the trend in the 1980s when they introduced their Chargecard; this operates in the same way as other credit cards such as Mastercard and Visa, and is clearly designed to encourage sales in their stores by providing a deferred payment method. At the same time, of course, the card provides a profit opportunity for

Marks and Spencer Financial Services, because interest is charged on monthly balances that are not paid within a certain period. In addition, the system provides marketing opportunities, because promotional material can be mailed to cardholders with their monthly statements. Marks and Spencer have since expanded into a range of financial services, including life assurance, pensions and unit trusts. For some years, Marks and Spencer refused to accept any credit card other than its own; this policy obviously contributed to the loss of sales the company has been suffering from and it has been reversed so that the store now accepts any generally acceptable credit or debit card.

Mainstream supermarket chains such as Sainsbury and Tesco (through the Royal Bank of Scotland) have established their own banking operations, offering savings and payment facilities. Such organizations are able to tap into a large base of regular customers, and can use the financial facilities as one of their devices for building up customer loyalty, while also making a profit from the diversification of product.

Banks and building societies have responded by considering how to make their products less formal and more accessible – but have not as yet as yet started selling groceries and clothing from their high-street branches! However, some banks have set up ATMs at the supermarket branches.

2.16 Trade Bodies and Associations

Within the financial services industry, as in all walks of life, people and organizations with things in common tend to group together for mutual assistance and protection.

A number of trade associations have sprung up over the years, the principal purpose of which is to represent the interests of their members to the government, the regulatory bodies and other organizations with a view to influencing policy development and legislative decisions. They are also concerned to an extent with consumer protection and they exercise some control over the way in which their members operate through the publication of codes of conduct and codes of practice (this aspect of their role is covered in Chapter 3).

We have already mentioned these trade associations in the relevant sections above. The main ones are described below, although the list is not exhaustive.

Association of British Insurers (ABI): The ABI is the trade association for insurance companies and represents virtually the whole of the UK insurance company market. It has around 450 members who between them transact over 96% of the business of UK insurance companies.

The ABI represents its members to government, parliament, civil servants, regulatory bodies and a number of other organizations, including some in the European Union. It provides its members with information on such things as technical matters, investment, training standards and accounting practice.

It promotes public understanding of insurance matters by contacts with the media and consumer bodies, and also provides classroom resources to schools in support of National Curriculum topics.

The Association of Friendly Societies is the official representative body for UK friendly societies. It represents the collective interests of its members to government and regulators and provides a public voice on matters of interest to the societies.

British Bankers Association (BBA): Founded in 1919 as a trade association for banks whose main business was in the UK, the BBA's role was broadened in 1972 to encompass all banks and discount houses operating in the UK. It is a member of the European Banking Association.

The BBA played a major role (along with the BSA – see below – and the Association of Payment Clearing Services) in the development of the Code of Banking Practice, which came into effect in 1992. The code, now known as the Banking Code, sets out standards for good banking practice by listing 11 key commitments that banks should make to customers about the way in which they provide their products and services.

It is the leading trade association in the banking and financial services industry representing banks and other financial services firms operating in the UK. It has 295 members as well as many associate members, which fund its not-for-profit activities. 85% of members provide wholesale banking services and 75% are of non-UK origin, representing 60 different countries. The BBA covers a wide range of European and international issues such as the prudential regulation of firms and the operation of international capital markets. It is closely involved with domestic UK concerns, such as the provision of basic bank accounts and promoting financial inclusion.

Building Societies Association (BSA): The BSA is the trade body for the UK's building societies. Dating back originally to 1869, it was established in its present form in 1936. Membership is open to any permanent incorporated building society, registered in the UK, which satisfies the authorization requirements of the Building Societies Act 1986 as amended by subsequent legislation. It acts as a central representative body for its members, putting the industry's views to government, the media and other interested bodies, and it provides information to its members.

The BSA has been closely involved over the years in negotiations with the Building Societies Commission (BSC) over all aspects of the regulation of building societies, including the increased scope of societies' permitted activities following the 1986 Act. It will continue this process with the Financial Services Authority, which took over the BSC's regulatory role in 2001.

The BSA monitors changes not only in building society legislation, but also in many other pieces of relevant legislation affecting the provision of the wide variety of financial services that societies can now offer – and it reports to its members on the impact of any such changes. In its advisory role, the BSA has also drafted model rules and memoranda to assist societies in their adoption of proper procedures.

In 1988, when diversification into new areas was becoming common in financial services, the BSA began to look at the possibility of representing a wider number of institutions operating in the housing finance field. As a result of this initiative, supported by the Association of British Insurers, the Finance Houses Association and others, the Council of Mortgage Lenders came into being in 1989.

Council of Mortgage Lenders (CML): The CML is the trade association for mortgage lenders in the UK. It has 134 members, including banks, building societies and other residential mortgage lenders, who together account for about 98% of residential mortgage lending in the UK. It also has 58 associate members who have an interest in the housing market. It represents the interests of its members to a range of relevant bodies.

It works closely with the BSA in representing the views of mortgage lenders to the Treasury, the Financial Services Authority, the Inland Revenue, the Land Registry and other relevant organizations.

The CML has issued a code of practice originally called the Mortgage Code, which sets out the standards to which mortgage lenders that subscribe to the Code must adhere. This Code came into force in July 1997. Details of the Code are given in Chapter 3.

Finance and Leasing Association is the trade body of finance companies (see Section 2.5) which represents the UK's asset finance and consumer credit sectors (including the financing of vehicles and other assets). It is the principal voice and self-regulator of the asset finance and consumer credit industries. Full members include banks, finance house subsidiaries of banks and building societies, independent finance companies and the finance arms of manufacturers and retailers. Full members provide consumer credit and finance, instalment finance or asset finance including leasing. Associate members are firms of lawyers, accountants, data providers, software houses and others who supply services to the asset finance and consumer credit industries.

The FLA influences the regulatory and legal framework in the UK and Europe. It undertakes work on issues of importance to members concerning financial, regulatory, accountancy, taxation, legal and commercial matters.

The National Association of Pension Funds is the principal UK body representing the interests of the occupational pensions movement. Its members include both large and small companies, local authorities and public sector bodies which together provide pensions for more than 7 million employees and 4 million retired people and account for more than £650 billion of pension fund assets. NAPF members also include businesses that provide professional services to pension funds such as consultancy, actuarial, legal, trustee, administration, IT and investment services.

NAPF leads the debate on pensions and campaigns on issues such as taxation, legislation and regulation, and aims to ease the administrative and financial burden on employer-sponsored pension schemes to ensure their continued success.

The National Association of Estate Agents has around 10,000 members and is the leading professional body in estate agency.

3

REGULATION OF THE FINANCIAL SERVICES INDUSTRY

3.1 Introduction

The latter part of the twentieth century saw a strong assertion, in Western societies, of the rights of the consumer. Although some people believe that this trend – notably in the USA – has gone too far, there is a general acceptance that protection for the consumer is both necessary and appropriate.

One of the primary objectives pursued by most modern governments is the establishment of an economic and legal environment in which a balance is established between the need for businesses to make a profit and the rights of customers to receive a fair deal. This has led to the regulation, to some degree, of most industries in the UK.

At the same time, governments wish to preserve confidence in the monetary system and to protect the creditors of financial institutions. And, because it deals with money – a vital common denominator both in the lives of individuals and in the national economy – the financial services industry has become perhaps the most regulated business sector of all. With the establishment by the government in April 1998 of the Financial Services Authority, and the passing of the Financial Services and Markets Act 2000, there is no sign of a slowing down in the trend to greater supervision of the industry.

Although governments try to foresee problems and to introduce legislation as a means of 'prevention rather than cure', it remains true that most regulatory legislation in the past has been reactive rather than proactive. Legislation has often resulted from:

● Particular scandals or crises: many such events have arisen over the years, from the crash of the Liberator Building Society in the 1880s to the events surrounding the Bank of Credit and Commerce International and the collapse of Barings Bank in the 1990s.

● An increase in consumers' financial awareness and a demand for a more customer-focused business approach: for instance, demands for a 'one-stop-shop' approach to financial services sales was instrumental in the move to deregulation of banks and building societies.

- The need to respond to changes in lifestyle: for instance, more relaxed attitudes to marriage and divorce in recent years have led to a strengthening of the rights of divorcees to share in former spouses' pension benefits.

- Developments in business methods: technological advance in particular has fuelled many changes in the last years of the twentieth century and the early part of the twenty-first; this is particularly true for banks and building societies, whose customers now can and do carry out many of their transactions electronically.

- Innovation in product design: rapid expansion has been seen in the ranges of certain products, particularly in mortgage products and in the derivatives market.

3.2 Government Policy

Government policy on the regulation of the financial services industry in the UK has, since the late 1970s, displayed what might at first glance appear to be something of a paradox. There have been specific moves in what seem to be two opposite directions:

- In some areas, **deregulation** as been the key development;

- At the same time, other parts of the industry have become more closely **regulated**.

This is not, however, the contradiction it may seem to be, because the aims of both developments have been to benefit the consumer through greater choice, better service and stronger protection.

Deregulation

Deregulation was experienced mainly in the worlds of banking and building societies. The Wilson Committee, which presented its findings in 1980, concluded that both banks and building societies were being prevented by existing legislation from operating in markets where genuine needs for their services existed. For example:

- Traditionally, banks were not active in the mortgage market because government credit controls had severely restricted their lending activities, while at the same time the increase in home ownership was creating a huge demand for mortgages.

- Similarly, building societies – operating under legislation which dated in some cases from as far back as the nineteenth century – were restricted to lending on mortgages and to offering simple personal savings products. Their research, however, had shown that their customers would be willing to buy a much wider range of banking products, such as unsecured loans, from them if societies were permitted to market and sell them.

The building societies established their own investigation by the Spalding Committee, which reported on the specific areas in which societies felt they could provide useful services if they were allowed to do so.

The deregulation which was introduced in the 1980s was designed to remove these barriers, enabling institutions to broaden their services and to move into new markets. The relevant changes were introduced largely through the Building Societies Act 1986 and the Banking Act 1987, both of which are described later in this chapter.

The increased competition was beneficial for customers, who, in addition to having a much wider choice of both products and providers, saw a reduction in the cost of many products.

Regulation

At the same time, it was beginning to become apparent that the rather haphazard collection of legislation by which the investment, savings and insurance industries were regulated was failing to provide customers with adequate protection against incompetence or fraud. For instance:

- Although the Insurance Companies Act 1982 had introduced rules regarding the authorization of life assurance companies, and their accounting procedures and solvency margins, it did not address the ways in which life assurance and investment products were sold.

- Similarly, although the Policyholders' Protection Act 1975 provided a form of compensation for policyholders in the event of an insurance company becoming insolvent, very little protection was available for those who put their money into other forms of investment.

The situation had been highlighted by a number of high-profile business collapses and prosecutions, some of which involved investment advisers who had accepted money from clients on the pretext of investing it on their behalf, but had in fact used the money for their own purposes.

The result was that in the mid-1980s a new and comprehensive set of regulations was developed, covering life assurance companies and other providers of investment products, as well as those who sell, or give advice about, investment products. The system, introduced by the Financial Services Act 1986, was based on the concept of **self-regulation**, with each part of the industry – although ultimately responsible to the Treasury – expected to monitor its own success in meeting the terms of the legislation, and to administer a system of penalties for failure to do so. The costs of compliance (ie systems to ensure adherence to the regulations) added considerably to the administrative costs of product providers and financial advisers.

By the mid-1990s, it was becoming clear that the self-regulation aspects of the system had not been wholly successful; and that led to the establishment of a single regulator, the Financial Services Authority (FSA), with regulatory responsibility for the whole of the financial services industry.

Full details of the power and responsibilities of the Financial Services Authority under the terms of the Financial Services and Markets Act 2000, and its relationship to other regulatory bodies, are included later in this chapter.

The regulatory framework

Regulation of the financial services industry in the UK is, broadly speaking, a four-tier process:

- **First level:** The Acts of Parliament that set out what can and cannot be done. Whenever reference is made in these notes to Acts of Parliament, it should be borne in mind that the effects of the laws are often achieved through subsidiary legislation – known as statutory instruments – which are made pursuant to the Act. These instruments, which are numerous, are not mentioned specifically in these notes.

  Examples of legislation that directly affects the industry are:

  – The Financial Services and Markets Act 2000;

  – The Banking Act 1987;

  – The Building Societies Act 1997.

- **Second level:** The regulatory bodies which monitor the regulations and issue rules about how the requirements of the legislation are to be met in practice. The main regulatory body is now the Financial Services Authority, which has taken over the regulatory responsibilities of a number of other bodies, including, for example:

  – The Bank of England;

  – The Building Societies Commission.

- **Third level:** The policies and practices of the financial institutions themselves, and the internal departments that ensure they operate legally and competently. For example:

  – The Compliance Department of a life assurance company.

- **Fourth level:** The arbitration schemes to which consumers' complaints can be referred. For example:

  – The Financial Ombudsman Service;

  – The Mortgage Code Arbitration Scheme;

These various components of the regulatory system are discussed in more detail later in this chapter.

3.3 The Role of the Bank of England

The Bank of England (often referred to simply as the Bank) was founded by a group of wealthy London merchants in 1694 and later granted a Royal Charter by William III. It developed a unique relationship with the Crown and Parliament, which was formalized in 1946 when it was nationalized and became the UK's central bank.

A central bank is an organization that acts as banker to the government, supervises the economy and regulates the supply of money. In the United States, for example, these tasks are the responsibility of the US central bank, which is known as the Federal Reserve. Within the Euro-zone of the European Union, the role of central bank for those states that have accepted monetary union is taken by the European Central Bank (ECB).

The level of independence of central banks varies from country to country. In the UK, the Bank of England has always worked closely with the Treasury on a range of economic matters. Since May 1997, however, the Bank has had a more independent role in the control of the UK economy, because the government has transferred to the Bank the responsibility for setting the level of interest rates in the UK.

A central bank may also act as supervisor and regulator of the country's banks and banking systems. This role was carried out in the UK by the Bank of England until 1998, when the responsibility was transferred to the Financial Services Authority (FSA).

The Bank of England has a number of important roles within the UK economy. Its main functions are:

- **Issuer of banknotes:** The Bank of England is the central note-issuing authority, and is charged with the duty of ensuring that an adequate supply of notes is in circulation.

  This function should not be confused with any action the Bank may take to control money supply as part of overall monetary policy. Notes and coins form only a very small proportion of the money supply.

- **Banker to the government:** The government's own account is held at the Bank of England. The Bank provides finance to cover any deficit by making an automatic loan to the government. One way of raising funds to finance the government's spending is through gilt-edged securities (see below). If there is a surplus, the Bank may lend it out as part of its general debt management policy.

- **Banker to the banks:** All the major banks have accounts with the Bank of England, for depositing or obtaining cash, settling clearing, and other transactions. In this capacity the Bank can wield considerable influence over the rates of interest in various money markets, by changing the rate of interest it charges to banks that borrow or the rate it gives to banks that deposit.

  Every authorized bank has to maintain at least one particular account with the Bank of England (clearing banks must maintain two, as explained below). Neither of these accounts earns any interest, this effectively representing the cost for being authorized. The accounts are:

– A non-operational account (for all banks): this is a deposit that cannot fall below a specified ratio (0.3% in 2001) of the authorized bank's eligible liabilities (essentially its deposits).

– An operational account to be used by clearing banks in the settlement of clearing.

● **Adviser to the government:** The Bank of England, having built up a specialized knowledge of the UK economy over many years, is able to advise the government and help it to formulate its monetary policy.

The Bank's role in this regard has been significantly enhanced since May 1997, with full responsibility for setting the base rate in the UK having been given to the Bank's Monetary Policy Committee (MPC). This committee meets once a month and its mandate in setting the base rate is to ensure that the government's inflation targets are met.

● **Foreign exchange market:** The Bank of England manages the UK's official reserves of gold and foreign currencies on behalf of the Treasury. It can influence the value of the pound in the foreign exchange markets by using foreign currency from its Exchange Equalization Account. For instance, if the pound is falling rapidly, the Bank can use foreign currency to buy sterling; the effect of this should be that the increased demand pushes up the price.

● **Lender of last resort:** The Bank of England traditionally makes funds available when the banking system is short of liquidity, in order to maintain confidence in the system. It does so mainly by dealing in the 'gilt repo' market. Under this system, banks, building societies and securities firms effectively sell gilt-edged stocks to the Bank, entering into a legally binding contract to repurchase equivalent gilts from the Bank on a specified date at a pre-determined price. Gilt repo is therefore a form of loan with gilts used as security. The rate of interest charged by the Bank is determined by the repurchase price in relation to the sale price – and it is through this mechanism that the Bank is able to influence the level of interest rates charged by the banks (and hence influence the state of the economy).

This process should not, however, be thought of as something that happens only when the banking system is in difficulties; the Bank acts almost daily to iron out shortages of liquidity, which can occur for all kinds of reasons. An example might arise on or around those dates in the year when people pay their tax bills: the banks' operational deposits are debited and the government's account is credited, so removing funds from the banking system. In general, this works in such a way that the banks have, on most days, a prospective shortage of funds. The Bank of England is then able to supply those funds (largely through gilt repo) at a rate of interest which it chooses – and thus can determine the level of interest rates generally.

In addition to the functions described above, the Bank of England was formerly charged with responsibility for the supervision and regulation of those institutions that make up the banking sector in the UK. This responsibility was transferred to the Financial Services Authority with effect from 1 June 1998. Details of this role and of its transfer to the FSA are included later in this chapter. However the Bank maintains its traditional responsibility for maintaining the stability of the financial system as a whole.

Management of the gilt-edged security market: The Bank of England was also formerly responsible for managing new issues of gilt-edged securities. This function has now been transferred to the Debt Management Office within the Treasury, in order to avoid conflicts of interest that might arise from the Bank's new responsibility for setting interest rates.

Gilt-edged securities, also known as **gilts**, are loans to the government. There is a wide variety of loans on different terms and for varying periods, including some with no fixed redemption date.

These securities are called **gilt-edged** because the income and the redemption amount are guaranteed by government.

Gilts are an important element of the investment spectrum, particularly for institutions such as life assurance and pension funds which are looking for secure longer-term investment. Further details of gilts from an investor's point of view are included in Chapter 4.

3.4 Banking Legislation

Before 1979, there had been no formal legal definition of what constituted a bank. This was an unsatisfactory state of affairs, because it meant that virtually anyone could set up in business to take deposits, with little or no requirement to safeguard customers' funds. That situation was rectified by the Banking Act 1979, the main purpose of which was to protect depositors' money through supervision of the institutions.

The Act set out certain criteria that an institution had to satisfy in order to be recognized as a bank by the Bank of England (and subsequently by the FSA). To be recognized as a bank, an institution had to:

● provide a wide range of banking services or a specialized service;

● have a high reputation in the financial community.

The clearing banks, discount houses and other major banks met these requirements. Most other institutions were required to obtain a licence from the Bank of England (by meeting certain financial requirements) before they could take deposits from the public.

There was also a third category – exempt institutions – for organizations considered to be adequately covered by other existing legislation (notably building societies).

In summary, the main consequence of the Banking Act 1979 was that an institution could not accept deposits from the public unless it was a recognized bank, a licensed deposit-taker or an exempt institution.

The Banking Act 1987

By the late 1980s, particularly following the collapse of Johnson Matthey, the authorities felt that the 1979 Act needed refining and updating in certain respects. This led to the introduction of the Banking Act 1987, which built on the 1979 Act and formalized several features of regulation.

One development in terminology was that recognized banks and licensed deposit-takers under the terms of the 1979 Act became known as authorized institutions. Only they and the exempt institutions are allowed to take deposits.

The authorization requirements of the 1987 Act are detailed below.

Capital adequacy

Broadly speaking, institutions must have sufficient capital to make it very unlikely that deposits will be placed at risk. Although a bank's lending is generally financed by deposits, any losses made (for instance if a loan is written off) should be borne by shareholders rather than by depositors. Minimum requirements for capital adequacy are therefore set, in order to protect a bank's depositors.

A bank's capital base is usually made up of three elements:

- **Tier 1 capital:** (also known as core capital): This comprises shareholder's equity and accumulated profits verified by auditors. Tier 1 capital must be at least 4% of risk-weighted assets. (Risk-weighted refers to a system, introduced by the EC Solvency Ratio Directive, of assigning different weights to different categories of a bank's assets according to relative risk. For example, cash is weighted at 0%, Treasury Bills at 10% and personal loans at 100%.)

- **Tier 2 capital:** (or supplementary capital): This includes general provisions against unidentified future losses, and medium- or long-term subordinated debt. (Subordinated debts are loans to a company provided typically by shareholders or a parent company; they rank behind other debts if a company is wound up, and would therefore normally receive a higher interest rate.) Tier 1 and Tier 2 capital together must be at least 8% of risk-weighted assets. In practice banks always keep more than the required 8%.

- **Tier 3 capital:** This includes certain other forms of subordinated debt, as well as profit arising from the bank's trading book. (The trading book relates to investment activities as distinct from a bank's more traditional activities such as loans and more liquid assets such as gilts, which are referred to as the banking book.)

Large exposures

Institutions are required to avoid putting all their eggs in one basket and risking losses if a particular customer should be unable to meet its commitments.

The 1987 Act requires large exposures to be reported, and the FSA takes the view that no individual customer's business should exceed 10% of the capital base without proper justification – and only in the most exceptional circumstances would exposure to one party or group of over 25% be acceptable.

The FSA also requires institutions to report their exposures to individual market sectors (eg manufacturing) and to individual countries, although no specific maximum levels have been set for these.

Liquidity

Banks never hold enough ready money to meet all their obligations at once, but they must maintain confidence that deposits can be repaid on demand. They are expected to maintain sufficient liquidity (cash and near-cash assets such as gilts) to meet cash withdrawals as they are required. This also means matching known future requirements with expected receipts, and also maintaining sufficient liquidity to meet unexpected demands.

There is no common liquidity requirement for all institutions. The FSA discusses with each institution its particular circumstances and sets appropriate levels accordingly. In practice, banks are encouraged to hold a wide range of liquid assets, and also to have a wide range of depositors.

Provision for bad debts

If an institution does not make adequate provision for bad or doubtful debts, it will overstate the value of its loans and therefore exaggerate the adequacy of its capital base.

Here again the FSA does not set the precise level of provision that must be made by each institution, but requires that it be shown to be adequate in the institution's particular circumstances.

Systems and controls

All institutions must have adequate systems for record-keeping, monitoring and control of transactions, to ensure that assets are safeguarded and commitments maintained within the management's defined limits.

They are required to commission **reporting accountants** to monitor systems and controls and to report on a regular basis. This task is usually carried out by the external auditors.

Directors and managers

Anyone occupying a senior position with an authorized institution, such as director or manager, must be acceptable to the FSA as a **fit and proper person to hold that office**. The FSA sets out statements of principle as to how it will interpret the term fit and proper, and the relevant qualities include competence, diligence and sound judgement.

Range of services

Institutions authorized under the terms of the 1987 Act (see also Section 2.3) are expected to offer all of the following facilities to customers:

● current and/or deposit account facilities to personal and/or corporate clients;

● loans and/or overdraft facilities;

● foreign exchange facilities;

● finance for foreign trade;

● financial advice to personal and corporate customers;

● investment management facilities;

● purchase/sale facilities for securities in sterling and foreign currencies.

The 1987 Act also restricted the use of the word bank in the name of an institution. In order to call itself a bank, an institution must be authorized as a deposit taker and have minimum capital of £5 million.

Other important provisions of the Act include:

● The power to veto undesirable take-overs of authorized institutions.

● Authorized institutions must notify the FSA of any loans to a single customer which exceed a specified percentage of their capital.

● Auditors of authorized institutions are required to disclose relevant information to the FSA.

The 1987 Act also addressed the question of investor protection by establishing a Deposit Protection Board to administer the already-established Deposit Protection Scheme. This scheme provided a fund from which it repaid individuals 90% of the first £20,000 in the event of the collapse of a bank. The fund was financed by levies from the authorized institutions. From December 2001, the Deposit Protection Scheme was replaced by the

Financial Services Compensation Scheme which, in the event of the collapse of a bank or building society, compensates the customer by an amount up to 100% of the first £2,000 plus 90% of the next £33,000 (ie a maximum of £31,700).

The Bank of England Act 1998

This Act came into force on 1 June 1998, and its effect was to transfer responsibility for supervision of the banking sector in the UK from the Bank of England to the newly-formed Financial Services Authority (FSA). The Bank of England was to continue its traditional responsibility for maintaining the stability of the financial system as a whole. This move was the first stage of the government's plan to bring together 'under one roof' the supervision and regulation of all aspects of financial services.

In taking over this role, the FSA took on the responsibilities for regulation and supervision which were placed originally on the Bank of England by the Banking Act 1987. It has stated that its primary aim will be to strengthen the protection of investors, although it stresses that it cannot ensure protection. Indeed, its statutory objectives include the aim of securing an 'appropriate' level of protection for consumers, allowing for the fact that consumers have different levels of knowledge and skill but should take some responsibility for their decisions. The meaning of the word 'appropriate' remains somewhat subjective, and this is likely to become a contentious area.

In order to become or to remain authorized by the FSA, a banking institution must satisfy the FSA that its business is conducted in a prudent manner. The main requirements to be met are explained above under the heading The Banking Act 1987.

3.5 Regulation of Building Societies

Building societies are mutual institutions owned by their members. They are subject to a wide range of statutory regulation, including the Financial Services Act 1986, the Data Protection Act 1998 and the Consumer Credit Act 1974.

In addition to this more general legislation, they have, since as far back as the nineteenth century, been subject to specific building society legislation. For example:

- The Building Societies Act 1874 was passed in response to the findings of a Royal Commission which recommended controls to regulate the two thousand or so societies active at the time.

- The Building Societies Act 1894 was in response to the crash in 1892 of the Liberator Building Society.

- The Building Societies Act 1939 introduced measures to clarify the validity of certain types of lending arrangement.

- The Building Societies Act 1960 introduced controls over corporate lending, effectively restricting societies largely to residential lending.

- The Building Societies Act 1962 consolidated those earlier Acts into one statute, and for over 35 years societies were subject to a highly restrictive regime which effectively confined them to making secured loans to members for property purchase, and raising funds for this purpose from members in the form of deposit accounts or shares.

The trend to deregulation, described earlier in this chapter, resulted in the passing of the Building Societies Act 1986 and led to fundamental changes in the activities of building societies.

The Building Societies Act 1986

This Act, which came into force on 1 January 1987, significantly expanded the powers of building societies, enabling them to diversify into new areas of business and to compete on more equal terms with retail banks.

The overall status of building societies remained unchanged. They were to continue to be mutual organizations owned by their investing and borrowing members, although the rights and powers of investors remained much greater than those of borrowers (a situation later rectified by the Building Societies Act 1997).

The fact that societies remain mutual organizations is an important factor in determining what restrictions are imposed on their lending. Their shareholders are depositors whose capital is expected to be secure, rather than equity shareholders (in a company) who are aware that the value of their capital investment could fall. The majority of societies' lending therefore remains on a strongly secured basis (ie mortgages – see below).

The 1986 Act repealed previous legislation, apart from a few sections of the 1962 Act. These, too, were later replaced by a Code of Practice.

Although the scope of societies' activities was greatly expanded, Section 5(1) of the 1986 Act requires that the principal purposes of a building society should still be accepting retail funds and making loans secured on residential land. This means that:

- At least 50% of the funds raised by societies had to be from the retail savings market (the Act originally stipulated 60%, but this was later amended to 50%).

- At least 75% of commercial assets had to be held as loans secured by first mortgage of an owner-occupied residential property (the Act originally stipulated 90%, but this was later amended to 75%.). Other loans secured on property can account for up to 25% of the total, while unsecured loans, together with investments in property or in subsidiaries, cannot exceed 10% (these two figures were originally 10% and 5%, respectively).

The Act automatically conferred on building societies certain basic powers, and other powers could be adopted by special resolution. The automatic powers were those that enable a society to carry out its mainstream business, and include the following powers:

● To raise funds by shares and deposits;

● To make loans secured on residential land;

● To hold land and premises for the purpose of conducting its business.

The powers that could be adopted cover a range of non-mainstream business, and include the power to make loans secured on land overseas, to make unsecured loans, and to offer a variety of financial products.

Schedule 8

Section 34 of the 1986 Act gave effect to the deregulation which societies had been seeking, by giving them the power to provide a range of financial services, which were listed in Schedule 8 to the Act.

However, it soon became clear that the practical effect of Schedule 8 was not at all what had been expected. The Schedule set out a detailed specification of those activities that were now permitted, but this turned out, paradoxically, to be rather restricting in practice, simply because things that were not specifically included could not be offered. For instance, it had been anticipated that Schedule 8 would permit societies to issue credit cards and to offer deposit pension plans, but this proved not to be so.

The Building Societies Commission and the Treasury quickly recognized and accepted that there was a problem, and instigated a review of the Schedule in October 1987. The result was that Schedule 8 was effectively replaced in its entirety, through the issuing of a series of new Orders in 1988.

The replacement was in fact contained in Schedule 5 of the Building Societies (Commercial Assets and Services) Order 1988, but the fundamental deregulation which the 1986 Act introduced is still commonly referred to as **Schedule 8**.

The revision was designed to avoid the technical difficulties from which the initial approach suffered, by setting out broadly defined powers and then listing any specific services which societies would not be allowed to provide.

The broad spread of services that could be offered was listed under six main headings. These are shown below, together with a few examples of typical services covered by each definition:

Banking services

● Deposit taking

- Loans other than mortgages
- Leasing and hire purchase
- Money transmission and cheque clearing
- Safe-deposit facilities

Investment services

- Unit trusts
- Pension management
- Portfolio management

Insurance services

- Life assurance
- General insurance
- Insurance broking and advice

Trusteeship

- Family trusts
- Corporate trusts
- Pension fund trusts

Executorship

- Arranging wills
- Acting as executor
- Administering estates

Land services

- Estate agency
- Surveys and valuations
- Conveyancing

Regulation of building societies

Section 1 of the Building Societies Act 1986 established the Building Societies Commission

(BSC) as the regulator of all registered building societies. The Commission, which was a corporate body accountable to the Treasury, also has a general supervisory and advisory role.

With effect from December 2001, the responsibilities of the Building Societies Commission were taken over by the Financial Services Authority (FSA). In order to ensure a smooth transition, many of the staff of the BSC were transferred to the FSA.

The FSA will continue to carry out the main functions of the former Building Societies Commission. These include:

- to promote the protection of investors' funds;

- to promote the general stability of building societies;

- to ensure that building societies fulfil their principal purpose (ie to provide loans secured by first mortgages on owner-occupied residential property, funded by the savings of individual members);

- to advise the government on building society matters.

In order to carry out its responsibilities, the Commission was given a range of powers, which the FSA will now be able to apply, including the power to:

- authorize societies and impose restrictions for continued authorization;

- advise on the purpose of societies;

- intervene in the event of a breach of the limits set down for assets and liabilities;

- control societies' advertising;

- deal with certain complaints and disputes.

These powers could be employed, for example, if it were learned that a society had taken on business in the new areas of activity beyond the limits laid down. The FSA could then require the society to initiate a restructuring that would bring its assets and liabilities back within the statutory limits.

Societies would generally approach the Commission for an opinion before launching any innovative scheme or product. This avoided the expense and embarrassment of having to withdraw it if the Commission ruled that it was beyond the society's powers. This approach will continue to be encouraged under the FSA, whose aim is to regulate where possible in a proactive rather than a reactive manner.

Capital adequacy

Financial institutions hold reserves to serve as a buffer in the event of loss and to encourage confidence in investors. All banks, licensed deposit-takers and building societies are required to hold specified minimum levels of reserves, or capital, to ensure that the interests of their customers are not compromised.

A deposit-taking institution needs capital for three main reasons:

- To meet expected or unexpected difficulties, for instance pressure on the interest-rate margin between deposits and lending, and to cover any losses due to bad debts.

- To avoid systemic risk, where the collapse of one financial institution could result in a 'domino' effect, with others also collapsing. This risk was illustrated by the banking crisis in Asia in the late 1990s.

- To provide a buffer against any difficulties experienced in offering other financial services either directly or through a subsidiary. This aspect became of greater significance following the deregulation introduced by the 1986 Act.

Capital adequacy requirements for building societies are determined by the Financial Services Authority (FSA) based on views originally set out by the Building Societies Commission in a Prudential Note in 1987. Historically, a flat-rate reserve requirement had been customary, but in the more sophisticated financial environment of today, it is acknowledged that appropriate levels of capital adequacy depend on how risky are the activities an institution carries out.

For instance, it is generally true for banks and building societies that the capital reserve required for mortgage loans is only half as much as the requirement for unsecured loans.

The FSA – using the BSC's original definitions) – actually defines two measures of capital requirement for each building society:

- **Minimum acceptable capital:** The level of capital, based on current business levels, below which a society would be at risk.

- **Desired capital:** Higher than the minimum level, this is the capital requirement that should be used when planning and budgeting – for instance when deciding whether to extend the range of activities of the society.

The pace of change in the business areas of building societies led the Commission – and later the FSA – to set two different levels of adequacy for the new types of activity: there is generally set an initial higher capital adequacy requirement for new societies (of which there are now very few) or for those gaining experience in new fields of operation, with a lower figure being allowed when sufficient experience has been gained. These two levels should not be confused with the two measures of capital adequacy described in the previous paragraph.

The Building Societies Act 1997

By the early 1990s, it was felt that the 1986 Act, despite the amendments and extensions that had been made to it, remained too restrictive to permit building societies to develop as they wished. Consequently, the government instigated a review of building society legislation in 1994, which culminated in the passing of the Building Societies Act 1997.

This new legislation does not replace the 1986 Act, but makes a number of important amendments to it.

The main purpose of the 1997 Act was to finally remove the prescriptive regime and replace it with a permissive regime. A building society can now pursue any activity permitted by the terms of its own memorandum (except for a few specified activities, mainly related to stock market trading and market making). It must, however, still have as its principal purposes the lending of funds on residential property and the accepting of investments from individual members:

● As regards a society's lending, this means that loans on residential property must still make up at least 75% of a society's assets. Residential property is now defined as being land which is at least 40% used for dwellings, and loans on residential property that is let can now also be included.

● Similarly, societies must still be funded substantially (at least 50%) by the savings in the form of shares held by individual members. Funds can be accepted from corporate bodies as deposits and loans, but not in the form of shares.

The 1997 Act also introduced changes in other areas:

● **Regulation:** the relevant regulator (at the time the BSC and later the FSA) was given powers to deal with a situation in which a building society does not comply with those restrictions that still remain under the new regime, for instance failure to stay within the lending or funding limits. The FSA can insist that such a society prepare a restructuring plan to remedy the failure or to take steps to cease to be a building society and become a company.

● **Accountability:** The Act increased the accountability of societies' boards to their members. One effect of this was to give members who are mortgage borrowers broadly the same voting rights as are enjoyed by investing members.

● **De-mutualization:** a number of measures were introduced to further protect members' interests in the event of a society changing its status to that of a bank.

Changes were also made to the rules under which an institution that was formerly a building society is protected from take-over for five years after its conversion. This protection is removed if over 75% of the shareholders vote to do so, or if the institution itself takes over another financial institution.

3.6 The Cheques Act 1992

Despite the trend to electronic payment methods, cheques are still a significant method of paying for goods and services, with around twelve million being processed through the UK clearing system every day.

Customers know that a cheque is basically an instruction to their bank to transfer some money from their account to another person's (or organization's) bank account, but most customers are unaware of the technicalities of how the system works, and therefore unaware of the protection which it does, or does not, offer them.

It may be useful, therefore, to begin with one or two definitions:

- A cheque, in the absence of indication to the contrary, is a **negotiable instrument**, which means that ownership of it passes to anyone who receives it in good faith and for value.

- A cheque is a form of **bill of exchange**, so we must first define a bill of exchange: this is an unconditional order in writing from (and signed by) one person (the **drawer**) to another (the **drawee**), requiring the drawee to pay on demand or on a fixed date a sum of money to another party (the **payee**), or to his order or to the bearer.

- A cheque is a bill of exchange payable on demand on which the drawee is a bank, the drawer is the person writing the cheque and the payee is the person specified as such on the cheque.

In the past, cheques were often received, in payment for goods or services, by people who did not themselves have bank accounts. If such a cheque was open (ie not crossed), it could be presented by the holder for payment at a bank counter. Crossed cheques cannot be presented for cash payment, but have to be paid into a bank account, thereby causing a problem for anyone without an account.

The nature of cheques as negotiable instruments, however, meant that such people could generally transfer the cheque to another person (who did have a bank account) in exchange for cash, having first endorsed it by signing it on the reverse. There was, as a result, a largely undocumented cheque-cashing market operating through corner shops, pubs and garages. Although the system provided a useful service, it was open to abuse, providing no real protection against the fraudulent exchange of, for example, stolen cheques for cash.

Cheques are sometimes crossed as not negotiable. This does not mean that the cheque cannot be transferred – it means that a person receiving the cheque cannot have (or pass on) a better title than the person from whom he received it. In the event of one defect in title (eg a cheque being stolen), all subsequent holders will not have good title.

The most recent development aimed at reducing the risk of cheque fraud was introduced by the Cheques Act 1992. The effect of this was that cheques which are crossed account payee (with or without the word 'only') become non-transferable instruments. In other words, they can be paid in to a bank only for the credit of the person named on the cheque as the payee.

3.7 The Financial Services Act 1986

The enormous increase in the volume of investment business during the 1960s and 1970s highlighted the fact that existing legislation was outdated and provided inadequate protection for investors.

Government concern led to the publication in 1984 of the Gower Report, which recommended sweeping changes and a much stricter regulatory environment. Many of the report's recommendations were incorporated in the Financial Services Act 1986.

The Act defined the types of investment affected by the legislation, and set down regulations about the way in which investment business must be conducted. Its main objective was to protect private investors from any people in the business of selling or advising on financial services who do not have the necessary skills or, worse still, may attempt to exploit or defraud the investor for financial gain.

The scope of the Act

The Act covered the activities of many individuals and organizations who:

- provide financial products, eg life assurance companies;

- sell financial products, eg financial advisers;

- deal in investments, eg stockbrokers;

- give advice on financial products, eg financial advisers;

- manage investment funds, eg pension fund managers.

Some of these individuals/organizations and their activities were already covered by elements of existing legislation. For example:

- Independent insurance brokers were regulated by the Insurance Brokers (Registration) Act 1977, but this did not cover other types of adviser, such as direct sales forces.

- The Prevention of Fraud (Investments) Act 1958, which was largely an amalgamation of pre-war legislation, had proved inadequate to deal with a now more sophisticated and competitive industry.

Not all investment products were covered by the Act, the main exceptions being the deposit and lending services of banks and building societies, which were considered to be adequately covered by their own existing legislation, and National Savings products. Tangible assets such as antiques and stamp collections are also excluded from the definition of investments within the meaning of the Act.

The main investment products regulated under the terms of the Financial Services Act 1986 are listed below (further details of financial services products are included in Chapter 4):

- Life assurance policies with an investment element: including whole of life assurance, endowment assurance, annuities.

- Pensions: including personal pensions, stakeholder pensions, executive pension schemes, additional voluntary contributions (AVCs) and free-standing AVCs.

- Company shares and loan stocks: including preference shares and convertibles.

- Futures, options, rights issues and other interests in shares.

- Collective investment schemes such as unit trusts and investment trusts.

- Personal equity plans (PEPs) and individual savings accounts (ISAs) except cash ISAs.

- Gilt-edged securities and similar local authority investments.

It can be seen that these are all products that could lead to an investment gain or loss, depending on a variety of factors including the quality of investment decisions, the length of time for which the investment is held, or the performance of the national or world economy. Even gilts, which are guaranteed by the government to be repaid on maturity, are included because buying and selling before the maturity date can result in a capital loss.

Overall responsibility for ensuring that the financial services industry complied with the terms of the Financial Services Act 1986 was given to a newly-established regulatory body, the Securities and Investments Board (SIB), although in practice, the SIB never regulated many businesses itself. It became in effect a powerful umbrella organization, presiding over the establishment, development and working practices of a number of independent subsidiary bodies known as Self-Regulatory Organizations, or SROs.

As their name suggests, these SROs authorized and regulated their own member firms. They were the Personal Investment Authority, regulating financial advisers and others who advise on and sell life assurance, pensions and investment products, the Investment Management Regulatory Organization, covering fund managers and portfolio managers, and the Securities and Futures Authority, which regulated firms involved in the stock markets.

The regulatory structure established under the Financial Services Act 1986 remained in place until December 2001, when the Financial Services and Markets Act 2000 came fully into force, and the Financial Services Authority became the sole regulator for the UK financial services industry.

Many of the regulations which came into force under the auspices of the 1986 Act form the basis of the regulatory regime which commenced in December 2001. This is described in the next section.

3.8 The Financial Services and Markets Act 2000

Although the regulatory regime introduced by the Financial Services Act 1986 – together with related measures such as the training and competence standards – went a considerable way towards meeting its main objectives, there was a growing feeling through the 1990s that the overall structure was still too fragmented for the increasingly integrated world of financial services in the UK. For example, many of the large banking groups were regulated by a number of different organizations, including the Bank of England and all of the self-regulatory organizations.

This led at times to confusion as to where the regulatory responsibility lay. The collapse of Barings Bank in 1992 highlighted many of the anomalies, with the roles of the Bank of England and the Securities and Futures Authority being criticized.

The Chancellor of the Exchequer announced in May 1997 that financial services regulation in the UK would be reformed again under the auspices of a single regulator, the Financial Services Authority (FSA). This new body came into existence almost immediately, and initially it was, in effect, the Securities and Investments Board under a new name. However, changes in the regulatory environment began almost immediately.

The first significant change occurred in June 1998, (the so-called N1 date) with the supervision of the UK banking sector being transferred from the Bank of England to the FSA.

To enable the transfer of regulatory power to be effected as smoothly as possible, the government introduced a draft Financial Services and Markets Bill in 1998. After a long passage through Parliament, the Financial Services and Markets Act 2000 (FSMA 2000) received Royal Assent in June 2000, and a date was set (1 December 2001 – known as the N2 date or simply N2) when the FSA would become the single regulator under the terms of the FSMA 2000.

With effect from December 2001, the FSA took over the Regulatory responsibilities previously carried out by:

● The self-regulatory organizations (PIA, IMRO and SFA);

● The Building Societies Commission;

● The Friendly Societies Commission;

● The Registrar of Friendly Societies (in relation to the regulation of credit unions);

● The Insurance Directorate of the Treasury.

The Financial Services Authority

The FSA is not a government department – it is in fact a limited company – but it does have statutory powers, given to it under the Financial Services Act 1986, the Banking Act

1987, the Financial Services and Markets Act 2000, and other legislation. The FSA Board – which makes its policy decisions – is, however, appointed by the Treasury, which has the overall responsibility for the UK financial services industry.

The scope of the FSA is demonstrated by the fact that it regulates around 10,000 organizations (largely investment firms but also including 1,000 insurance companies and over 600 banks) and about 180,000 individuals. It has well over 2,000 staff and an annual budget approaching £170 million.

The importance of having adequate safeguards for financial services customers is highlighted by the FSA's own statistics: over 80% of UK households have a bank or building society account, 70% make investments in pensions or life assurance, and over a quarter of all adults own shares directly or through unit trusts, PEPs and ISAs.

The FSA has the following statutory objectives:

- Maintaining confidence in the UK financial system (including financial markets, exchanges, and regulated activities). The aim is to ensure that markets are 'fair, efficient and transparent';

- Promoting public understanding of the financial system (including public awareness of the benefits and risks of different forms of financial transactions);

- Securing an appropriate level of protection for consumers. An 'appropriate' level may depend on:

  - the different level of risk that relates to different investments;

  - the different experience/expertise of different consumers;

  - the consumers' need for accurate advice and information;

  - the principle that consumers should take responsibility for their decisions.

- Reducing the scope for financial crime. The three main areas of financial crime which the FSA seeks to control are:

  - money laundering;

  - fraud and dishonesty, including e-crime;

  - criminal market conduct, such as insider dealing.

The FSA believes it can work simultaneously towards all these objectives, but has warned that it may sometimes have to make choices about how to strike a balance between them.

The performance of the FSA in regulating the industry will be judged against a set of 'principles of good regulation'. For instance it must be seen to be:

- allocating its resources in the most efficient and economic way;

- ensuring that the costs of regulation are in proportion to the benefits;
- taking proper account of the responsibilities of those who manage authorized firms;
- facilitating innovation and maintaining industry competitiveness;
- taking into account the international character of financial services and the UK's competitive position;
- facilitating, and not having an unnecessarily adverse effect on, competition.

Following the practice established by its predecessor the SIB, the FSA's regulatory regime is based on a set of eleven Principles for Business, from which all the more precise rules and regulations follow. They are:

1. Integrity

A firm must conduct its business with integrity.

2. Skill, care and diligence

A firm must conduct its business with due skill, care and diligence.

3. Management and control

A firm must take reasonable care to organize and control its affairs responsibly and effectively, with adequate risk management systems.

4. Financial prudence

A firm must maintain adequate financial resources.

5. Market conduct

A firm must observe proper standards of market conduct.

6. Customers' interests

A firm must pay due regard to the interests of its customers, and treat them fairly.

7. Communications with clients

A firm must pay due regard to the information needs of its clients, and communicate information to them in a way which is clear, fair and not misleading.

8. Conflicts of interest

A firm must manage conflicts of interest fairly, both between itself and its customers and between one customer and another.

9. Customers: relationship of trust

A firm must take reasonable care to ensure the suitability of its advice and discretionary decisions for any customer who is entitled to rely on its judgement.

10. Clients' assets

A firm must arrange adequate protection for clients' assets when it is responsible for them.

11. Relations with regulators

A firm must deal with its regulators in an open and cooperative way, and must disclose to the FSA appropriately anything relating to the firm of which the FSA would reasonably expect notice.

These principles, and the rules which follow from them, are contained in the FSA Handbook. This large and complex document sets out the standards, rules and regulatory processes in a number of areas, including the authorization of firms and individuals, the conduct of business rules, compliance procedures, and the processes for complaints, the resolution of disputes and compensation arrangements.

Authorization and control

Following the passing of the FSMA 2000, firms need 'permission' before they can carry out 'regulated activities' (unless they are exempt). These regulated activities are listed in a piece of subsidiary legislation, the Financial Services and Markets Act 2000 (Regulated Activities) Order 2001, and include the following:

● Accepting deposits;

● Effecting and carrying out insurance contracts;

● Dealing in and arranging deals in investments;

● Managing investments;

● Advising on investments;

● Establishing collective investment schemes;

● Establishing stakeholder pension schemes;

● Mortgage products (with effect from 31 August 2002).

Permission is given in the form of a list of the regulated activities which the firm may carry out. The relevant section of the FSMA 2000 under which permission is granted is Part IV – as a result this form of permission is often referred to as 'Part IV Permission'.

Similarly, individuals will need 'approval' before they can carry out certain functions in relation to a firm's regulated activities. These are known as 'controlled functions' and permission to carry them out is given by the FSA under Section 59 of the FSMA 2000. There are two kinds of approved persons:

- Those who carry out senior or supervisory functions, and are said to have 'significant influence' over the firm;

- Those who act in a customer-related field – typically in the role of adviser.

All approved persons must comply with four Statements of Principle in carrying out their controlled functions. They are required to:

- act with integrity;

- act with due skill, care and diligence;

- observe proper standards of market conduct;

- deal with the FSA in an open and cooperative way.

Approved persons who exercise 'significant influence' are also required to specifically comply with three other Statements of Principle, which relate to the implementation of systems, controls and compliance standards. The FSA considers this aspect of regulation to be very important: senior managers are expected to take responsibility for the effective management of firms, developing clear reporting lines and ensuring that risks are properly identified and managed. Firms are required to establish controls and reporting systems appropriate to the size, complexity and risks of the business.

The FSA will authorize only those firms and individuals who satisfy the necessary criteria (known as threshold conditions) to engage in regulated activities. These conditions include honesty, competence and financial soundness.

To ease the process of changeover to the new regulatory regime, a 'grandfathering' system was employed under which firms, persons and products that were authorized under previous legislation (such as the Financial Services Act 1986) received equivalent authorization under the FSMA 2000 without having to reapply for 'permission' or 'approval'.

An exception is made for professional firms – such as solicitors and accountants – who provide investment services only as an incidental part of (and subordinate to) their normal professional work. Such firms are exempt from regulation by the FSA provided that they do not receive payment for the service, other than from their clients (so they could not, for instance, receive commission from a life company for selling an endowment policy).

Conduct of business rules

A set of 'core Conduct of Business Rules' applied under the Financial Services Act 1986. These were rules, laid down by the FSA, which had to be incorporated in the rulebooks of all the self-regulating organizations (SROs). The SROs also developed detailed rules which applied specifically to their own membership. Many of the detailed rules for financial advisers remain broadly the same under the FSMA 2000, having been adapted and amalgamated to form the backbone of the FSA's Conduct of Business Sourcebook.

Some of the important of the rules for financial advisers are described below:

Know your customer: An adviser must not give investment advice to a client unless he has fully ascertained the client's personal and financial circumstances.

This process is carried out by the completion of a confidential client information questionnaire, commonly known as a **factfind**. The information gathered includes the following details about the client, spouse, children and other dependants:

- **Personal information:** name, address, date of birth, marital or relationship status, state of health.

- **Employment details:** occupation, employer details, income and benefits, pension arrangements.

- **Assets:** property, personal belongings, savings and investments, policies.

- **Liabilities:** mortgage, other loans, credit cards.

- **Expenditure:** household expenses, loan repayments, regular savings, holidays, luxuries.

- **Attitudes and objectives:** including attitude to investment risk.

Suitability and best advice: An adviser's recommendations must be based on the information gathered in the fact-finding process, and must be framed solely in the best interests of the client. This means that:

- No account may be taken of the commission that would be received.

- Churning is prohibited (churning is the cancellation of a client's existing product in order to replace it with a similar product for which commission is received).

Disclosure: An adviser must supply the client with sufficient information to enable him to reach a decision. This includes details of the adviser's status (see notes on polarization, below), of costs and charges, of likely maturity or cash-in values, and of the client's statutory rights.

Clients must be given certain important documents, including:

- **Terms of business letter:** All new clients must receive this document before any information is sought or advice given. It sets out the basis on which any business will be transacted, and must include a description of the adviser's status – independent or tied (see below).

- **Key features document:** This includes full details of the product being recommended, including a statement of the risk factors involved. It also includes client-specific quotations of expected future values of the product, based on growth rates determined by the regulatory body.

- **Reason why letter:** This must be issued shortly after the product comes into force. As its name suggests, it explains to the client precisely why the particular product has been recommended.

- **Statutory cancellation notice:** Sometimes known as a cooling-off notice, this reminds clients of their right to withdraw from the contract within 14 days of receiving the notice.

Polarization: One of the most important concepts introduced by the Financial Services Act 1986 was polarization. Prior to the 1986 Act, clients were often not aware whether investment sales staff were recommending the best product available in the marketplace or whether they were merely able to sell the products of one company. This problem was tackled by the concept of polarization, which means that all advisers have to be either independent or tied, and that they must make their status clear to clients before giving any advice.

- **Tied** advisers are appointed representatives advising on, and selling, the products of only one company (or group of related companies). Legally, tied agents operate as agents of the product provider to which they are tied, but they still have a responsibility to their clients to provide suitable and appropriate advice.

- **Independent** financial advisers (often known as IFAs) are intermediaries acting on behalf of the client, and are in legal terms agents of their clients. They give advice across the whole financial services market, and must select not only a suitable type of product for the client but also the most appropriate product provider.

Both types of advisers must explain to all new clients – verbally and in writing – the difference between independent and tied advice, and must state whether they are independent or tied.

By the end of the 1990s it was becoming clear that the polarization regime was no longer the ideal way of protecting the customer against the danger of 'commission bias' (ie the tendency of advisers to recommend products which pay larger commissions). In fact situations were arising in which polarization seemed to be against the customer's interest.

In March 2001, the polarization rules were modified, to introduce a 'half-way house' between tied and independent. This allows tied agents, whose product provider does not offer stakeholder pensions, to recommend another provider who does – so-called 'multi-tied' agents.

In January 2002, the FSA issued a consultation paper (no. 121: 'Reforming Polarization – Making the Market Work for the Consumer') which signalled the end of polarization by suggesting that the status of advisers should simply be a matter of disclosure to the customer. Those advisers wishing to be considered truly 'independent' would have to negotiate a fee-paying arrangement with clients (though they could rebate commission to offset this). The rules preventing product providers from taking large stakes in adviser firms would be removed. At the time of going to press, these suggestions remain the subject of heated debate throughout the industry.

Training and competence

The competence of financial services staff at all levels in all organizations is of paramount importance, and depends to a large extent on the quality of the training and development which they receive.

The FSA has published a Training and Competence Sourcebook setting out rules and guidance for firms in the attainment and maintenance of the competence of employees. Firms must ensure that employees become and remain competent for the work they do, by regularly reviewing competence and by appropriate supervision.

The sourcebook sets out detailed rules for the training and competence of:

● financial advisers and those who deal in or manage investments;

● 'back office' supervisors who oversee certain administrative functions.

It is a firm's responsibility to assess an employee's competence before permitting him or her to carry out activities regulated by the FSA. This means that:

● the employee must be assessed as competent to carry out the activity without supervision;

● the employee must have passed an appropriate approved examination (for instance, the main appropriate examination for financial advisers are the Financial Planning Certificate (FPC) and the Certificate for Financial Advisers(CeFA)).

Firms must maintain records showing how employees' competence has been and is being assessed. All records relating to training and competence of individual employees must be retained for at last three years after they leave the firm – for pension transfer specialists, records must be kept indefinitely.

Money laundering

One of the FSA's statutory objectives is to reduce financial crime. A significant area of this responsibility relates to the prevention of money laundering, which is the process of filtering the proceeds of criminal activity through a series of accounts or other financial products in order to give it an apparent legitimacy or to make its origins difficult to trace.

Legislation to deal with money laundering was first introduced in the Criminal Justice Act 1993, which required all firms and individuals authorized under the then-current legislation (ie the Financial Services Act 1986) to:

- establish accountabilities and procedures to prevent money laundering;

- educate their staff about potential problems;

- obtain satisfactory evidence of identity for transactions over ECU 15,000 (about £10,000);

- report suspicious circumstances;

- refrain from alerting persons being investigated (this is considered particularly important, and failure to comply can lead to criminal prosecution and possible imprisonment).

These regulations have been continued and reinforced under the FSMA 2000. In particular:

- Firms must appoint a Money Laundering Reporting Officer, who must be a person of 'appropriate seniority'. This officer must report to the firm's senior management at least once a year on the firm's compliance with the rules.

- Firms must ensure that their procedures are up-to-date, reflecting any findings published in reports by the government or the Financial Action Task Force.

- In assessing a firm's compliance, the FSA will check whether the firm has followed the guidelines of the Joint Money Laundering Steering Group.

Complaints and compensation

New rules on complaint-handling arrangements were introduced by the FSMA 2000, consolidating and enhancing the arrangements under the previous regulatory regime. The rules require firms to deal properly and promptly with consumer complaints. The key requirements for firms' complaints procedures are that firms must:

- have appropriate and effective complaint-handling procedures;

- make consumers aware of these procedures;

- aim to resolve complaints within 8 weeks;

- notify complainants of their right to approach the Financial Ombudsman Service if they are not satisfied;

- report to the FSA on their complaint handling, on a regular 6-monthly basis.

The FSMA provides for a mechanism under which 'certain disputes may be resolved quickly and with the minimum of formality by an independent person'. Of course, the concept of an ombudsman, as a person or organization providing an independent facility for the resolution of complaints and disputes relating to public bodies and commercial organizations, has been with us for many years. Indeed, in the past, a number of separate ombudsman bureaux have operated in the financial services marketplace, each dealing with problems arising in a particular sector. These included the Banking Ombudsman, the Building Societies Ombudsman, and many more relating to insurance, investment, pensions and other areas.

The FSA recognized that such a fragmented system was neither helpful nor efficient, and the framework for an integrated body, the Financial Ombudsman Service (FOS), was established by the FSMA 2000.

The FOS took over from the existing financial services ombudsman schemes in December 2001, with the aim of having a single organization with a consistent set of rules to deal with complaints and disputes arising from virtually any aspect of financial services. Note that the rules mentioned here are rules about dealing with complaints – the FOS stresses that it does not make the rules under which firms are authorized, nor can it give advice about financial matters or debt problems.

Although now a single organization the FOS does acknowledge that different types of problems may arise from different areas, so it has established three different divisions within the service, namely:

● Banking and Loans Division;

● Insurance Division;

● Investment Division.

The Financial Ombudsman Service is free to customers and is open to all private individuals and small businesses. It is funded by the firms who are members of the FOS; membership is compulsory for all firms authorized under the FSMA 2000.

Complainants must first complain to the firm itself, and the FOS will become involved only when a firm's internal complaints procedures have been exhausted without the customer obtaining satisfaction.

Compensation arrangements for customers who have lost money through the insolvency of an authorized firm have been coordinated under a single scheme with effect from December 2001. The Financial Services Compensation Scheme is made up of a number of sub-schemes relating to different default situations, as follows:

● Default of an insurance company: compensation of at least 90% of the value of the policy.

● Loss due to insolvency of a firm carrying out investment business regulated under FSMA 2000: 100% of the first £30,000, plus 90% of the next £20,000 (ie a maximum of £48,000).

- Loss of deposited funds due to the default of a bank or building society: 100% of the first £2,000, plus 90% of the next £33,000 (ie a maximum of £31,700).

Claims cannot be made against the Financial Services Compensation Scheme for other losses – for instance, losses due to negligence, poor advice, or simply due to a fall in stock market values. In some cases, however, the customer may be able to sue for compensation through the civil courts.

Compliance

The FSA has stated that its approach to supervision and enforcement of compliance will be somewhat different from that of its predecessors. It intends to take a risk-based approach to supervision; this means that it will make – on an on-going basis – risk assessments of each authorized firm, making judgements about the probability of any particular risk occurring within a particular firm. This in turn will be based on the FSA's view of the firm's strategy, business risk, financial soundness, systems, controls, organization and management. The frequency and investigative depth of compliance visits by the FSA's officers will depend on this assessment of risk. Firms are also required to keep the FSA informed of anything which the FSA might reasonably expected to want to know.

When a firm is judged to have failed to comply in any way with the requirements of the regulatory regime, the FSA has a range of disciplinary powers, including:

- private warning of a firm or individual;
- public censure;
- financial penalties;
- suspension or withdrawal of authorization.

Firms that have breached regulations can also be required to compensate customers for any losses resulting.

3.9 Regulation of Mortgage Business

Specific regulation, by the FSA, of mortgage provision is not expected to be introduced until September 2002 (known as the N3 date).

However, regulation of mortgage advice and mortgage provision has been in place for some while on a voluntary basis, through the Code of Mortgage Lending Practice, now known as the Mortgage Code (see Section 3.12). Although this is a voluntary code, almost all mortgage lenders do subscribe to it.

The Code has been in force for lenders since July 1997, and it was extended to intermediaries in May 1998. Although it is voluntary for intermediaries too, most do subscribe to it, for the simple reason that lenders who subscribe to the Code will not (under the terms of the Code itself) accept business from intermediaries who do not.

Compliance with the Code is monitored by a body known as the Mortgage Board (formerly the Mortgage Code Compliance Board). Firms that are registered with the Mortgage Board are required to meet certain 'fit and proper' criteria in relation to senior staff, controllers and supervisors. These criteria are similar to those which apply under FSA authorization rules; in order to avoid duplication of administration, FSA-authorized firms will be exempt from meeting these Mortgage Board requirements.

The Mortgage Board has also introduced training and competence requirements – in particular, registered firms must ensure that, by the end of 2002, all their advisers who provide an advice and recommendation service (as defined by the Mortgage Code) have acquired an appropriate qualification. The acceptable qualifications are the Certificate in Mortgage Advice and Practice (CeMAP) or the Mortgage Advice Qualification (MAQ).

The FSA will also take steps towards an appropriate involvement in the regulation of the mortgage industry with effect from September 2002. Its draft rules have been published; their aim is to ensure that a more balanced approach is adopted towards the giving of information to customers. In particular, features that might be considered to be the more negative aspects of mortgage deals – such as redemption penalties and compulsory insurances – will have to be given greater prominence in advertisements. In addition, clients will have to be given a 'pre-application illustration', which must also give prominence to such factors as redemption penalties and fees paid to intermediaries.

It was initially suggested that the FSA's regulation would cover mortgage lending only and not advice, although lenders would be given the responsibility for ensuring that intermediaries from whom they accept business do in fact comply with the rules. This caused considerable concern within the industry, because it was feared that the system might force lenders to transact business with a much smaller number of intermediaries – thus causing a contraction in the number of intermediaries providing mortgage advice. As a result, the decision was reversed by a Treasury announcement in January 2002. It is likely that in the short term the Mortgage Code will continue to form the basis of this regulation, although in the longer term the FSA will no doubt issue its own rules.

3.10 The Pensions Act 1995

Pension provision in the UK is a complex mix of two types of state scheme, a diverse range of occupational schemes and a very wide choice of private pension arrangements. Although some aspects of occupational and personal pensions were covered by the provisions of the Financial Services Act 1986 and other legislation (and continue to be regulated under the Financial Services and Markets Act 2000), it had become clear by the early 1990s that new legislation was required to deal with a number of developments.

The Pensions Act 1995 introduced changes to several aspects of pension provision and supervision.

Security of occupational pensions

Public confidence in occupational pension scheme security had been severely dented by the Maxwell affair, where pensioners' funds were used to meet the companies' general obligations. The government sought to restore confidence with measures designed to prevent fraud and to improve the administration of occupational schemes.

Following a recommendation from the Pension Law Review Committee, the Occupational Pensions Regulatory Authority (OPRA) was created in 1996 and given overall responsibility for the regulation of occupational pension schemes.

The former OPB (Occupational Pensions Board) was abolished from 6 April 1997, and OPRA took over its role as Registrar of Occupational and Personal Pension Schemes and its responsibility to assist with the funding of the Occupational Pensions Advisory Service (OPAS).

OPRA is responsible for ensuring compliance with legislation relating to occupational schemes, operating generally in a reactive rather than proactive way. This means that although it is able to initiate investigations, and does carry out spot checks, it works primarily by investigating reports of non-compliance and acting to ensure that matters are put right.

Equalization of pension age

Currently in the UK the state pension age is 65 for men and 60 for women. EC directives require that men and women must be treated equally by pension schemes, and the UK government has decided to implement this in relation to state schemes by equalizing the retirement age at 65.

This change will be phased in between 2010 and 2020, so that women born before 6 April 1950 will continue to be eligible for state pensions at age 60, while those born after 5 April 1955 will qualify at age 65. For those born between 1950 and 1955, their state retirement age will be determined by a sliding scale between 60 and 65.

Contracting out of SERPS

Two important changes were made to the rules for contracting out of the State Earnings Related Pension Scheme (SERPS). Employed people are contracted in to SERPS (and both they and the employer pay full Class 1 National Insurance contributions) unless they or their employer choose to contract out.

The changes introduced by the Pensions Act 1995 are:

- Employers wishing to contract their staff out of SERPS through an occupational scheme used to have to ensure that their scheme provided a guaranteed minimum pension (GMP) which was equivalent to the benefits that would have accrued if members had remained in SERPS. That rule has been superseded by a new formula based on a statutory benchmark of an accrual rate of 1/80ths of final remuneration per year of service, and a retirement age of 65.

- Changes were also introduced to the system of National Insurance rebates available to individuals who contract out of SERPS by taking out a personal pension plan. A flat-rate rebate was replaced by a sliding scale giving larger rebates to those nearer to retirement age.

The purpose of this change was quite simply to encourage older people to contract out or to remain contracted out of SERPS. It is generally accepted that the costs of running state pension schemes will increase sharply as more people live longer in retirement, and governments have for some time been seeking to shift the burden of pension provision to individuals and the private sector. Recently the government took a further determined step in that direction by announcing that, from April 2002, no further contributions to SERPS would be allowed, with the scheme being effectively replaced by a new arrangement known as the Second State Pension, or S2P.

3.11 Consumer Protection and other Legislation

In addition to the legislation already described, the interests of financial services customers are safeguarded by aspects of a range of other laws and regulations. Some of these relate closely to financial services, whereas others are aimed more broadly at the rights of consumers in general.

The Consumer Credit Act 1974

The purpose of the Consumer Credit Act 1974 is to regulate, supervise and control certain types of lending to individuals, and to provide borrowers with protection from unscrupulous lenders. The provisions of the Act are regulated by the Office of Fair Trading.

There are many types of lender in the market for financial services, ranging from large multinational banks to individual moneylenders. The Act sets out standards by which all lenders must conduct their business. It includes a number of safeguards under which potential borrowers must be made aware of the nature and conditions of a loan, and of their rights and of their obligations.

The Act affects most aspects of bank lending activities, including personal loans and revolving credit such as credit cards. However, not all loans are covered by the Act:

- Loans up to and including £25,000 are regulated by the Act unless they are exempt, but those in excess of £25,000 are not.

- Loans for the purchase of a private dwelling are exempt; further loans for the improvement or repair of a private dwelling are also exempt, provided that they are from the same lender as the original mortgage loan. However, loans raised on the security of a dwelling, but used for other purposes, are not exempt.

The main elements of the Act's provisions are:

- Suppliers of loans and credit as defined in the Act have to be licensed by the Office of Fair Trading.

- Clients must receive a copy of the loan agreement for their own records.

- Prospective borrowers have a cooling-off period during which they can review the terms of the loan and, if they wish, decide not to proceed with the transaction. This applies to all loans regulated by the Act, unless the loan agreement is signed on the lender's premises.

- Undesirable marketing practices are forbidden: for instance, advertisements must not make misleading claims.

- Credit reference agencies must, on request, disclose information held about individuals, and must correct it if it is shown to be inaccurate.

- One of the Act's most significant innovations was a new system for comparing the price of lending. This is the annual percentage rate (APR) which must be quoted for all regulated loans. The APR allows not only for the rate of interest, but also for other charges involved in setting up the loan (such as legal costs and arrangement fees).

The Data Protection Act 1984

This Act provided protection for individuals in relation to information about them stored by electronic or mechanical means. Basically this meant data held on computer files; paper-based records were not covered by the 1984 Act.

All businesses which held computer-based information about individuals were required to register with the Data Protection Registry.

The Act prescribed the uses to which data could be put:

- It must be used in a lawful manner.

- It must not be used for any purpose other than that for which it is kept.

- It must not be held for longer than is necessary to complete the purpose for which it was originally obtained.

- It must not be disclosed to anyone not connected with its purpose.

Individuals have various rights related to computer-held information about themselves:

- Individuals must be given access to data about themselves on request, although it is permissible to make a charge to cover the costs of supplying the information.

- Data must not be accessible by unauthorized persons.

- Data must be kept accurate and up-to-date.

- If incorrect, data must be corrected when the inaccuracy is pointed out.

The Data Protection Act 1998

As the result of a European data protection directive, the UK government prepared this new data protection legislation, which, though dated 1998, was actually implemented in 2000.

The new Act builds on the 1984 legislation and its main data principles are based on the rules described above. However, the 1998 Act expands and strengthens the regulations in many areas, including:

- Paper-based and other manually-held information is now included.

- Data cannot be transferred outside the EU unless the country to which it is sent has adequate data protection regulations. Since the law results from an EU directive, it can be assumed that other EU states do have adequate data protection.

- Every organization must have a **data controller** with responsibility for ensuring that its systems comply with the rules. Organizations will, for instance, have to make their computer data systems secure from hackers and system faults that corrupt data.

- Data controllers have to notify the data protection commissioner on an annual basis of the types of personal data being processed and the purposes of the process.

- Individuals also have the right to be told the purposes for which data about themselves is being used, and in the case of certain types of data known as **sensitive data** (about race, sexual behaviour and physical and mental health), explicit consent to the use of the data must be obtained.

The Supply of Goods and Services Act 1982

The Supply of Goods and Services Act applies to all contracts involving the supply of services, including those for the supply of financial services. Its terms mean that, in the absence of anything specific, the following provisions are automatically deemed to be included in all such contracts:

- The service will be performed with reasonable care.

- The work will be done within a reasonable time.

- A reasonable charge will be made.

3.12 Codes and Statements of Practice

The Fair Trading Act 1973 was introduced to protect customers against unfair trading practices. It attempted to bring together the previously fragmented protection legislation by creating the Office of Fair Trading. The Director General of Fair Trading has adopted a number of approaches to promoting consumer protection: one of these is to encourage the development, by various industry groups and trade associations, of codes of practice and statements of practice.

These are a form of self-regulation, issued by the appropriate trade body as a guide to recommended practice. They may be non-statutory or they may have statutory backing (for example, some acts of parliament have provided that codes of practice should be drawn up). In either case they are not themselves law. However, if it were established that one party had disregarded a code of practice, that fact would be taken into account in any legal proceedings.

A number of codes and statements of practice are operative in the financial services industry. **Codes of practice** are voluntary statements by a trade association setting out the standards of business it expects from its members. Examples of codes of practice are:

The Banking Code

In January 1987, the Treasury and the Bank of England initiated an independent review of banking services law, which culminated in the issuing of the Jack Report in February 1989. Its key recommendation was the introduction of an element of non-statutory regulation within the bank and building society industries, in order to develop a clear and fair relationship between institutions and their customers.

The result was the Code of Banking Practice (now more commonly known as the Banking Code), drawn up by the British Bankers Association and the Building Societies Association, which came into effect in March 1992.

The aim of the code is to set out good standards of banking practice. It is not considered to be best practice: subscribers to the code can if they wish adopt different standards if they believe them to be better than those in the code.

The code relates to dealings with **personal customers**, which covers private individuals, executors and trustees, but not clubs, societies, companies, sole traders or partnerships. It covers the following products and services:

- Current accounts;

- Deposit and savings accounts;

- Cash mini-ISAs and TESSA-only ISAs;

- Card services and cash machines;

- Loans and overdrafts, but not mortgages;

- Payment systems;

- Foreign exchange transactions;

- Electronic purse.

The standards of the code are set out in ten **key commitments** which apply to the conduct of business for banking products and services. These commitments specify that banks and other organizations which subscribe to the code will:

- act fairly and reasonably in all dealings with customers;

- ensure that all services and products comply with the code;

- supply customer information in plain language, and offer help if the customer does not understand;

- help customers to understand the financial implications of products and services;

- have secure and reliable banking and payment systems;

- ensure that the procedures followed by their staff reflect the commitments set out in the code;

- deal with complaints and correct errors speedily;

- consider sympathetically and positively any cases of mortgage arrears or financial difficulty;

- ensure that all services and products comply with relevant laws and regulations;

- explain if products and services are offered in more than one way (eg branch/Internet).

The main provisions of the Code are that providers of banking services (including building societies) should:

- initiate procedures to check the identity of new customers;

- describe the terms and conditions of banking services in plain language;

- explain how variations can be made in terms and conditions, and give reasonable notice before such variations are made;

- explain to customers the basis for its charges, and publicize changes to charges and interest rates;

- establish an internal procedure for dealing with customer complaints;

- belong to an external complaints scheme, such as the ombudsman scheme;

- exercise restraint in the direct marketing of their services;

- advertise credit responsibly in accordance with all relevant laws, regulations and codes of practice;

- keep customers' information confidential;

- refrain from passing information to third parties (including related companies) without a customer's specific consent;

- provide prospective guarantors with details of their rights and obligations, and advise them to seek independent legal advice.

An independent body, the Banking Code Standards Board, is charged with the responsibility of reviewing the operation of the code at least every two years to ensure that its provisions keep up with current developments. The Board also checks on compliance with the code, and on receipt of complaints about non-compliance, takes up the matter with the bank or building society concerned.

The Mortgage Code

This code sets out the terms of the relationship between mortgage lenders and borrowers, and is designed to help borrowers to understand how lenders are expected to deal with them.

The code – published by the Council of Mortgage Lenders – came into force on 1 July 1997, and applies to all loans to personal customers secured on owner-occupied property. It does not apply to overdrafts, loans regulated by the Consumer Credit Act 1974 or the selling of investments regulated by the Financial Services and Markets Act 2000 (even where those investments are linked to mortgage repayment).

As with the Banking Code, an independent review body (the Mortgage Board, formerly known as the Mortgage Code Compliance Board) monitors compliance with the code, and reviews the code from time to time.

The standards of the code are set out in ten key commitments which apply to the conduct of business for mortgage products and services. These commitments specify that lenders will:

- act fairly and reasonably in all dealings with customers;

- ensure that all services and products comply with the code;

- supply customer information in plain language, and offer help if the customer does not understand;

- help customers to choose a mortgage appropriate to their needs;

- help customers to understand the financial implications of a mortgage;

- help customers to understand how a mortgage account works;

- ensure that the procedures followed by their staff reflect the commitments set out in the code;

- deal with complaints and correct errors speedily;

- consider sympathetically and positively any cases of mortgage arrears or financial difficulty;

- ensure that all services and products comply with relevant laws and regulations.

The Mortgage Code also contains detailed provisions relating to a range of practical aspects of mortgage lending, including:

- **Marketing:** Advertising and promotional material must be clear, fair and reasonable, and must not be misleading.

- **Mortgage choice:** To enable customers to make an informed choice they will be given full details of mortgage methods, including interest rates, tax relief, charges, the effect of early repayment, associated insurance.

- **Borrowing capacity:** Borrowers must be made aware that all lending is subject to an assessment of ability to repay, which may include credit references.

- **Charges:** A tariff of charges must be given to customers at the start of a mortgage and at any other time on request.

- **Confidentiality:** All personal information must be treated as private and confidential, and can be disclosed only with the customer's consent, except in cases where the lender is legally obliged to disclose the information.

- **Complaints:** Lenders must have specific internal procedures for handling complaints fairly and speedily. They must also belong to an independent ombudsman scheme.

Other codes and statements of practice

There are also codes of practice within other areas of financial services. For instance the Association of British Insurers (ABI) has codes relating to the selling of insurance products that are not covered by the Financial Services and Markets Act 2000.

They cover matters such as general sales principles; the need to explain the contract; disclosure of underwriting information; and how to deal with claims.

Statements of practice are voluntary agreements signed by various organizations involved in a particular industry. They offer some consumer protection, but not to the same extent as does a code of practice. Examples of statements of practice are:

- **Statement of Practice on Transfers of Mortgages:** Portfolios of mortgages can be sold by one lender to another in just the same way as other investments can be sold. This statement, adopted by many lenders, aims to safeguard the rights of borrowers when their mortgages are transferred to a third party.

  Under the terms of the statement, a lender is required to obtain a borrower's consent before his mortgage can be transferred.

- **Statement of Practice on Arrears and Possessions:** This statement, which became operative in January 1997, gives an overview of mortgage lenders' good practice when dealing with mortgage arrears and possession cases. It stresses that, since all cases are different, lenders must adopt a flexible approach and assist each borrower according to his or her particular circumstances.

  Possession of property will be sought only as a last resort when all other reasonable solutions have been explored. Lenders will not seek to take possession where borrowers have suffered a significant reduction in income but are making reasonable regular payments, nor where mortgage interest payments are covered by income support.

3.13 The Advertising Standards Authority

In addition to abiding by the rules laid down in industry-specific regulations, advertisements for financial services and financial products have to meet the standards laid down in the British Code of Advertising under the supervision of the Advertising Standards Authority (ASA).

The ASA was set up in 1962 and is an independent self-regulatory body which administers the British Codes of Advertising and Sales Promotion.

It covers all non-broadcast advertisements, ie those which appear in:

- the national and regional press, magazines and free newspapers;
- posters, hoardings and transport sites;
- direct mail leaflets, brochures, catalogues and circulars;
- cinema commercials, videos, viewdata, CD-ROMs and the Internet;
- pack promotions, competitions and prize draws.

The ASA can take action against individuals and organizations whose advertising contravenes the code. The first step is usually to discuss the offending advertisement with the advertiser, and – if an acceptable explanation is not given – to require the advertisement to be changed or withdrawn.

Details of the ASA's adjudications of complaints it has received are made public, for instance on its Internet web site. A quick look at the list of adjudications covering the financial sector shows that advertisements from many banks and other institutions have been referred to the ASA over the years. For example, one bank advertised a fixed-rate mortgage without saying that there was effectively a tie-in period for the product. A member of the public complained that this wrongly implied there was no tie-in, and the complaint was upheld by the ASA.

A number of sanctions are used against offenders, ranging from the adverse publicity generated by its adjudications to legal proceedings in the case of persistent or deliberate offenders. This legal action is available through a referral of the advertiser, agency or publisher to the Office of Fair Trading.

The Advertising Code requires that advertisements should be prepared with a sense of responsibility to consumers and society, and should respect the generally accepted principles of fair competition in business. Specifically the Code requires that all advertisements should be:

- **Legal:** Advertisements should contain nothing that breaks the law or incites anyone to do so; nor should they omit anything that the law requires.

- **Decent:** Advertisements should not contain anything which is likely to cause serious or widespread offence, judged by current prevailing standards of decency. Account is taken of the context of the advertisement, the medium used and the likely audience. Particular care should be taken with sensitive issues such as race, religion, sex or disability.

- **Honest:** Advertisers should not exploit the credulity, lack of knowledge or inexperience of consumers.

- **Truthful:** Advertisements should not mislead by inaccuracy, ambiguity, exaggeration, omission, or any other means.

   Advertisers are permitted to express opinions, including opinions about the desirability of their products, provided that it is clear that it is opinion and not a statement of fact. Assertions or comparisons that go beyond subjective opinion must be capable of being objectively substantiated.

3.14 European Legislation

Financial services institutions operating in the UK are affected by European Union (EU) legislation in a number of ways. For instance, such legislation may define the way in which regulation is applied to overseas institutions with operations in the UK, or to UK institutions transacting business in other European states. Similarly, domestic UK legislation may – in financial services as in other areas – be passed to implement directives from the European Parliament.

The European Community (EC), as it was originally known, was established by the Treaty of Rome in 1957. The founder members were Belgium, France, Germany, Italy, Luxembourg and the Netherlands. Membership now also includes Denmark, Ireland, Greece, Portugal, Spain, Finland, Austria (but not Switzerland), Sweden, and of course the UK. It was renamed the European Union following the Treaty of Maastricht in 1993.

The European Economic Area (EEA), which includes all EU members plus Iceland, Norway and Liechtenstein, came into being on 1 January 1994.

The aim of the European legislation is to increase market freedom across the EU by allowing credit institutions, insurance companies and investment firms which are authorized in one member state to carry on business in other member states without having to seek separate authorization in each country.

This aim is achieved by issuing a number of directives which are expected to be imported into each member state's domestic legislation, thereby facilitating the harmonization of regulatory standards. These directives are based on a mutual recognition of the standards imposed in the member states and an agreement on specific minimum criteria. The aim is to create a balance between the different demands of widely varied markets, thereby creating a single European market that offers customers greater choice and the benefits of increased competition.

Some examples of relevant EU directives are given below.

The Second Banking Directive

This directive was adopted in 1989 and member states were required to implement its provisions by 1993. Its purpose was to permit credit institutions to carry out in the EU any of the activities listed in the directive, provided it is permitted to carry out those activities in its home state. Member states are not compelled to allow all the listed activities, so an activity permitted in one country may not necessarily be permitted in another.

The Second Banking Directive was implemented in the UK by the Banking Co-ordination (Second Council Directive) Regulations 1992. Some of the activities listed in the Second Directive are activities also regulated by the Financial Services Act 1986, so amendments were required not only to the Banking Act 1987 but also to the Financial Services Act. Some regulations in the Consumer Credit Act 1974 were also affected.

Institutions operating directly, or by setting up branches, in another state can do so without local authorization in that state, although they are expected to conform to local conduct of business rules. If an institution wishes to set up a subsidiary in the other state, that would require authorization by the host state.

The Third Life Directive

Sometimes known as the Life Framework Directive, this was adopted in November 1992 and came into force on 1 July 1994. Its provisions were incorporated into the Insurance Companies Act 1982 via the Insurance Companies (Third Insurance Directive) Regulations 1994.

This directive introduced the concept of a single licence for insurance companies that provide life assurance, to operate across the EU while being supervised by their home state. If operating in another state, either directly or through a branch network, the regulatory authorities in the other state must be informed, but authorization and regulation remain with the company's home state, which has responsibility for monitoring companies' solvency.

In order to gain authorization, an insurance company must:

● limit its operations to insurance only;

● submit a scheme of operations;

● be run by persons of high standing;

● have a minimum guarantee fund.

Local legislation of the states in which the company operates also apply, where they relate to advertising, marketing and contract matters. Similarly, any premium taxes applied are those of the host state rather than the company's home state, and insurers must comply with local provisions for collecting taxes.

The directive covered a number of matters which required harmonization if the directive's principles were to work smoothly throughout the EU. These included:

● The types of assets that could be used to represent a company's solvency margin.

● Actuarial principles related to the calculation of assets and liabilities and the matching of assets to the type of business carried on.

● Notification to host states of policy conditions and the methods of calculating premium rates.

● Requirements for disclosure of information to the policyholder. In the UK, for instance, the **key features document** meets the requirements for information to be given to a policyholder before a life assurance policy starts.

Investment Services Directive

The Investment Services Directive (ISD) was established in May 1993 and became effective from 1 January 1996. Its aim is to enable investment firms to operate in different European states in much the same way as the Second Banking Directive and Third Life Directive broadened the markets for banks and life assurance companies, respectively.

In aiming to provide direct access to well-regulated markets across the EU, it established the following basic requirements:

● Firms that provide certain specified investment services in the EU must obtain authorization in their home state.

● Firms authorized in that way can then operate in other EU states.

● There are specified minimum standards for the prudential rules (ie about accounting, administration, record-keeping etc.) applied in the home state, and for the rules relating to conduct of business in other member states in which firms operate.

There are specified reporting requirements for all authorized firms.

The core activities to which the ISD relates are broadly similar to those under the UK's Financial Services Act, ie dealing as an agent, discretionary portfolio management and underwriting issues.

The ISD does not apply to:

● Insurance companies and friendly societies;

● Investment services provided to parent or subsidiary companies;

● Investment services that are incidental to a firm's main activity;

● Employee share schemes.

Capital adequacy ratio

The capital adequacy ratio was introduced by the Basle Committee in 1988 to ensure international banks maintain adequate capital to absorb any losses they may incur and to promote competitive equality (a 'level playing field') among them. Also by ensuring that all banks maintain adequate capital this will help to minimize the systemic risk, ie the risk that the collapse of one bank results in the collapse of other banks.

The capital adequacy ratio requires that a bank must have sufficient (Tier 1 + Tier 2) capital to match at least 8% of its risk-weighted assets.

Assets are weighted as follows;

- Cash   0%
- Gilts or other OECD government debt   20%
- Mortgages to owner occupiers   50%
- Commercial loans   100%

In addition, account must be taken of 'off-balance-sheet' items such as guarantees or foreign-exchange risks

Capital is split into two types

- **Tier 1 Capital:** Shareholders equity and disclosed reserves.

- **Tier 2 Capital:** Undisclosed reserves, revaluation reserves, subordinated debt, general provisions.

- Bank of International Settlements (BIS) regulations require that at least 50% of the capital must be Tier 1 capital.

- Banks must report their exposures under both the Banking Book (lending) and Trading book (derivatives, securities, etc).

A recent application of the capital adequacy ratio has been in determining the future of troubled banks in South Korea and Japan. Many banks in both countries suffered significant losses due to the collapse of corporate customers and resultant bad debts in the late 1990s.

In order to restore confidence in their financial systems, it will be necessary to either close banks or inject capital to meet the minimum solvency requirements. The capital ratio can be improved by selling off performing assets, merging with another financial institution or seeking government assistance.

Capital Adequacy Directive

The Capital Adequacy Directive (CAD) is complementary to the ISD and applies to the trading book of credit institutions and to investment firms that are subject to the provisions of the ISD. The trading book relates to a banking institution's investment activities, as distinct from its more traditional banking activities, such as deposits and loans, which are covered by the banking book.

The three main objectives of the CAD are:

- To protect investors in the European market.

- To establish **a level playing field** between credit institutions and non-bank investment organizations.

- To enhance the standing of the EU as a financial centre.

The CAD establishes minimum capital requirements (known as own-fund requirements) to cover market risks arising from debt, equity and related derivatives in an institution's trading book. The directive sets different levels of own-fund requirements, according to whether the institution is permitted to hold clients' money, and whether it deals on its own account and/or underwrites issues.

Market risk is divided into two areas of risk:

- **Specific market risk:** This is risk related to a particular security or issuer.

- **General market risk:** This covers wider risks such as interest-rate changes or stock-market movements.

Practical application of the ISD and CAD in the UK were implemented through the Investment Services Regulations 1995, through amendments to financial services legislation and changes to the rules and working practices of the regulatory bodies.

As an example, in relation to the recognition in the UK of European investment firms, the Financial Services Authority (FSA) will, in its capacity as host state regulator, receive notification from the firm's home state that the firm wishes to operate in the UK. The FSA then has a duty to inform the firm of the relevant laws and regulations that apply.

The FSA has powers to prohibit or restrict the provisions of investment services in the UK by a European firm if it believes that the firm is likely to contravene the UK's financial services legislation. It must first request the firm in writing to remedy the situation, and if this does not result in satisfactory action, the FSA will inform the firm's home state. Action by the FSA will then follow only if the measures taken by the home state fail.

New Basle Accord

The Basle Committee on Banking Supervision, acting under the Bank for International Settlements, published a consultative document in January 2001 with suggestions for a new capital adequacy framework to replace the 1988 Accord. The Committee wants to develop more risk-sensitive standardized and internal approaches to capital adequacy, aligning capital adequacy assessment more closely to the key elements of banking risk. This should provide banks with more incentive to enhance their risk measurement and management capabilities.

At the time of writing (early 2002), the proposals are still under discussion.

The proposed new framework will be based on three 'pillars', which will be mutually reinforcing:

- **Minimum capital requirements:** The main changes to the minimum capital requirements set out in the 1988 Accord are in the approach to credit risk and in the inclusion of explicit capital requirements for operational risk. Otherwise, the primary goal is to deliver a more risk-sensitive approach which will on average neither raise nor lower the level of regulatory capital for banks.

The definition of capital is not being changed and the minimum ratios of capital to risk-weighted assets, including operational and market risks, will remain at 8% for total capital. Tier 2 capital will continue to be limited to 100% of Tier 1 capital.

In the standardized approach to credit risk, exposures to various types of counterparties (eg banks, corporates) will be assigned risk weights based on assessments by external credit assessment institutions. This approach will be extended to internal-ratings approaches on a foundation level and on an advanced level, with banks playing a greater role in making their own assessments of the probability of default by their customers.

- **A supervisory review process:** This will ensure that each bank has sound internal processes for assessing capital adequacy based on a thorough evaluation of its risks.

- **Effective use of market discipline:** This is achieved through enhanced transparency when banks make meaningful disclosures to inform market participants of the scope of their application, the composition of their capital, their risk exposure assessment, management processes and capital adequacy.

4

THE PERSONAL FINANCIAL SERVICES MARKET

4.1 The Customers

The UK economy can be thought of as being made up of four main areas of activity: the personal sector, the public sector, the company sector and the overseas sector.

These notes will look in detail at the personal sector only. They will describe:

- the individuals and groups that make up the sector;

- the factors that affect financial needs within the sector;

- the products that can meet those needs;

- the ways in which people gain access to those products.

The personal sector includes the affairs of individuals, households, unincorporated businesses, private trusts and some private non-profit making bodies such as charities and clubs. These notes will, however, concentrate on the matters affecting individuals and their immediate households.

There is a well-established pattern to the way in which most savers and investors build up and hold their assets. It begins with savers' attitudes to the need for liquidity and safety and then, as incomes and savings grow, moves gradually away from liquidity and towards an acceptance of greater risk.

- The first stage is cash, which is by definition perfectly liquid. After that, a current account with a guarantee card is virtually as good as cash. People do not generally hold any other form of asset until their cash requirements are met.

- The next stage is secure, short-term investments such as instant access (or short-notice) bank and building society deposits.

- With a sufficient balance in short-term savings, investors look next at products with less flexibility but a greater return, such as fixed-term bonds.

- Further down the line, individuals may be attracted to products that offer greater

---

long-term potential but at the risk of short-term loss. Shares and other equity-linked investments such as unit trusts are good examples.

It is also well-established that the financial needs of individuals and families change and develop as people pass through the different stages of life. While accepting that everyone is different, there are some broad statements that can be made about a typical 'financial life-cycle':

- **School-age young people:** They may be attracted by small lump-sum or regular savings schemes, perhaps with incentives such as free money boxes. Banks and building societies are no doubt hoping to build customer loyalty from an early age by offering such schemes, but this may be largely illusory!

  It is typical for accounts to be opened for young people by grandparents or other relatives, at birth or later as birthday gifts. National Savings (including Premium Bonds) and building societies are popular homes for such savings. Stakeholder pensions can even be opened on behalf of children, from birth onwards.

- **Teenagers and students:** At this stage, few young people have any surplus income, although some who have started to work full-time or during holidays may be able to accumulate savings.

  Some may borrow to purchase a car or to fund a holiday. Many students now have to borrow to finance their college or university studies, mainly through special schemes established for that purpose.

- **Post-education young people:** The ability to save increases for those in employment, with the possibility of higher incomes as careers progress. If they establish a home of their own (often initially by renting), their savings may be modest at first.

  Some may decide to save towards a deposit for their first house purchase. Short-term accessible saving schemes are their most likely choice. Many telephone-based and Internet-based financial services are aimed at this market.

- **Young families:** Although statistics indicate that fewer young people today get married, many still form relationships and raise families. This often leads to increased borrowing, particularly for a mortgage. At the same time, income may be reduced if one partner gives up work to look after children, or alternatively outgoings may increase if a childminder is employed. Similar factors affect the growing number of one-parent families. Whatever the situation, there is often little scope for savings at this stage.

  Protection of the earners' income against illness or death becomes very important. Young people should also begin to think about pension provision, though in practice few do.

- **Established families:** As families settle into an established lifestyle, they tend to become better off financially. There may be a return to a two-income situation.

  People often trade up to a larger house, increasing their borrowing accordingly. Creditworthiness may improve, enabling greater borrowing for cars and household goods.

  This is also the beginning of the time when wealth may be increased by the receipt of inheritances from the estates of parents or other relatives.

- **Mature households:** This is generally the period of highest earning potential, and outgoings may also decrease as children leave home and mortgages may be paid off.

  At this stage, pension provision becomes a priority for many people as they begin to realize that they may not be going to have as high an income in retirement as they had hoped.

- **Retirement:** Prior to retirement, most people's financial planning is centred on converting income into lump sums (or lump sums into bigger lump sums). At retirement, when income from employment ceases, the focus changes: the requirement is now to produce income from capital.

  Other factors also become more relevant. For instance, the need to prepare for possible inheritance tax liabilities should be considered. Similarly the cost of health care, and possibly long-term care in old age, may become an issue.

4.2 The Range of Products

The financial services industry has developed products to meet all the needs likely to be encountered by individuals and families at the various stages of life.

Such products fall broadly into four types:

- Those that provide protection against the financial effects of unforeseen or unfortunate events which may befall individuals, their families and other organizations. These products are normally provided by insurance companies.

- Those that enable people to save money and invest for short-term or long-term financial goals.

- Those that are designed for the specific – and vitally important – goal of planning for an adequate income in retirement.

- Those that enable people to borrow money to make purchases they cannot afford from their current savings.

To cover such a wide range of products in great detail is beyond the scope of this book, but the main groups of products are described generically in the following sections.

4.3 Protection Products

Most people have some form of insurance to protect them against the financial effects of adversity. In some cases it is compulsory – for instance for drivers of motor vehicles on public roads. In many other cases it is wise to insure against the loss of (or damage to) items that are too valuable to replace out of normal income, such as a house and its contents.

The examples mentioned above relate specifically to general insurance; here, however, we shall discuss insurance products that fall within the overall definitions of life assurance and sickness insurance, ie those that protect against the adverse financial effects of someone's death or their longer-term illness.

Life assurance

Life assurance policies pay out a lump sum (or sometimes a series of payments) in the event of the death of a specified person who is known as the **life assured**. If there is more than one life assured on a policy, it is known as a joint life policy and it will specify whether the policy benefit (which is known as the sum assured) will be paid out on the first death, on the second death or in some other circumstance.

If a policy is taken out by someone who is not the life assured, it is known as a **life-of-another** policy. In all such cases – except where the life assured is the applicant's spouse – it is necessary to prove that insurable interest exists before the policy can commence. Broadly speaking this means that the person taking out the policy (the applicant or proposer) must prove that he or she would suffer a quantifiable financial loss in the event of the death of the life assured; and the sum assured cannot exceed that loss. An example, is a lender whose loan would not be repaid if the borrower died: in that case, the lender could insure the borrower's life for the amount of the loan.

The need for life assurance protection is found in many different circumstances. Some of the most common are:

- **Family protection:** The death of a breadwinner can leave a family with large debts and no income to support their standard of living. The surviving spouse may have to return to work, leaving young children with relatives or with a childminder. The situation may be just as severe on the death of a dependent spouse, because this could leave the breadwinner with the choice of giving up work to look after the children or meeting the expense of hiring someone to look after them.

- **Debt protection:** When a mortgage or other loan is being repaid largely from the income of one individual, the death of that individual can result in failure to make the repayments, possibly leading to the loss of any property used as security for the loan. This could, for example, leave a wife and children with the problem of finding somewhere else to live, on top of the trauma of the loss of a husband and father.

- **Tax mitigation:** In circumstances where an individual dies and leaves a substantial estate to a relative or to someone else, the recipients of the inheritance may find that they have to pay inheritance tax out of the value of the estate; the only exception to this is when the estate is left to the deceased's spouse. This can often be achieved only by selling some or all of the assets which form the estate, for instance a house. For sentimental or practical reasons, however, the recipients may be unwilling or unable to dispose of the estate's assets in order to pay the tax. A suitable life policy, of sufficient size to pay the tax, would have prevented the assets from having to be disposed of to obtain the necessary cash.

- **Business protection:** The death of a key employee could have a devastating effect on the profits of a company. Employees who fall into that category might be, for example, a charismatic managing director; a product designer; or a sales manager with a host of personal contacts. Protection against the financial consequences of losing such an employee should be part of a company's planning. Policies designed to provide this protection were originally called key man insurance, but they are now normally, and more appropriately, referred to as key person policies.

  Another work-related circumstance is the desire of business partners to be able to buy out the share of a partner who has died, without having to realize partnership assets in order to do so. In fact, a large part of the value of many partnerships, such as solicitors and accountants, is made up of that intangible asset goodwill, which takes account of the reputation of a business and its personnel; this could be realized only by selling the business as a whole – the very action the remaining partners will wish to avoid. Life assurance on each of the partners' lives can provide a solution.

Life assurance protection policies fall mainly into two categories: whole of life assurance and term assurance.

Whole of life assurance:

The sum assured is payable on the death of the life assured whenever that death occurs. The policy therefore has no fixed time limit and remains in force – provided that premiums continue to be paid – until it is brought to an end by the payment of a death claim, or until it is surrendered (cashed in) by the policyholder for a reduced sum.

Premiums are often payable throughout the lifetime of the policy, although they can be limited to a particular term or to some fixed age, such as 60 or 65.

Whole of life policies can be issued in a number of different formats: non-profit, with-profit, unit-linked or unitized with-profit. The characteristics of these different formats are described in the section on life assurance-based investment products (Section 4.5).

The unit-linked format is particularly useful for whole of life assurance, because it provides the flexibility to change the level of cover on a policy as an individual's financial situation changes. Since the cost of the cover is taken each month by cashing in an appropriate number of the policy's fund of units, changing the level of cover can be achieved by increasing or decreasing the number of units cashed.

As an illustration, consider a young family for which substantial life cover is a priority. The policy could be set up to give the maximum cover for the amount of premium they could afford, in which case the cost of the cover would use up all or most of the units being allocated. After a while, as the children get older, the need for life cover on the parents' lives will probably reduce; they might, however, wish to begin to make some savings towards the children's higher education. At that point, the policy's life cover element could be decreased, leading to a smaller number of units being cashed each month. The result is that a fund of units develops, building up an investment which can be cashed in at a later date.

Some unit-linked whole of life policies include additional benefits such as total and permanent disability benefit, and waiver of premium in the event of sickness. Such policies are often referred to as universal whole of life contracts.

Term assurance:

In the case of term assurance the sum assured is payable only if the life assured dies before the end of a specified term. If the life assured survives the term, the cover ceases and no payment or refund of premiums is made. Similarly, if the policy is cancelled part way through the term, it has no cash surrender value. The term can be from one month to 30 years or more, although if a very long term is required, it may be better to consider a whole of life assurance.

A number of different varieties of term assurance have been developed over the years in order to satisfy a range of different needs. They include:

- **Level term assurance:** The sum assured remains level throughout the term.

- **Decreasing term assurance:** The sum assured reduces over the term of the policy, but the premiums usually remain level, although they may be restricted to a shorter period such as two-thirds of the term.

  The sum assured may reduce by equal annual amounts, or in some other specified manner. The most common form is a policy where the sum assured reduces in line with the outstanding capital on a repayment mortgage of a given term and specified rate of interest. This policy is often known as a mortgage protection assurance; it should not be confused with the type of short-term accident sickness and unemployment cover which is often sold to protect mortgage repayments against illness and redundancy, which may also be referred to as 'mortgage protection'.

- **Family income benefits:** This policy is different in that the sum assured is payable not as a lump sum but as a series of regular monthly or quarterly instalments from the date of death until the end of the policy term. As an alternative to the instalments, however, the beneficiaries can, in the event of a claim, choose to receive a discounted lump-sum payment.

- **Increasing term assurance:** Some people feel that the sum assured should increase over the term of the policy to provide a hedge against inflation. Increasing term assurance provides cover that increases each year at a specified simple or compound rate of interest.

- **Convertible term assurance:** This is a term assurance (normally a level term assurance) that includes an option to convert the policy into a whole of life or endowment policy of the same sum assured without further evidence of health. The cost of the option is usually an additional 10% or 15% of the premium. If the option is not exercised during the term of the policy, the option lapses with no refund of the extra premiums paid.

- **Renewable/increasable term assurance:** This term assurance includes an option, that can be exercised at the end of the term, to renew the policy for an additional term and to increase the sum assured by a specified amount, again without further evidence of health.

- **Pension term assurance:** People who are eligible to take out a personal pension plan or stakeholder pension are also permitted to effect a term assurance policy in conjunction with their pension plan. The main advantage of doing so is that the premiums paid on pension term assurance attract tax relief whereas conventional term assurance premiums do not. However, the maximum premium that is allowed is 10% of the contributions being paid to the pension plan.

Permanent health insurance

Death is not the only event which can cause severe problems to a family's or a business's financial situation. The effect of serious or long-term illness can be equally devastating. Indeed it can lead to even more severe financial problems in a family situation, because, in addition to the loss of the income of the person who is ill, there may be the increased costs of treatment, medication and care.

Permanent health insurance (PHI) is designed to provide replacement income in the event of an individual being unable to work due to illness, disability or accident. Each insurance company has its own definition of what 'unable to work' actually means, but a typical policy might require that a person be 'unable to carry out his own occupation or any other occupation for which he is suited by reason of training, skill and experience'.

The term of a PHI policy cannot extend beyond the person's intended (or actual) retirement date, and there is a maximum permitted benefit level which most companies set at around 60% of earnings, less the basic state incapacity benefit. The maximum benefit rule is enforced by the companies to prevent the excessive claims that would no doubt ensue if policyholders could receive more income when sick than they would if they returned to work!

Each PHI policy is subject to a deferred period, which is the time which must elapse after the policyholder falls ill before benefit payments can commence. The minimum deferred period is four weeks, or the policyholder can choose 13 weeks, 26 weeks, one year or even two years. The longer the deferred period, the lower the premium, simply because fewer claims are likely to arise if the time period for most common illnesses is excluded.

When payments do commence, they are paid monthly until the claimant recovers, reaches retirement age, or dies. The word permanent in the policy title refers to the fact that – provided premiums are paid – the insurance company cannot cancel the policy simply on the grounds of heavy claims experience.

The level of premiums payable on a PHI policy depend not only on age, policy term and benefit amount – but also vary according to the occupation of the policyholder. People whose jobs are more dangerous, physically demanding or mentally stressful generally have to pay higher premiums. Gender is also a factor in PHI premium levels: statistics show that women spend, on average, more time off work due to illness than men, and they are likely to pay as much as 50% more for PHI cover than their male colleagues.

Group PHI: Some employers arrange PHI cover for their employees on a group basis. As well as the individual's maximum permitted benefit, the employer could cover the cost of National Insurance and pension contributions. One advantage for group scheme members is that they can normally be accepted for some or all of their cover without medical evidence.

Taxation: Benefits from individual PHI policies are not subject to tax. Benefits from group schemes are paid to the employer and taxed as a trading receipt; the employer passes the benefits to the employee as earnings, which are taxed under PAYE as normal.

Critical illness cover

Critical illness cover (CIC), sometimes also known as dread disease cover, was first developed in South Africa and the USA in the early 1980s. Although the benefit payments from critical illness policies relate to sickness rather than death, they are very different from permanent health insurance (PHI) policies. The most significant differences are:

● The benefit is payable on the diagnosis of one of a specified range of illnesses and conditions. It is not necessary for the claimant to be off work, and the benefit is paid irrespective of whether the claimant subsequently recovers.

- The benefit is in the form of a tax-free lump sum, not a regular income. Once the benefit has been paid, the policy ceases, and the sum assured would not be paid again, even if the policyholder subsequently suffered another of the specified illnesses.

Each company that offers CIC policies has its own list of the illnesses that are covered, but they normally include: most forms of cancer; heart attack; stroke; coronary artery disease requiring surgery; major organ transplants; multiple sclerosis; total and permanent disability. Some critical illness cover policies also include payment of the sum assured on death if it occurs before a claim has been paid for diagnosis of a specific disease.

Private medical insurance

Private medical insurance (PMI) provides an individual with access to private medical treatment rather than being dependent on the National Health Service (NHS).

Traditionally this type of cover has been provided by specialist organizations such as BUPA, and it was viewed mainly as an occupational benefit, purchased by employers as a benefit for senior staff. In recent years, however, the well-publicised concern about the finances of the NHS and its consequently lengthening waiting lists have broadened the appeal of this type of cover, and conventional insurers are entering the market.

PMI policies are suitable for people who wish to ensure speedy treatment for acute but not life-threatening illnesses, and also for those who want to be able to choose the hospital, the consultant, and the most convenient time for treatment. The benefits provided by PMI policies normally include: ambulance fees; hospital charges; specialists' fees; nursing care. Prospective policyholders will be required to declare any pre-existing conditions – which will then normally be excluded from cover, as will routine check-ups.

4.4 Savings and Investment Products

There are no formal definitions of the terms savings and investment, or of the difference between them. It is generally accepted that the terms can be used interchangeably to refer to any scheme where money is put away with a view to receiving income from it and/or increasing its capital value, although some people prefer to reserve the word savings for schemes which involve putting aside smaller regular amounts.

The financial services industry provides a very extensive range of savings and investment products to meet the needs of a wide spectrum of customers. The products can be categorized in a number of different ways. Some of those categories are mentioned here, together with a few illustrative examples (details of the various products mentioned are included later in the chapter):

- **Regular savings or lump sum:** Most people build up their savings by small regular amounts from their disposable income. They may use regular savings schemes into deposit accounts or unit trusts, or pay regular premiums to endowment policies, or contributions to pension plans.

The need to invest a lump sum may arise from the receipt of a legacy or other windfall, or it may reflect the desire to move money from one form of investment to another. Lump-sum investments are found in a wide variety of forms, including:

– Bank and building society term investments, often with a minimum balance, usually offering higher returns for longer periods.

– National Savings products such as National Savings Certificates and Pensioner's Bonds.

– Gilt-edged securities: these are interest-bearing loans to the government which can be traded on the stock market.

– The purchase of shares, either directly or indirectly via unit trusts or investment trusts.

Many schemes, such as unit trusts, offer the choice of regular saving or lump-sum investments.

● **Level of risk:** This ranges from products where there is no risk (or virtually no risk) to the capital, such as bank deposit accounts, to those where the customer accepts the risk of loss of some or all of the capital in order to speculate for higher returns: most stock market-related investments fall into the latter category to some degree.

As a general rule, products that carry a greater risk also have a greater potential for high returns.

● **Accessibility:** Many deposit accounts have instant access or require only short notice of withdrawal. At the other end of the scale, some investments are not directly accessible until a fixed maturity date: gilt-edged securities fall into that category, although they can be sold prior to their redemption date (but without any guarantee as to what price may be obtained).

● **Taxation:** The main UK taxes affecting investors are income tax and capital gains tax. Descriptions of these and other taxes are given later in this chapter.

With many investments, tax is payable by investors both on the income received and on any capital gain made on eventual sale. Shares and unit trusts fall into this category. Some investments, for instance gilt-edged securities, are taxed on income but exempt from capital gains tax.

The government has in recent years tried to encourage savings by offering tax-free investment schemes, including:

● **National Savings:** some products, including National Savings Certificates and Children's Bonus Bonds, are tax-free.

- **Personal equity plans (PEPs):** Introduced in the late 1980s to encourage greater share ownership, PEPs were free of tax on income and capital gains. Investment was in shares and similar securities either directly or through unit trusts. They were replaced by ISAs (see below) from April 1999.

- **Tax exempt special savings accounts (TESSAs):** The deposit-account equivalents of PEPs, offering tax-free interest over a fixed five-year period, they were also replaced by ISAs from April 1999.

- **Individual savings accounts (ISAs):** Available from April 1999, ISAs offer a tax-efficient savings environment by combining a number of the characteristics of PEPs and TESSAs. They are available through retail shopping venues as well as the usual financial outlets.

Further details of these products are given later in this chapter.

4.5 Life Assurance-based Investment Products

The most common form of savings contract offered by life assurance companies is the endowment assurance, which is, broadly speaking, a policy on which the sum assured is paid out at the end of a specified term or on the earlier death of the life assured (though some policies are open-ended and allow the policyholder to choose when to receive the proceeds of his or her investment). The client's investment is made in the form of regular premiums to the life assurance company throughout the term of the policy. There are a number of variations, the most common of which are:

Non-profit endowment

This policy has a fixed sum assured, which is payable on maturity (ie at the end of the policy term) or on earlier death. Because the return is fixed and guaranteed, the investor is shielded from losses due to adverse stock market movements; on the other hand, he or she is equally unable to share in any profits the company might make over and above those allowed for in calculating the premium rate (hence the name: non-profit). For that reason, non-profit policies are rarely used today.

With-profit endowment

Like its non-profit equivalent, a with-profit endowment has a fixed basic sum assured and a fixed regular premium. The premium, however, is greater than that for a non-profit policy of the same sum assured, and the additional premium (sometimes called a bonus loading) entitles the policyholder to share in the profits of the life assurance company.

The company distributes its profits among policyholders by annually declaring bonuses which become part of the policy benefits and are payable at the same time and in the same circumstances as the sum assured. There are two types of bonus:

- **Reversionary bonuses:** These are normally declared each year, and once they have been allocated to a policy they cannot then be removed by the company. Some companies declare a simple bonus, where each annual bonus is calculated as a percentage of the sum assured; others declare a compound bonus, with the new bonus being based on the total of the sum assured and previously declared bonuses. Most companies set their reversionary bonuses at a level that they hope to be able to maintain for some time, in order to smooth out the short-term variations of the stock market; however, with the level of interest rates and other investment yields falling in recent years, bonus rates in general have also been falling. In spite of this, with-profit policies have in the long run produced much better returns than non-profit.

- **Terminal bonuses:** A terminal bonus is a bonus that may be added to a with-profit policy when a death or maturity claim becomes payable. Unlike reversionary bonuses, it does not become part of the policy benefits until the moment of a death or maturity claim, thus allowing the company to change the terminal bonus rate – or even remove the terminal bonus altogether – if it wishes to. Terminal bonuses are intended to reflect the level of investment gains that the company has made over the term of the policy, so the rate of bonus often varies according to the length of time that the policy has been in force.

A variation of the with-profit endowment, known as a low-cost endowment, is often used for mortgage repayment purposes. This policy is described in the section related to mortgages (Section 4.11).

Unit-linked endowment

The first unit-linked policies were issued in the late 1950s, and represented a revolutionary change in the way in which policies were designed. The development reflected the desire of many policyholders to link investment returns more directly to the stock market, or even to specific sectors of the market.

Unit-linked endowments work as follows: when a premium is paid, the amount of the premium – less any deductions for expenses – is applied to the purchase of units in a chosen fund; a pool of units gradually builds up, and at the maturity date the policyholder receives an amount equal to the total value of all the units then allocated to the policy. Most unit-linked endowments also provide a fixed benefit on death before the end of the term. The cost of providing this cover is taken from the policy each month by cashing in sufficient units from the pool of units.

Over the longer term, the most successful unit-linked endowments have shown better returns than with-profit endowments. Unlike with-profit endowments, however, unit-linked policies do not provide any guaranteed minimum return at maturity; they are, therefore, a good illustration of the maxim that greater potential return generally goes hand-in-hand with the acceptance of greater risk.

Unitized with-profit endowments

These policies have been available since the late 1980s, when they were introduced in an attempt to combine the security of the with-profit policy with the greater potential for reward offered by the unit-linked approach. As with unit-linking, premiums are used to purchase units in a fund, and the benefits paid out on a claim depend on the number of units allocated and the then-current price of units.

The difference from a standard unit-linked policy lies in the fact that unit prices increase by the addition of bonuses which, like the reversionary bonuses on a with-profit policy, cannot be taken away once they have been added. This means that unit prices cannot fall and the value of the policy **if it is held until death or maturity** is guaranteed. If the policy is surrendered (ie cashed in before its maturity date), however, a deduction is made from the value of the units. This deduction, the size of which depends on market conditions at the time of the surrender, is known as a market value adjustment.

4.6 National Savings and Gilt-edged Stocks

The British government offers two main investment channels through which it seeks to fund the public sector net cash requirement (PSNCR). The PSNCR represents broadly speaking the excess of government and public sector spending over its income from taxation and national insurance. Its primary source of borrowing from individuals is through the various National Savings schemes, whereas gilt-edged securities (gilts), although they are available to the general public, are purchased mainly by institutions such as banks, life assurance companies and pension funds.

National Savings

A broad range of schemes is available, with almost every type of savings and investment need catered for. It is important that investors should be aware of the characteristics of each product in relation to interest rates, investment term, accessibility, taxation, and minimum and maximum investments.

The main products are listed and described below. Where interest rates are quoted for illustrative purposes, these are the rates applicable in early 2002, which are of course subject to change.

Ordinary account

This is an instant access deposit account available to anyone aged 7 or over, with most transactions being carried out in cash through a Post Office. Interest rates are very low (maximum 0.6%), but the first £70 of interest each year is tax-free.

Investment Account

This is a deposit account which offers a stepped interest scale from 2.6% for balances under £500, to 3.6% for £50,000 and above. Access to cash is subject to one month's notice (or shorter notice with an interest penalty). Interest is credited to the account gross, but it is taxable.

Fixed-Interest Savings Certificates

These are lump-sum investments which pay a guaranteed rate of interest over two or five years – the current issues offer 2.95% and 3.25% per annum respectively. The interest is not paid out but accumulates to increase the value of the certificate. They are completely free of income tax and capital gains tax, which makes them particularly attractive to higher rate taxpayers, who, based on 3.25%, obtain an equivalent gross yield of 5.42%. The maximum holding is £10,000. Certificates can be cashed in before the end of the 5-year term, but this will result in a lower rate of interest being paid.

Index-Linked Savings Certificates

Like the fixed-interest certificates, these are tax-free and must be held for two or five years in order to obtain the full guaranteed rate of interest. Index-linked certificates are different in that their value increases with inflation as well as offering interest. The guaranteed interest rate is lower than that on fixed-interest certificates: on the current 2-year and 5-year issues, it is 1.3% and 1.4% respectively.

Children's Bonus Bonds

These are long-term tax-free investments for children. Interest rates are guaranteed for five years at a time (currently 4.05% if held for 5 years) and a special bonus is added at each 5th anniversary of purchase. A further bonus is added on the child's 21st birthday, but no further interest is added after that – so it is usual to cash in the bond at that point.

Income Bonds

National Savings Income Bonds pay a regular monthly income, offering competitive variable interest rates (currently up to 3.8%) on lump sum investments from £500 to £1 million. The monthly interest payments are made gross (ie without deduction of tax) direct to a bank or building society account. The interest is, however, taxable and must be declared by taxpayers to the Inland Revenue.

Pensioners' Bonds

People aged 60 or over (the same age applies to men and women) can invest between

£500 and £50,000 to obtain monthly interest payments which are guaranteed for 1, 2 or 5 years at a time: the current 5-year bonds pay 4.3%, with lower interest rates on the shorter terms. The interest is paid gross, but is taxable. The bonds can be cashed in at the end of the term, subject to 60 days notice; they can also be cashed in at other times, but this will result in an interest penalty.

Fixed-Rate Savings Bonds (1-, 3- or 5-year terms)

Interest is at a guaranteed rate (currently up to 4.45% gross), after which the bond can be cashed in or left for a further period at a new guaranteed rate. These bonds therefore appeal to people who do not wish to commit their capital investment for a long period. They are available for investments of between £500 and £1 million. Interest is credited net of basic rate tax, so higher rate taxpayers will have an additional tax liability.

Capital Bonds

Like savings certificates, capital bonds are for people who are willing to tie up their investment for a five-year period in return for a guaranteed interest rate (currently 4.4% gross). The interest is not paid out but accumulates to increase the value of the bond. However, the interest is taxable and it suffers a rather eccentric taxation regime: the holder of the bond is taxed on the interest each year when it is credited to the account, even though he or she cannot receive it until the end of the five years.

Premium Bonds

A purchase of Premium Bonds (minimum investment £100, maximum £20,000) provides an investor with a regular draw for tax-free prizes, while retaining the right to cash in the bond for its face value. In effect, all the investors agree to pool the interest (currently 2.4%) which they would otherwise receive on the investment, and hold a monthly lottery for the right to receive a large prize – up to £1 million depending on interest rates – and a range of smaller prizes.

Gilts

Gilt-edged securities (gilts) are fixed-interest loans to the government. The name of each gilt specifies the rate of interest payable on the loan (known as the coupon rate) and the year in which the loan will be repaid (the redemption date). For example, a typical gilt might be named Treasury 8% 2013: this would mean that the holder of £100 nominal value (or par value) of the stock would receive interest of £8 gross per annum – normally payable half-yearly – until the nominal principal of £100 is repaid by the government in the year 2013. In this context, therefore, 'fixed interest' refers to the fact that a regular fixed amount of interest is paid to the holder of a given nominal amount of stock. The market rate of interest available to someone buying this stock may vary from day to day, as explained later in the notes on price and yield.

Gilts are categorized primarily according to the length of time remaining until redemption. Some gilts have a spread of redemption dates, indicating that the government may redeem them, at its own discretion, at any time between the two dates shown. The categories of gilts are:

- **Short-dated gilts** (or shorts) have five years or less to run.

- **Medium-dated gilts** (mediums) have between five and fifteen years to run.

- **Long-dated gilts** (longs) have fifteen years or more to run.

- **Undated gilts** have no specified redemption date and can be redeemed by the government at any time: there is no obligation ever to redeem them.

- **Convertible gilts** are shorts that provide the holder with options on certain specified dates to convert into a longer-dated gilt.

- **Index-linked gilts** are gilts on which the capital value and the interest payments move in line with the retail price index (RPI).

Gilts are always redeemed at par, ie at £100 for every £100 nominal value. Prior to the redemption date, gilts cannot be sold back to the government, so investors wishing to cash in their investment must sell the stocks to another investor. Gilts are traded on the Stock Exchange and there is a large and active secondary market. The current prices of gilts are always quoted per £100 par value.

The price at which a gilt can be bought and sold depends on a number of factors:

- Market rates of interest, both actual and anticipated. Broadly speaking, if market rates rise gilt prices fall because purchasers wish to obtain a higher yield from the same fixed coupon rate.

- Supply and demand. As with most products, financial and otherwise, increased demand can push up prices, and vice versa.

- Length of time to redemption. Since gilts are always redeemed at par, the price inevitably approaches £100 as the redemption date nears.

Interest on gilts is paid half-yearly, so it builds up, or accrues, between payment dates. If a gilt changes hands between interest payment dates, the purchaser pays for the accrued income along with the market price of the gilt, and therefore has the right to receive the next half-yearly payment in full.

Gilt yields Two different yield figures are quoted for gilts, the initial yield (or interest yield) and the redemption yield.

- The initial yield simply relates the income an investor will receive to the current price he would pay to purchase the stock. Thus:

Initial yield = Coupon x (Redemption price/Current price)

So, an investor purchasing our hypothetical Treasury 8% 2013 at a price of 133.3 (gilt prices are always quoted per £100 par value) would have an initial yield of 8% x (100/133.3) = 6%.

- The redemption yield also allows for the fact that an investor who holds the stock until it is repaid will receive a return of 100 whatever the price paid, and the gain or loss sustained will affect overall yield. Thus, in the above example, the redemption yield is less than 6% because the investor would suffer a loss of a quarter of the capital value over the period to redemption.

Taxation of gilts As with all investments, potential investors should consider the tax position when selecting gilt-edged stocks:

- **Income tax:** Interest from gilts is paid gross, but is subject to tax at an investor's highest rate. Payment for accrued interest on the sale of a gilt is also taxed as income.

- **Capital gains tax:** Gilts are exempt from tax on capital gains.

4.7 Shares

It was a stated aim of the government in the 1980s that Britain should become, to a much greater extent than previously, a share-owning democracy. Although it is true that the public has on the whole become more aware of the nature of investment in shares, any increase in share-related investment by individuals has been mainly through indirect channels such as unit trusts rather than the direct purchase of company shares. Direct investment in shares remains, for the most part, the territory of the large institutions such as pension funds, unit trusts and life assurance companies, who between them hold over 70% of the shares in issue. The main exception to this was in the privatization issues such as British Telecom which, perhaps partly due to their novelty value, did catch the attention of the investing public.

Ordinary shares

The most common form of shares are ordinary shares, also known as equities because they represent a direct investment in the equity of a company: this means that holders of ordinary shares are in effect part-owners of a company. Ordinary shares normally confer the following rights:

- To participate in the distribution of the company's profits in the form of dividends.

- To contribute to decisions about how the company is run, by voting at shareholders' meetings and electing a board of directors.

The one significant right that shareholders do not have is, of course, the right to ask the company to return their investment. They have in effect traded that right for a share in the ownership and the profits of the company. Shares are, therefore, irredeemable, and shareholders who wish to cash in their investment must sell their shares to someone else. The price at which shares change hands (the market price) depends on a number of factors, including:

- The current and expected future profitability of the company itself;

- The quality and track record of the management;

- The economic prospects of the industry in which it operates, and of other related industries;

- The state of the national and international economy;

- Supply and demand.

The market price is not the same as a share's nominal value or face value, which is usually equal to, or related to, the price at which the share was originally issued.

A full discussion of share investment is beyond the scope of these notes, but it may be useful to briefly introduce one or two basic concepts and to mention some of the more common terminology.

Risk and reward: Shareholders in a limited liability company do not have a liability for the debts of the company. The company has a separate legal identity and is itself liable for its debts. Shareholders do, however, run the risk that the value of their investment in the company could go down or even, in the event of a liquidation, be lost altogether. In line with the broad rules of risk and return, therefore, it would be expected that the potential for high returns would also be a feature of the share market. It is certainly true that, on average and over the longer term, equity markets have far outpaced the returns available on secure deposit-based investments.

Earnings per share: This is equal to the company's net profit divided by the number of shares, but it is not the amount of dividend to which a shareholder is entitled on each of his or her shares. This is because a company may choose not to distribute all of its profits: some may be retained in the business to finance expansion, for instance. This leads to the concept of:

Dividend cover: This factor indicates how much of a company's profits are paid as dividends in a particular distribution. If, for example, 50% of the profits is paid in dividends, the dividend is said to be covered twice. Cover of 2.0 or more is generally considered to be acceptable by investors, whereas a figure below 1.0 indicates that a company is paying part of its dividend out of retained surpluses from previous years.

Price/earnings ratio: As its name suggests, the P/E ratio is calculated as the share price divided by the earnings per share. It is generally considered to be a useful guide as to a share's growth prospects: a ratio of 20 or more, for example, indicates that a share is doing well and can be expected to increase in value in the future. Such a share is likely, as a result, to be relatively more expensive than others within the same market sector. A low ratio – less than about 4 – indicates that the market feels that the share has poor prospects of growth.

When assessing P/E ratios, it is important to compare them with those of companies within the same sector. For example, in the latter part of 1998 Marks and Spencer's share price and P/E ratio fell back sharply as investors were concerned about future profitability, given the uncertain economic climate and the company's poor sales performance compared to its competitors.

Taxation: Dividends are received by shareholders net of 10%, with a tax credit equal to the amount deducted. Lower rate and basic rate taxpayers have no further liability, but higher rate taxpayers have to pay sufficient additional tax to bring their tax paid up to the special higher rate applicable to dividends, which is 32.5% of the grossed-up dividend. (This extraordinary system was introduced to smooth out the effect of the abolition of advance corporation tax (ACT) from 6 April 1999.)

Gains realized on the sale of shares are subject to capital gains tax.

Ex-dividend: Dividends are usually paid half-yearly. Because of the administration involved in ensuring that all shareholders receive their dividends on time, the payment process has to begin some weeks before the dividend dates. A 'snapshot' of the list of shareholders is made at that point, and anyone who purchases shares between then and the dividend date will clearly not receive the next dividend (which will be paid to the previous owner of the shares). During that period, the shares are said to be ex-dividend (or xd). The share price would normally be expected to fall, on the day it becomes xd, by approximately the dividend amount.

Rights issue: Stock exchange rules require that when an existing company that already has shareholders wishes to raise further capital by issuing more shares, those shares must first be offered to the existing shareholders. This is done by means of a rights issue, offering for example one new share per three existing shares, generally at a discount to the price at which the new shares are expected to commence trading. Shareholders who do not wish to take up this right can sell the right to someone else, in which case the sale proceeds from selling the rights compensate for any fall in value of their existing shares (due to the dilution of their holding as a proportion of the total shareholding).

Scrip issue: Also known as a bonus issue or a capitalization issue, this is an issue of additional shares, free of charge, to existing shareholders. No additional capital is raised by this action – it is achieved by transferring reserves into the company's share account. The effect is to increase the number of shares and to proportionately reduce the share price.

Other shares and related securities

Preference shares: Like ordinary shares, preference shares are entitled to dividends payable from the company's profits. Preference dividends are generally at a fixed rate; in the payment hierarchy, they rank after loan interest but ahead of ordinary share dividends. Many preference shares are cumulative preference shares, which means that if their dividends are not paid, entitlement to them is accumulated until such a time as they can be paid. Preference shares do not normally carry voting rights, but in some cases they may acquire voting rights if their dividends have been delayed.

In the event of the winding up of a company, preference shares again rank behind loans but ahead of ordinary shareholders' claims.

Convertibles: These are securities, issued by companies to raise capital, which carry the right to be converted at some later date to ordinary shares of the issuing company. Traditionally they were issued in a form that effectively made them a loan (with a lower rate of interest than conventional debt because of the right to convert to equity), but in recent years they have been increasingly issued as convertible preference shares.

Derivatives: A derivative is a financial product that is indirectly based on – or 'derived' from – another financial product. It is usually related to a commitment to buy or sell that other product at a fixed price on a future date or between two dates. The most common products dealt with in this way are ordinary shares, interest rates and exchange rates. The main forms of derivatives are described below:

Options: Options are the best-known form of derivative. An option is the right (but not the obligation) to buy or sell a specific amount of an asset (which could be a certain number of ordinary shares) at a specified price (the exercise price) within a specified period. An option to buy is known as a call option, whereas the equivalent right to sell is referred to as a put option. The buyer of an option contract pays a purchase price, or option premium, to the seller (also known as the writer) of the contract.

Futures: Futures are similar to options, except that with futures there is an obligation to buy or sell at the specified price on a specified date. Futures are available in a range of financial products as well as commodities (eg coffee) and currencies, for which they can be used as a hedge against movements in exchange rates.

Warrants: Warrants are similar to call options, except that they are generally issued by companies and give the holder the right to purchase that company's ordinary shares, thus raising new capital for the company.

4.8 Collective Investments

Collective or pooled investments are arrangements whereby individual small investors can contribute – by means of lump sums or regular savings – to a large investment fund. Pooled investments offer a number of advantages to individual investors:

●   The services of a skilled investment manager are obtained at a cost that is shared among the investors. Individual investors do not need to research particular companies, or to understand and deal with occurrences such as rights issues.

- Investment risk can be reduced because the investment manager 'spreads' the fund by investing in a large number of different companies – so that if one company fails the whole investment is not compromised. Such a spread could not normally be achieved with small investment amounts.

- Fund managers handling investments in millions of pounds can negotiate reduced dealing costs for their investors.

- There is a wide choice of investment funds, catering for all investment strategies, preferences and risk profiles.

Investment funds can be categorized in a number of ways, for example:

- By location: eg UK, Europe, America, Far East, International;

- By industry: eg technology, energy;

- By type of investment: eg shares, gilts, fixed interest, property;

- By other forms of specialization: eg recovery stocks, ethical investments.

Most companies also offer one or more managed funds. This is an unfortunate choice of name, since it seems to imply that other funds are not managed! Nevertheless, the name has become accepted as applying to the type of fund where the managers invest in a range of the company's other funds in such proportions as they feel is appropriate from time to time to meet the managed fund's objectives. Most managed funds are middle-of-the-road in terms of risk profile, and are often chosen by people seeking steady market-related growth in situations where risk of loss needs to be kept to a minimum, such as pension provision or mortgage repayment.

A further categorization is possible, into funds that aim to produce a high level of income (perhaps with modest capital growth), those that aim for capital growth at the expense of income, and those that seek a balance between growth and income.

The main forms of collective investment are unit trusts, investment trusts and investment bonds. Although they may appear broadly similar to the unsophisticated investor, they are in fact very different, both in the way they operate and in the taxation treatment of the fund managers and of investors. Unit trusts have been particularly successful in attracting investment from individuals in the UK, with total funds under management of the order of £200 billion.

Unit trusts

Unit trusts are collective investments established under a trust deed. The deed is entered into between the promoters of the unit trust, known as the managers, and the trustees; each of them undertakes certain obligations under the terms of the deed:

- **The managers** are responsible for investing the funds, valuing the assets, fixing the prices of units, offering the units for sale and buying units back from unit-holders. They must comply in all respects with the terms of the trust deed, and with the rules of the Department of Trade and Industry (DTI) and the Financial Services Authority (FSA). For example, in order to be authorized by the FSA, a unit trust must not own more than 10% of the share capital of any one company; similarly, the managers must not invest more than 5% of the total fund in any one company's shares (there is a small exception to this rule which permits holdings in up to six companies to be as high as 7.5% of the total fund).

- **The trustees** must ensure that the managers comply with the terms of the trust deed. They also hold and control the trust's assets on behalf of the unit-holders, collect income from these assets and distribute it to the unit-holders.

Unit trusts are **unitized** funds, with each unit representing a proportion of the fund's total asset value. Unit trusts are also **open-ended** funds: this does not refer to time limits on the investment, but to the fact that when more money is invested, more units are created. In these respects they are similar to investment bonds, but different from investment trusts.

The prices at which units are bought and sold are calculated by the managers on a daily basis, using a method specified in the trust deed. The unit prices are directly related to the value of the underlying securities that make up the fund. There are three important prices in relation to unit trust transactions:

- The **offer price** is the price at which investors buy units from the managers.

- The **bid price** is the price at which the managers will buy back units from investors who wish to cash in all or part of their unit-holding. On any given day, the bid price is of course less than the offer price.

- The **cancellation price** is the minimum permitted bid price, taking into account the full costs of buying and selling. At times when there are both buyers and sellers of units, the bid price is generally above the minimum, since costs are reduced because underlying assets do not need to be traded.

Most unit trusts still use bid and offer prices, with the difference between them (known as the **bid-offer spread**) being of the order of 5% or 6%. Some unit trust managers, however, are moving to a single-price system, because they believe that this is better understood by investors. In that case, they may impose an exit charge if units are sold within, say, three or five years of purchase.

Unit trust managers are obliged to buy back units when investors wish to sell them. There is therefore no need for a secondary market in units, and they are not traded on the Stock Exchange. This adds to the appeal of unit trusts to the ordinary investor, for whom the buying and selling of units is a relatively simple process:

- Units can be bought direct from the managers or through intermediaries. They can be purchased in writing or by telephone: all calls to the managers' dealing desks are recorded as confirmation that a contract has been established.

● Purchasers receive two important documents from the managers:

  – **Contract note:** This specifies the fund, the number of units, the unit price and the amount paid. It is important because it gives the purchase price, which will be needed for capital gains tax (CGT) purposes when the units are sold.

  – **Unit certificate:** This specifies the fund and the number of units held, and is the proof of ownership of the units.

● In order to sell some or all of the units, the unit-holder signs the form of renunciation on the reverse of the unit certificate, and returns it to the managers. If only part of the holding is to be sold, a new certificate for the remaining units is issued.

Historic and forward pricing: A significant change in the pricing of units took place in July 1988. Prior to that, clients bought or sold at prices determined before the start of the dealing period – typically the previous day's valuation. (If a fund's daily valuation takes place, for example, at 12 noon, the dealing period is from mid-day on one day to mid-day on the following working day.) This system, known as historic pricing, was considered unacceptable because prices clearly do not reflect what is happening in the market, so that – for instance – an investor could telephone for a price just before the newly-calculated daily price was published, knowing that the market had risen in the meantime.

Concern about historic pricing led to the introduction of the system known as forward pricing, which is now standard practice for unitized funds. Under forward pricing, clients buy or sell in a given dealing period at the prices that will be determined at the end of the dealing period. The prices published in the financial press are therefore only a guide to investors, who do not know the actual price at which their deal will be made.

Fund managers are still permitted to use historic pricing if they wish, subject to the proviso that they must switch to forward pricing if an underlying market in which the trust is invested has moved by more than 2% in either direction since the last valuation.

Taxation of unit trusts: Income received by unit trust managers from the fund's investments is distributed to the unit-holders. These distributions are subject to income tax in the hands of the unit-holders, who receive them net of 10%, with a tax credit. As with share dividends, lower rate and basic rate taxpayers have no further liability, but higher rate taxpayers are liable for the balance of 32.5% of the grossed-up distribution (see Section 4.7).

The fund managers are exempt from tax on capital gains within the fund, but unit-holders are subject to CGT on gains made on the sale of units – normal CGT rules and exemption limits apply.

Investment trusts

Investment trusts are collective investments but, unlike unit trusts, they are not unitized funds. Furthermore – despite their name – they are not even trusts. They are in fact public limited companies whose business is investing (in most cases) in the stocks and shares of other companies. Investing in an investment trust is achieved by purchasing shares of the investment trust company on the Stock Exchange; similarly, in order to cash in the investment, it is necessary to sell these shares to another investor. As with all companies, the number of shares available remains constant, so an investment trust is said to be closed-ended (in contrast to the open-ended nature of unit trusts).

The share price of an investment trust obviously depends to some extent on the value of the underlying investments, but not directly so as in the case of a unit trust. The price can depend on a number of other factors, including supply and demand. In many cases the share price of an investment trust is less than the net asset value per share; this situation – referred to as being at a discount – means that an investor should achieve greater income and growth levels than would be obtained by investing in the same underlying shares through a unit trust or directly in the shares themselves.

One advantage of being constituted as a company is that an investment trust can benefit from gearing: this means that, like all companies, it can borrow money in order to take advantage of business opportunities (in their case, investment opportunities). This avenue is not open to unit trusts, which are not permitted to borrow. Gearing enables investment trusts to enhance the growth potential of a rising market, but investors should be aware that it can equally accentuate losses in a falling market.

Taxation of investment trusts: The taxation situation is the same as that described for unit trusts. At least 85% of the income received by investment trust fund managers must be distributed as dividends to shareholders, who receive them net of 10%, with a tax credit. As with all share dividends, lower rate and basic rate taxpayers have no further liability, but higher rate taxpayers pay the balance of the special rate of 32.5% of the grossed-up dividend.

Fund managers are exempt from tax on capital gains, but investors are subject to capital gains tax on the sale of their investment trust shares.

Split-capital investment trusts: Sometimes known as split-level trusts or splits, these are fixed-term investment trusts offering two or more different types of share. The most common forms of share offered by split-level investment trusts are:

● Income shares, which receive the whole of the income generated by the portfolio, but no capital growth.

● Capital shares, which receive no income, but which – when the trust is wound up at the end of the fixed term – share all the capital growth remaining after fixed capital requirements have been met.

Recent innovations have seen the introduction of intermediate types of shares, offering different balances of capital and income.

Investment bonds

Investment bonds, sometimes also known as insurance bonds, are collective investment vehicles based on unitized funds. Because of the unitized structure of their funds, they may seem at first sight to be similar to unit trusts, but they are actually very different.

Investment bonds are available from life assurance companies and are set up as single-premium unit-linked whole of life assurance policies. Investing in a bond is achieved by paying the single (lump sum) premium to the life company, and the investor receives a policy document which shows that the premium has been applied to purchase (at the offer price) a certain number of units in a chosen fund and that those units have been allocated to the policy. In order to cash in the investment, the policyholder takes the surrender value of the policy, which is equal to the value of all the units allocated, based on the bid price on the day when it is surrendered.

Investors are attracted by the relative ease of investment and surrender, by the simplicity of the documentation, and also by the ease of switching from one fund to another: companies generally permit switches between their own funds without charging the difference between bid and offer prices.

In the event of the death of the life assured, the policy ceases and a slightly enhanced value (often 101% of the bid value on the date of death) is paid out.

The funds in which the premiums are invested are internal life company funds, and their tax treatment is very different from that of unit trusts. In particular, they attract tax at 22% on capital gains, whereas unit trust funds are exempt, and this tax is not recoverable by investors even if they themselves have a personal exemption from capital gains tax. The taxation system for policy proceeds in the hands of the policyholder is complex, but, broadly speaking, because gains have been taxed at 22% within the fund, tax on the gain is payable only by higher-rate tax-payers, and then only at 18% – the excess of the higher rate over 22%.

Unlike investment trusts and unit trusts, investment bonds do not normally provide income in the form of dividends or distributions, but it is possible to derive a form of 'income' from them by making small regular withdrawals of capital (by cashing in units). These withdrawals are tax-free to basic rate taxpayers, and even higher rate taxpayers can withdraw up to 5% of the original investment each year without incurring an immediate tax liability.

Open-ended investment companies

Open-ended investment companies (OEICs) are a form of pooled investment which is popular in continental Europe, but which has not so far gained much acceptance in the

UK. Unit trusts are permitted to convert into OEICs if they wish, but as yet few have chosen to do so.

The format of an OEIC is rather like a cross between a unit trust and an investment trust, in that it has a corporate structure but with a variable number of shares, which can be created or liquidated according to the number of buyers or sellers in the market. Investors buy participating redeemable preference shares in the company; shares are traded at a single price (ie there is no bid-offer spread), but initial charges are made.

The company often acts as a sort of umbrella fund, split into a number of lesser funds, each specializing in a particular category of investment. New funds can be easily created, and switching between funds is simple and cheap.

4.9 Tax-efficient Investment Schemes

Personal equity plans

Personal equity plans (PEPs) were introduced in the 1986 Budget, and first became available in 1987. They were designed to encourage individuals to invest directly or indirectly in shares, by offering a tax-free environment, within certain limits, for investments which met specified criteria.

Investments held within PEPs are free from tax on income and on capital gains. Similarly, investors are not subject to tax on income received from PEPs or on gains made when cashing in a PEP investment.

In 1997 the government announced that it would dispense with PEPs and replace them with a new tax-free scheme, the Individual Savings Account (ISA) with effect from 6 April 1999. Existing PEPs can remain in existence, but no new investment into them was permitted after 5 April 1999.

One important development was the use of PEPs for mortgage repayment purposes: the availability of a tax-free fund meant that the monthly payments needed to build up a specified repayment amount were less than the equivalent figures for a taxed fund such as an endowment policy. Since 1999, ISAs can be used for this purpose.

PEPs can be held only by individual UK residents (ie they cannot be held jointly), and, like ISAs, they must be managed by an approved investment manager – although self-select PEPs, where the investments are chosen by the investor, are permitted.

Investment can be directly in the securities, or indirectly via unit trusts or investment trusts.

PEP investments had originally to be in UK or EU ordinary or preference shares, or UK corporate bonds or convertibles. The geographical restriction was later removed to bring PEPs into line with ISAs.

Tax-exempt special savings accounts

Following the introduction of PEPs, it was felt in some quarters that it was inappropriate to offer a tax-free scheme for people willing to invest in market-related securities without providing similar facilities for those who prefer to take a more cautious deposit-based approach.

This point of view was accepted by the government, and it led to the introduction from 1 January 1991 of tax-exempt special savings accounts (TESSAs), which are five-year deposit accounts offered by banks and building societies. TESSAs provide tax-free interest, subject to certain rules and restrictions:

● Maximum investment in the first year was £3,000, and in subsequent years is £1,800 pa, subject to an overall limit of £9,000.

● Capital cannot be withdrawn until the end of the five-year period. If capital is withdrawn, the account reverts to being an ordinary taxable account.

● 80% of the interest can be withdrawn without losing the tax-free status. The remaining 20% – equivalent to the basic rate of income tax – is not lost, but has to remain within the TESSA until the end of the five-year term.

The interest rates on TESSAs may be variable or fixed, at rates determined by individual banks and building societies.

New TESSAs have been unavailable since 5 April 1999. However, TESSAs that commenced on or before that date will be permitted to run their full course of five years, with their normal annual and overall investment allowances. Investors will be permitted to pay into these continuing TESSAs in addition to any investment into individual savings accounts (ISAs). At the end of the five years, the capital (but not the interest) from a TESSA can be re-invested into an ISA without affecting the normal ISA investment limits.

Individual savings accounts

Following a change of government in 1997, ministers felt that the existing tax-free savings schemes, particularly PEPs, were not sufficiently accessible to a large proportion of the population. It is estimated that 50% of the population of the UK have less than £200 in savings, with about 25% having no savings at all. The government therefore introduced, from 6 April 1999, the individual savings account (ISA). Its stated objectives are to develop the savings habit and to ensure that tax relief on savings is fairly distributed.

The government has stated that ISAs will be available in their initial form for at least ten years (until 2009), with a review being held after seven years to consider possible changes to the scheme.

ISAs can be marketed directly by financial institutions, or by independent intermediaries.

The government hopes that the accessibility of the scheme will be increased by it becoming available not only from conventional financial outlets, but also from supermarkets and other retail stores. There is, however, little evidence to suggest that buying an ISA along with your groceries will become part of the shopping scene of the twenty-first century, except perhaps at those supermarkets which have developed their own banking and finance subsidiaries.

There are three possible components of ISAs:

- Stocks and shares: this component can include:

  - Shares and corporate bonds issued by companies listed on stock exchanges anywhere in the world (this is much broader than the original PEP limits – the broader limits now also apply to PEPs).

  - Gilt-edged securities and similar stocks issued by governments of countries in the EEA.

  - UK-authorized unit trusts which invest in shares and securities.

  - UK open-ended investment companies (OEICs).

  - UK investment trusts – except for those investing in property.

- Cash, including:

  - bank and building society deposit accounts

  - taxable National Savings accounts – but not investment accounts or pensioners' bonds.

- Single-premium life assurance policies (schemes for regular premiums must be set up as recurring single premiums so that savers are under no obligation to maintain premium payments in order to obtain policy benefits). These can include with profit and unit-linked products.

Tax reliefs: Investors are exempt from income and capital gains tax on their investments. Prior to 5 April 2004, fund managers can reclaim the 10% deduction from share dividends, but this benefit will then be withdrawn. Fund managers are exempt from tax on other income and gains received for the benefit of investors.

Subscription limits: The maximum overall subscription is £7,000 per tax year, of which up to £3,000 can be in the cash element, and up to £1,000 in the life assurance element. The full £7,000 can be placed in the stocks and shares element (provided that this done through a maxi-ISA – see below). There is no statutory minimum investment, but individual ISA providers may set their own minimum levels.

The government initially decided to impose an overall ceiling of £50,000, but this was later abandoned and there is now no overall investment limit.

Withdrawals: There is no minimum period for which an ISA must be held. Withdrawals can be made at any time without jeopardising the tax-free status.

Choice of managers: Each year, savers have two options: either to take an ISA with a single manager who offers an account that can accept the full subscription (a maxi-ISA), or to go to separate managers for each of two or more components (mini-ISAs). The rules surrounding these choices are complex, and seem to detract from the government's stated aim of making the scheme more accessible to less sophisticated investors.

Cost, access and terms standards

The government has also introduced a set of standards (known as cost, access and terms, or CAT, standards), intended to help less knowledgeable investors choose a suitable deal.

In order to meet the CAT standards, ISAs must be simple clear and fair. They must not be restricted to certain customers, such as existing customers or those willing to purchase their ISA in conjunction with another product. Providers of CAT-standard ISAs must also be committed to continuing to provide ISAs to those who have bought them.

Specific additional standards apply to the different ISA components, for example:

- Cash ISAs must:
  - have no regular or one-off charges, or restrictive conditions;
  - have a minimum transaction size no greater than £10;
  - pay interest no lower than 2% below base rate;
  - increase rates within one month of an increase in base rate.

- For stocks and shares ISAs:
  - fund charges must not exceed 1% of net asset value per annum;
  - minimum investment levels must not exceed £50 per month or £500 per lump sum payment;
  - unit trusts, investment trusts and OEICs must have at least 50% of their funds invested in stocks and shares listed on EU stock exchanges;
  - units and shares must be single-priced (ie no bid-offer spread);
  - investment risk must be highlighted in the literature.

- For insurance ISAs:
  - annual fund charges must not exceed 3%;
  - minimum premiums must not exceed £25 per month or £250 for a lump sum;
  - surrender values from three years onwards must not be less than the total premiums paid.

ISAs that meet the standards will be CAT-marked. The government has stressed that the CAT mark is not a seal of approval, and it seems likely that many ISAs, particularly those investing in the stocks and shares component, will be marketed without being CAT-marked. This is because the cost restrictions are so tight that they may preclude schemes that allow for the cost of giving advice to potential investors.

4.10 Pensions

State pension arrangements and employers' occupational pension schemes are described in Chapter 2.

Here we shall concentrate on individual arrangements which are mainly intended for people who, for whatever reason, are not members of an occupational scheme. However, with the advent in 2001 of stakeholder pensions, private pension provision is also available to certain members of occupational schemes.

Successive governments have offered tax benefits and other incentives to encourage people to fund adequate retirement pensions for themselves rather than depending on state retirement provision and other social security benefits. Financial services companies from life assurance companies to banks and building societies have not been slow to enter this potentially very large market.

The industry's reputation in this field was, however, somewhat tarnished by the so-called 'pensions mis-selling scandal' of the late 1990s: it was discovered that people had been wrongly advised to take out personal pensions rather than joining, or remaining in, an occupational scheme. The Personal Investment Authority instituted a compulsory review of all such cases by advisers and pension providers, which has already resulted in some clients receiving substantial compensation. Responsibility for this review has been taken over by the Financial Services Authority (FSA).

Personal pensions

Personal pension plans were introduced in the Finance Act 1986, and have been available since 1 July 1988. They are individual pension arrangements for people who have relevant earnings from non-pensionable employment. This includes self-employed sole traders, business partners, employees whose employers do not provide a pension scheme, and employees who choose not join their employers' scheme. Unemployed people, and others who have no earned income, are not eligible to take out personal pensions but may be able to contribute to a stakeholder pension (see later); similarly, unearned or investment income does not count towards eligibility for personal pensions.

Retirement benefits can be taken from a personal pension plan at any chosen age between 50 and 75. It is not necessary to actually retire in order to take the benefits. Special rules apply to certain occupations: for instance the Inland Revenue's rules allow the benefits for professional sportsmen and sportswomen to be taken at much younger ages, in some cases as low as 35.

Personal pensions are always money-purchase arrangements, which means that the amount of pension payable depends on the level of contributions paid, the investment performance of the fund, and the pension annuity rates available on retirement. Most pension providers offer a wide choice of funds. The pension is not in any way directly related to the client's income at retirement, as it would be in a final-salary occupational scheme.

The main tax advantages associated with personal pensions are broadly in line with those for occupational schemes and other pension arrangements:

- Contributions (within permitted limits) attract tax relief at the client's highest rate of tax.

- The invested funds are exempt from tax on capital gains.

- Up to 25% of the accumulated fund can be taken as a tax-free lump sum at the time when the pension payments commence. (At least 75% of the fund must be taken in the form of a regular lifetime income, which is taxed as if it were earned income.)

Because of the beneficial tax treatment of personal pensions, strict limits are imposed on the amount that can be contributed each year. Maximum contribution rates are set as a percentage of net relevant earnings, the percentage depending on the individual's age at the start of the tax year. The percentages range from 17.5% of earnings at ages up to 35, to 40% at ages over 60.

Even these contribution limits were not, however, sufficient to prevent what the Inland Revenue considered to be abuse of the system, particularly by certain people (notably in the entertainment industry) whose annual relevant earnings could be very large indeed. As a result, the concept of the earnings cap was introduced in 1989. The earnings cap sets an upper limit to the amount of net relevant earnings that can be taken into account in determining maximum contributions; it is £95,400 pa in the 2001/2002 tax year. The maximum contribution for a 65-year-old person with £1 million earnings would therefore be 40% of £95,400, or £38,160.

It was also possible, prior to 2001, for people to make use, in each tax year, of unused contribution allowances from earlier years, but this facility has now been withdrawn.

Although the bulk of a personal pension fund must be used to purchase an annuity, it is not essential to buy this annuity from the company that supplied the pension plan. By making use of a facility known as the open-market option, an individual's fund value can be transferred to another annuity provider of his or her choice. It may be possible in this way to obtain a higher annual pension figure.

In spite of the open-market option facility, one problem that has faced retiring personal pension holders in recent years is that annuity rates (the rates which determine how much pension can be purchased by the accumulated fund) have been very low. In part this reflects the fact that people are on average living longer, but the main cause has been the lower interest rates and investment yields that have been available.

A partial solution to this problem was introduced by the Finance Act 1995 and the Pensions Act 1995 in the form of an income withdrawal (or income draw-down) facility. This enables an individual to receive an 'income' by making small regular withdrawals of capital from the fund (within certain limits) while deferring the purchase of a pension until later when, hopefully, annuity rates might have increased.

One answer to the potential problem of low annuity rates at retirement is for pension policies to be written with guaranteed minimum annuity rates. This may be good for sales, but can put pressure on profit margins if annuity rates are low when policyholders reach retirement. A controversy arose in 1998 when at least one insurance company (Equitable Life) applied differential (ie lower) terminal bonus rates to policies with guaranteed annuities, as a means of funding the additional costs of providing pensions at the guaranteed levels. A court ruling that this was illegal has led to serious financial problems for the insurer.

Pension term assurance: People who are eligible for a personal pension or a stakeholder pension can also take out term assurance cover and receive full tax relief on the premiums. The idea is to enable those who are not in an occupational scheme to be able to provide for themselves life cover similar to that normally offered by employers' schemes – although they have to pay for it themselves, whereas 'death-in-service' cover within a scheme is normally free to the employees. The maximum cover permitted for any individual is determined by a limit on the amount that can be paid for the cover: premiums cannot exceed 10% of the contributions to the related personal or stakeholder pension.

Contracting out through personal pensions: There is only one situation in which an employee who is a member of his employer's occupational pension scheme can take out a personal pension in relation to his earnings from that employment (although some scheme members may be able to take out a stakeholder pension). That situation arises when the occupational scheme is contracted in to SERPS (the state earnings-related pension scheme) and the employee wishes to individually contract himself out of SERPS. Similarly, employees who are not in an occupational scheme – and would therefore be in SERPS – may wish to contract themselves out of SERPS.

In those circumstances, the employee continues to pay full Class 1 National Insurance contributions, but a contributions rebate is paid each year direct to a personal pension provider of the employee's choice. These rebates must be used to set up a personal pension plan for the employee to replace the benefits lost by opting out of SERPS: these special plans, known as appropriate personal pensions, are subject to certain additional restrictions which ensure that the benefits they provide are similar in nature to the SERPS benefits which they replace.

Retirement annuity contracts: Prior to the introduction of personal pensions, the only type of pension plan available for an individual to effect independently was a retirement annuity contract, sometimes known as a Section 226 contract because the legislation which initially governed the use of the plans was included in Section 226 of the Income and Corporation Taxes Act 1970. They were broadly similar in nature to the personal pensions which succeeded them, but the details (such as maximum contribution levels and possible retirement ages) were different.

Although no new retirement annuity contracts could be issued following the introduction of personal pensions, existing contracts can be maintained and contributions to them increased. This can be a significant factor for a person with a large income, because the earnings cap, which limits contributions to a personal pension, does not apply to retirement annuities provided that they are a person's sole source of individual pension planning.

Stakeholder pensions

This new form of private pension became available from 6 April 2001. The government's aim in introducing it was to take some of the pressure off the state provision of pensions by encouraging more individuals to contribute to their own pension arrangement. They felt that this could be achieved by organizing a scheme which is simple and has lower costs.

Although stakeholder pensions are available to most people, they were intended to be particularly attractive to people at lower earnings levels, who traditionally do not have pension provision and who rely on the state pension. Early indications suggest that this move to include the lower paid has largely failed, with the majority of stakeholder pensions being purchased by the financially more sophisticated, who would have been making pension provision anyway – by means of personal pensions or additional voluntary contributions (AVCs) – and can do so more cost-effectively through stakeholder pensions.

One common misconception is that stakeholder pensions are state pensions. They are in fact private pensions, although there are certain circumstances in which the government makes it compulsory for stakeholder pension facilities to be provided by employers.

Stakeholder pensions are similar to personal pensions in many ways, for instance:

● They are money purchase schemes;

● The pension can be commenced between 50 and 75;

● 25% of the fund can be taken as a tax-free lump sum;

● Tax relief on contributions is available;

● They can be used to contract out of SERPS.

There are also some fundamental differences, for example:

● It is not necessary to have earned income: up to £3,600 pa can be contributed by persons with no earnings (contributions can even be made on behalf of children);

- Tax relief on contributions will be available at the basic rate, even to non-taxpayers;

- Members of occupational schemes who earn less than £30,000 can contribute up to £3,600 gross pa, and it seems likely that stakeholder pensions will replace additional voluntary contributions as the main means by which employees within that earnings range purchase additional pension benefits.

- Charges cannot exceed 1% of the fund value pa, and entry and exit charges are not permitted. One effect of this particular restriction (rather like the similar limit on CAT-standard ISAs) is that the low limit on charges precludes the payment of commission to independent financial advisers – and this may result in people finding it difficult to obtain advice on stakeholder pensions. To overcome this problem, the government has prepared a set of decision-making flow-charts, known as decision trees, which people can use to determine whether stakeholder pensions are appropriate to their own circumstances.

Employers with five or more employees, if they do not provide an occupational pension scheme, must make a stakeholder scheme available to all their employees who meet certain criteria. The employees are not obliged to join, but the employer must provide a payroll deduction system for those who do join, and pay the employees' contributions to a stakeholder pension provider. The employers themselves are not obliged to contribute to the scheme.

Stakeholder pension schemes must be registered with the Occupational Pensions Regulatory Authority (OPRA), and can be run by a board of trustees or by stakeholder scheme managers.

4.11 Mortgages

Mortgages are the most common method of purchasing residential property in the UK. Historically, building societies were the main providers of mortgage loans. Since the deregulation of the financial markets in the 1980s, banks and specialist mortgage finance companies have also offered mortgages and a range of related products.

House purchase loans are usually known as mortgage loans because the borrower mortgages the property, in other words creates a legal charge over the title deeds to the lender as security for the loan. The full name of this type of mortgage is charge by deed expressed to be by way of a legal mortgage. A legal charge is referred to in Scotland as a standard security.

The borrower, who mortgages the property, is known as the mortgagor, and the lender, who takes an interest in the property for the duration of the loan, is referred to as the mortgagee.

Prior to 1925, land was mortgaged by a transfer of ownership of the property to the lender (known as a mortgage by demise), but this is no longer the case. A legal charge does not involve transfer of the property, but is effected by a deed which states that the property has been charged with the debt (the mortgage loan) as security for the lender.

A lender with such a charge is to all intents and purposes in just as strong a position, and is given rights over the property. If the borrower defaults on mortgage repayments, the lender is entitled to take possession of the property and to sell it to recover the money owed. That step is, however, normally taken only as a last resort. Under the terms of a statement of practice established by the Council of Mortgage Lenders, problems of arrears – which generally arise from unforeseen circumstances such as redundancy or family breakdown – should be treated sympathetically and positively. Before resorting to possession, lenders explore all avenues by which an arrangement could be reached, taking into account the borrower's circumstances. There are, in any case, a number of drawbacks for a lender in possessing a property, for instance the difficulty of obtaining a good price, the administrative costs and the lack of goodwill.

At the same time, borrowers retain certain rights, in particular:

- They have the legal right to repay the loan at any time (although this may be subject to an early repayment penalty if the borrower has chosen a fixed-rate, capped-rate or discounted mortgage).

- Borrowers whose properties have been taken into possession by a lender are still entitled to repay the loan right up to the time when the property is sold.

- Borrowers are entitled to the remainder of the sale price after a loan has been repaid, so if the lender sells the property to repay the loan, any surplus remaining after the first and any subsequent charges have been met must be paid over to the borrower.

Mortgages are long-term loans, normally for between 10 years and 30 years, with the most common terms being 20 or 25 years. The amount of the loan can be anything up to 100% of the property value, although it is more common today to advance a lower percentage, due to problems experienced during the property slump of the 1990s. If the value of a property falls, a lender could find that the amount outstanding on the mortgage loan is greater than the value of the asset on which that loan is secured. This is known as negative equity, and can bring problems for both the lender and the borrower. If the borrower, for example, defaults on the payments and the property is taken into possession, the lender may be unable to sell the property for a sufficient amount to repay the loan.

Other factors also affect the amount a lender may be prepared to lend, particularly the lender's assessment of the borrower's ability to repay the loan over the specified period. Factors affecting this assessment include:

- The borrower's income and outgoings;
- The nature and stability of the borrower's employment;

● The borrower's previous history of credit repayments.

Second mortgages

A second mortgage is one that is created when the borrower offers the property for a second time as security while the first lender still has a mortgage secured on the property. The new lender takes a second charge on the property; the original lender retains the deeds, and his charge takes precedence over subsequent charges. This means that in the event of a sale due to default, the original lender's claims will first be met in full; if sufficient surplus then remains, the second mortgagee's charge comes into play.

Clearly, a lender will only offer a second mortgage if there is sufficient equity in the property: in this context, equity refers to the excess of the value of the property over the outstanding amount of any loans secured on it.

Since second mortgages represent a higher risk to the lender, they are likely to be offered at higher rates of interest than first mortgages.

Repaying a mortgage loan

There are two fundamentally different methods of repaying a mortgage loan. These are the repayment mortgage, sometimes also called a capital and interest mortgage, and the interest-only mortgage. Traditionally, mortgages were of the repayment type, but since endowment mortgages (the earliest form of interest-only mortgage) began to become popular in the 1960s, controversy has raged about which is the better option for borrowers. In fact, the costs are generally not dissimilar, and each type has advantages and drawbacks, so the most appropriate choice depends on the circumstances and preferences of individual borrowers.

Repayment mortgages

With a repayment mortgage, the borrower makes monthly payments to the lender, with each monthly amount consisting partly of interest and partly of capital repayment. The amount of capital outstanding therefore reduces over the period of the loan until it is fully repaid at the end of the term.

The monthly amount is calculated in such a way that – provided interest rates do not change – it remains the same throughout the term of the loan. This means that the relative proportions of capital and interest in the payment amount vary throughout the term, being mainly interest towards the beginning of the term, and changing steadily to mainly capital towards the end of the term. The effect of this is that the outstanding capital amount reduces slowly in the early years of the loan, but falls at an increasing rate as time passes. If interest rates go up or down, the repayment amount is increased or decreased, or alternatively the mortgage term could be extended or shortened.

One advantage of this method is that – provided repayments are fully made and account is taken of all changes in interest rate – the loan will be fully repaid by the end of the term.

However, if the borrower – or any other person whose income contributes to the repayments – should die before the end of the mortgage term, the surviving family may have difficulty in maintaining the payments and, at worst, may have to sell the property and find somewhere else to live. Separate life assurance protection can be taken out to cover this eventuality. The policy should be arranged to pay out on the death of the borrower or on the first death of joint borrowers. The most appropriate policy is a decreasing term assurance policy on which the amount payable on death (the sum assured) reduces over time in line with the amount of capital outstanding on the mortgage. Such policies are traditionally known as mortgage protection policies; some confusion has, however, arisen in recent years following the introduction of policies offering short-term sickness, accident and redundancy cover for mortgage repayments, which are often also referred to as mortgage protection.

Interest-only mortgages

In the case of an interest-only mortgage loan, the monthly payments to the lender are made up solely of interest on the loan. No capital repayments are made to the lender during the term of the loan, and the capital amount outstanding does not reduce at all. The gross monthly interest amount therefore changes only if the mortgage interest rate is increased or decreased.

Of course, the borrower still has the responsibility of repaying the amount borrowed at the end of the term. This is normally achieved through the borrower making regular payments to an appropriate savings scheme, although the loan could be repaid out of other resources, for instance from the proceeds of a legacy. Lenders generally require some confirmation that a repayment vehicle is in place: this may mean, for instance, that an endowment policy is legally assigned to them, or simply that they hold the policy, certificate or other documents relating to the savings plan together with a letter confirming that they are to retain them until the debt is repaid. This latter system is known as an equitable arrangement rather than a legal arrangement.

The main schemes used for this purpose are endowment assurance policies, personal pensions, stakeholder pensions and individual savings accounts (ISAs).

Details of the use of the main savings schemes for mortgage repayment purposes are given below.

Endowment assurances

Both with-profit and unit-linked endowments can be used for mortgage purposes. In each case, special adaptations have been developed to take account of the particular needs of mortgage repayment.

One feature of life policies is that they can be legally assigned to a third party, who effectively becomes the owner of the policy and is entitled to receive the benefits in the event of a claim. Many lenders require the endowment to be assigned to them as part of the mortgage deal; others may simply require that the policy document be passed into their possession, without a formal assignment.

Low-cost endowment: Borrowers prefer to use with-profit policies rather than non-profit, because of the potentially better returns (for details, refer to Section 4.5 on life assurance-based investment products). The problem is, however, that the premiums are higher – an important consideration for most borrowers, who are seeking to minimize their mortgage costs.

The low-cost endowment provides a suitable compromise by basing premiums on a sum assured that is lower than the mortgage loan amount, but which will, including the bonuses which are expected to be declared over the policy term, become sufficient to repay the loan. Since bonuses are not guaranteed, the basic sum assured is calculated using a conservative estimate of future bonus rates – often around 75% of the company's current reversionary bonus rate. Terminal bonuses are not taken into account.

If the borrower were to die before the bonuses had reached the required level, the amount paid out would be insufficient to repay the loan. To cover this shortfall, a decreasing term assurance is added to the policy, the additional benefit being calculated as just sufficient to make up the difference between the mortgage amount and the current level of sum assured plus reversionary bonuses. Some companies add a level term assurance, or even a level convertible term assurance, in place of the decreasing term assurance.

If the total of sum assured plus bonuses does not reach the amount of the loan at the end of the term, it is – of course – the borrower's responsibility to fund the difference. Life companies assist their policyholders to avoid this by including regular reviews of the progress of their mortgage-related endowments to check whether the policy is on target to reach the required amount by the end of the term. If the policy does not seem to be on target, the company may recommend an increase in premium, possibly without further medical evidence being required, or may suggest other ways of addressing the problem.

On the other hand, if the total benefit at maturity, including bonuses, is greater than the amount required to repay the loan, the surplus provides a tax-free windfall for the borrower.

Unit-linked endowment: When used for mortgage purposes, the premium required is calculated as the amount which, if unit prices increase at a specified conservative rate of growth, will provide a fund sufficient to repay the loan at the end of the term. Policyholders can choose which fund or funds to use for their investment, but it is usually recommended that premiums be invested in a managed fund: it would certainly not be wise to use a very speculative fund for mortgage repayment purposes.

The growth rate is not guaranteed, and it is the borrower's responsibility to ensure that the policy will provide sufficient funds to repay the loan. Regular reviews, by the life company, of the policy's progress enable the borrower to increase the premiums if the policy is not on target. Most companies also provide the facility to switch to a cash fund, or similar, in order to protect the policy value from sudden market falls towards the end of the term.

One advantage of the unit-linked policy as a repayment vehicle is that, in a strongly rising market, the value of the policy may reach the required amount before the end of the term. In that event, the policy can be surrendered and the loan repaid early – thus saving on future interest, and freeing the repayment amounts for the client to use for other purposes.

However, the actual performance of endowment plans (especially with-profit plans) during the 1990s has led to a major review of this area of financial advice, and during 1999 the regulatory authorities instructed providers of endowment plans to review the actual performance of these products. This was for three main reasons:

- Poor performance of endowment plans during the 1990s;

- Concern over the standard of advice provided by financial advisers in making sure customers understood the risks involved with investment-backed schemes;

- Concern that holders of endowment mortgages would be faced with a large shortfall on the maturity proceeds, leaving them unable to repay their mortgage debt.

Pension mortgages

One of the attractive benefits of a personal pension plan or stakeholder pension is that up to 25% of the accumulated fund can be taken as a tax-free cash sum when the pension payments commence. This fact means that these plans have the potential to be used as mortgage repayment vehicles, with the loan being repaid out of the cash lump sum.

This method of mortgage repayment is clearly available only to individuals who are eligible to take out a personal pension plan or a stakeholder pension – but for those who are, the method has considerable financial benefits:

- Regular mortgage repayments, because they take the form of pension contributions, qualify for tax relief at a person's highest rate of tax. The practical effect of this for a higher rate tax-payer, for instance, is that each £100 of contribution costs him or her only £60. (This is in contrast to endowment policy premiums, on which there is no tax relief.)

- The fund in which the contributions are invested is not subject to tax on capital gains, which means that it should grow faster than an equivalent endowment policy fund, which is taxed on both income and capital gains.

On the other hand, there are a number of factors a borrower might feel are possible drawbacks to the use of a pension plan for mortgage repayment purposes:

- There is a minimum age at which the lump sum can be taken: in most cases this is

50, although it can be earlier for some occupations in which a lower normal retirement age is common. This means, in effect, that the term of the mortgage must run until at least age 50, and the mortgage could not be paid off earlier, even if the fund had grown to a sufficient value.

- Because only 25% of the fund can be taken in cash, a fund of four times the loan value must be built up, which means that contributions must be four times what is actually required to repay the loan. The remaining 75% is not wasted, of course, because it will provide a retirement pension – nevertheless, it may mean that total contributions are more than the borrower can afford, or more than are permitted by the regulations.

- A personal pension or stakeholder pension, unlike an endowment assurance, does not automatically carry with it any life assurance, so a separate policy will be required to cover the repayment of the loan in the event of premature death. It should be possible to use a pension term assurance for this purpose, thereby obtaining tax relief on the premiums.

There is a further characteristic of the use of a pension plan that might be considered a disadvantage by the lender: as with all pension contracts, personal pensions and stakeholder pensions cannot be assigned to a third party as security for a loan or for any other purpose. The lender cannot therefore take possession of the plan or become entitled to receive benefits directly from it. This fact has not, in practice, prevented the majority of lenders from moving into the pension mortgages market.

Individual Saving Accounts (ISAs)

Like PEPs before them, ISAs are recognized as an attractive means of repaying an interest-only mortgage. All managers allow investments to be made on a regular monthly basis, provided, of course, that the overall annual limits are not exceeded.

The ISA managers calculate the amount of regular investment that would be required to produce the necessary lump sum at the end of the mortgage term, based on an assumed growth rate and on specified levels of costs and charges.

The main benefits of using an ISA as a repayment vehicle are:

- The funds grow free of tax on capital gains, thus reducing the cost of repaying the mortgage. Prior to April 2004, funds will also be free of all tax on income, but after that date fund managers will no longer be able to reclaim tax deducted at source from share dividends.

- If the fund's rate of growth exceeds that assumed in the initial calculations, the mortgage can be repaid early.

One drawback to the use of ISAs is that they may not be available in the longer term. Since mortgages are generally long-term contracts, this could lead to many borrowers having to change their repayment vehicle 'mid-stream', as happened when PEPs were withdrawn in 1999.

Other drawbacks associated with the use of ISAs (and other similar investment schemes) are:

- If growth rates do not match the initial assumptions, the final lump sum will fall short of the mortgage amount – unless additional investments have been made.

- In the event of premature death, the value of the ISA investment is unlikely to be sufficient to repay the loan. Additional life assurance cover is required to meet this eventuality.

Mortgage interest options and other schemes

Most mortgage lenders offer a range of options for the payment of interest. The main options are:

- **Variable rate:** This is the basic method, with monthly payments going up or down without limit, broadly in line with changes in the Bank of England base rate. One disadvantage of a variable rate mortgage is that borrowers cannot easily predict the level of future payments, which can lead to budgeting problems.

- **Tracker mortgage:** Similar to the variable-rate mortgage, tracker mortgages are more directly linked to the Bank of England base rate, the rate being specified as (say) 1% above base rate

- **Flexible mortgage:** Flexible mortgages take a number of different forms, but they are generally repayment mortgages. An important common feature is the facility for the borrower to increase or decrease his or her mortgage payments; this may include, at one extreme, the ability to make lump-sum payments, and at the other to take short payment holidays. Some flexible mortgage schemes offer other additional features such as drawdown of extra funds, chequebook facility, or credit and debit cards.

- **Fixed rate:** The interest rate is fixed for a specified period, usually between one and five years, after which interest reverts to the lender's prevailing variable rate. There is often a substantial arrangement fee, charged to offset the lender's costs of reserving money market funds at a fixed rate for a fixed period. There may also be restrictions or penalties on redeeming the mortgage before the end of the fixed-rate period. In some cases the penalties may even extend beyond the end of the period.

- **Capped rate:** The interest rate is the normal variable rate, but subject to an upper limit known as the cap. If there is also a lower limit below which the rate cannot fall, it is known as a cap and collar mortgage. In either case the limits normally apply for a limited period and there is usually an arrangement fee.

- **Discounted mortgage:** This refers to a genuine discount off the normal variable rate (eg 2% off for three years), after which interest reverts to the variable rate. There are generally restrictions or penalties for redeeming the mortgage within a specified period, which may extend beyond the discount period. In the highly competitive mortgage market of recent years, offers of discounted mortgages have been used not only to attract new borrowers, but also to tempt borrowers to transfer from other lenders (or conversely to persuade existing customers not to transfer).

● **Deferred interest:** In the early years of the mortgage, some of the interest is not paid but is added to the outstanding capital. This system may be appropriate for borrowers who expect their income to increase, but both lenders and borrowers should be wary of using it at times when house prices are falling, because it brings an increased danger of negative equity.

● **Low start:** On a repayment mortgage, it may be possible to reduce repayments in the early years by deferring the capital portion of the instalments for the first few years. Borrowers need to be aware that payments will increase at the end of the initial period, and that no capital will have been repaid.

The regulators have in recent times criticized mortgage lenders for aggressively marketing low initial-cost mortgages (such as discounted, deferred interest and low-start mortgages). The principal concern is that when the initial period expires, borrowers will incur a sudden increase in payments, which could lead to a higher rate of defaults.

● **Equity share mortgages:** Developed in the 1980s, these schemes enable borrowers to trade a lower repayment on their mortgage (by paying a lower interest rate on part of the loan) in return for the lender taking a percentage stake in the ownership of the property.

● **Shared ownership mortgages:** Not to be confused with equity share mortgages, these schemes, which also date from the 1980s, were developed mainly by housing associations. They combine rental with owner-occupation by enabling a borrower to buy a stake in a property while renting the remainder of it. Typically, a borrower might initially buy a 25% stake, funded by a mortgage, with the option of buying subsequent 25% shares.

Mortgage interest relief

Tax relief on mortgage interest was originally introduced to encourage people to buy their own homes. In recent years its value had been reduced, first by restricting relief to the basic rate of tax even for higher rate taxpayers, and more recently by detaching the rate of relief from tax rates altogether, so that it was more correctly referred to as interest relief. The government finally withdrew the relief altogether with effect from 6 April 2000 as part of its desire to distribute tax relief more fairly.

Related products

Buying a house with a mortgage loan is a substantial long-term transaction which carries with it a number of responsibilities for a borrower. There are various related financial products which can help people to ensure that those responsibilities are met.

For instance, lenders generally insist that their security – the property itself – is protected by insurance against damage and other perils. In fact, lenders are permitted by law to:

● insist that a property subject to a mortgage is continuously insured by means of a policy that is acceptable to the lender;

● have its interest as mortgagee noted on the policy;

● secure a right over the proceeds of any claim, and to insist that the proceeds be applied to remedy the subject of the claim or to reduce the mortgage debt.

There are two forms of personal insurance protection that are closely related to mortgages, and are therefore appropriate to mention here:

● **Mortgage protection assurance** is a form of decreasing term assurance designed specifically to provide the life cover required to pay off the outstanding capital on a repayment mortgage. Many lenders have special block (bulk purchase) arrangements with insurers for these policies, sometimes branded under the lender's name. This benefits borrowers, who receive streamlined underwriting procedures and very competitive premiums which can be collected along with mortgage repayments. Borrowers are not, however, obliged to accept the lender's choice of insurance.

● **Sickness, accident and redundancy policies** are not restricted to use in mortgage situations, but they are particularly appropriate for protecting borrowers against those three events which can threaten their ability to maintain their mortgage repayments. A typical policy would protect payments for up to two years, although the first three or six months would normally be excluded.

According to statistics from the Council of Mortgage Lenders (CML), unemployment and divorce/separation are the major cause of mortgage arrears. In 1995 the rules under which mortgage interest can be paid by social security benefits (Income Support) were tightened; this has increased the need for individuals to make their own arrangements to cover such eventualities, and there has been a strong lobby for sickness, accident and redundancy cover to be made compulsory.

4.12 Secured and Unsecured Personal Lending

With a secured loan, the borrower offers something of value so that in the event of default, the lender can take the asset and sell it (realize the security) and be repaid out of the proceeds.

The major form of secured personal lending is of course the mortgage loan for house purchase, the security being a first charge on the borrower's private residence. Lenders may grant additional loans for other purposes, secured on the equity in a borrower's property. Other lenders may also be willing to lend money against a second, subsidiary, charge on the property.

By contrast, an unsecured loan relies on the personal promise, or covenant, of the borrower to repay. Unsecured loans are therefore generally higher risk than secured lending, with the consequence that they are subject to higher rates of interest and are normally available only for much shorter terms. For example, whereas mortgages secured on property are available for 25 years or even longer, personal loans are rarely offered for much more than six or seven years.

Unsecured loans have long been available from banks and finance houses, but it was not until the passing of the Building Societies Act 1986 that building societies were able to move into that area of business. Initially they were restricted to no more than 5% of their commercial assets being in the form of unsecured loans, although this has since been increased to 15%.

Unsecured personal lending takes a number of forms, the most common being:

- **Personal loans:** These are offered by banks, building societies and some finance houses. They are normally for a term of one to five years, and the interest rate is generally fixed at the outset and remains unchanged throughout the term.

  Many of the larger lenders operate a centralized assessment of loan applications through telephone call-centres, using a form of credit scoring to assess the suitability of the borrower.

  The loans can be used by the customer for any purpose – typically they are used to purchase cars, fund holidays or consolidate existing higher cost borrowings such as credit card balances.

  The purpose of the loan determines whether it is regulated under the terms of the Consumer Credit Act 1974 (see Chapter 3). Most such loans under £25,000 are regulated by the Act unless they are for house purchase or home improvement.

- **Overdrafts:** An overdraft is a current account facility, offered by all retail banks and some building societies, which enables the customer to continue to use the account in the normal way even though its funds have been exhausted. The bank sets a limit to the amount by which the account can be overdrawn. An overdraft is a convenient form of short-term temporary borrowing, with interest calculated on a daily basis, and its purpose is to assist the customer over a period in which expenditure exceeds income – for instance, to pay for a holiday or to fund the purchase of Christmas gifts.

Because it is essentially a short-term facility, the agreement is usually for a fixed period, after which it must be renegotiated or the funds repaid. Overdrafts that have been agreed in advance with the institution are normally an inexpensive form of borrowing, although there may be an arrangement fee. Unauthorized overdrafts, on the other hand, attract a much higher rate of interest.

Overdrafts are regulated by the Consumer Credit Act 1974, but exempt from the documentary requirements although the annual percentage rate (APR) does have to be shown, to enable customers to make comparisons with alternative borrowing methods.

● **Revolving credit:** This refers to arrangements where the customer can continue to borrow further amounts while still repaying existing debt. There is usually a maximum limit on the amount that can be outstanding, and also a minimum amount to be repaid on a regular basis.

The most common way of providing revolving credit is through credit cards (see below), although some institutions do provide revolving personal loans which allow the borrower to draw down funds as the original debt is repaid.

4.13 Credit Cards, Debit Cards and Charge Cards

It is hard to believe that plastic cards, now an integral part of most people's financial affairs, have been around only for the last 30 years. Their development and their impact have gone hand-in-hand with the rapid advance of the electronic processing technologies on which their systems now largely depend. Many cards can now hold a wealth of information about cardholders and their accounts, and can therefore interact directly with retailers' and banks' electronic equipment; these cards are often referred to as smart cards.

Cards are an extremely convenient way to buy goods and services, and their development has led to a considerable reduction in the use of cash and cheques. Initially restricted mainly to the purchase of petrol and major household items such as electrical goods, they are now acceptable in a wide range of locations, including most major food retailing chains. They come in a number of different forms:

Credit cards

Credit cards enable customers to shop without cash or cheques in any establishment that is a member of the credit-card company's scheme. There are two main credit card companies operating worldwide. Most credit cards issued in the UK are branded to banks, building societies or retail stores, but are basically either Mastercard or Visa. There are exceptions, one of which is Marks and Spencer, which runs its own credit card through a subsidiary finance company.

Originally all credit-card transactions were dealt with manually at the point of sale, but most retailers now have terminals linked directly to the credit-card companies' computers, enabling on-line credit limit checking and authorization of transactions.

As well as providing cash-free purchasing convenience, credit cards are a source of revolving credit. The customer has a credit limit and can use the card for purchases or other transactions up to that amount, provided that at least a specified minimum amount (usually 3% of the outstanding balance) is repaid each month. The customer receives a monthly statement, detailing recent transactions and showing the outstanding balance. If the balance is repaid in full within a certain period (usually 25 days or so), no interest is charged; if a smaller amount is paid, the remainder is carried forward and interest charged at the company's current rate.

Credit cards are an expensive way to borrow, with rates of interest considerably higher than most other lending products; rates vary but some are still over 20%. There is also normally a charge if the card is used to obtain cash either over the counter or from an automated teller machine (ATM). In addition, some credit-card companies charge card-holders an annual fee of around £12.

Credit card companies charge a fee to the retailers for their service. This is deducted as a percentage (typically around 3%) of the value of transactions when settlement is made by the credit card company to the retailer. There are, however, a number of advantages to retailers, in addition to the fact that more customers may be attracted if payment by credit card is available. For instance, payment is guaranteed if the card has been accepted in accordance with the credit card company's rules. Furthermore, the retailer can reduce his or her own bank charges because the credit card vouchers paid into a bank account are treated as cash.

Charge cards

Although used by the customer in the same way as a credit card to make purchases, the outstanding balance on a charge card must be paid in full each month. The best known examples are American Express and Diners Club.

Debit cards

An innovation introduced in the late 1980s, debit cards – such as Switch and Delta – enable cardholders to make payments for goods by presenting the card and signing a voucher, in just the same way as with credit cards or charge cards. In the case of debit cards, however, the effect of the transaction is that funds equal to the amount spent are transferred electronically from the cardholder's current account to the account of the retailer. This is known as EFTPOS (electronic fund transfer at point of sale) although at present the funds are not transferred instantaneously. The system therefore effectively replaces the use of cheques, and should in the longer term reduce handling costs.

Debit cards can also be used to withdraw cash from ATMs, and many debit cards now also act as cheque guarantee cards.

Electronic purse

A more recent innovation – introduced in the 1990s and still at the pilot stage – is the electronic purse, pioneered by Mondex. This is a system designed to enable customers to make purchases using a smart card that can be electronically topped up with funds. It is aimed not so much at the medium to large transactions (for which there are already a number of electronic payment methods) as at the type of small transactions for which cash is still the normal payment medium.

Trials of the electronic purse system were held in 1998 in the UK (Swindon) as well as the USA, Hong Kong and Japan. First reports suggest that the initial response in New York was not favourable, with stores finding the smart card machinery difficult to use, and customers showing reluctance to use their cards regularly. At present it is not clear how this market will develop.

One of the major problems related to plastic cards is the fraudulent use of stolen cards, particularly credit cards and cheque guarantee cards. Although cardholders are warned to sign their cards as soon as they receive them, the presence of a signature on the card makes fraudulent use a possibility. A number of initiatives have been undertaken in an attempt to reduce opportunities for fraud: publicity campaigns have aimed to make customers and retailers more aware of the need to be more vigilant; lists of stolen cards are sent to retailers; some card companies have experimented with card-holders' photographs on their cards, but the quality of the picture reproduction was so poor that the experiment was not a success. However, most companies still deliver new and replacement credit cards to their customers by ordinary mail!

4.14 Sources of Advice

It will be clear – even from the brief outline of financial products given in these notes – that the financial services marketplace is not only extremely complex but also changing and developing at an increasingly rapid pace.

It is not surprising, then, that members of the public should increasingly feel that they need the advice and guidance of professionals in order to find their way through the financial jungle. This is particularly true in the areas of investment, mortgages and pensions – not least because those transactions often involve large amounts of money and long timescales.

Fortunately there is plenty of help available, and the work of the regulatory bodies increasingly means that customers should receive advice only from suitably knowledgeable and skilled practitioners.

It is important that customers should know where they can go for advice, and that they should be made aware of any potential limitations to the advice they are given.

Information about some of the possible sources of advice is given below.

Banks and building societies

Traditionally, banks were thought of as giving advice only on the products they themselves supplied, such as deposits and loans, and on related matters – for instance business advice to customers seeking a business loan. Similarly, building societies would advise on their own savings schemes and on mortgage loans.

Since deregulation, that situation has considerably changed, with banks and building societies moving into many other business areas and offering advice on a wide range of financial products.

Customers now turn to their bank or building society for advice on life assurance and pensions, on regular savings and lump-sum investments, on mortgage repayment methods, on unit trusts and ISAs. Banks and building societies employ financial advisers who have to meet the same qualification and skills requirements as their counterparts in life offices, investment companies, insurance brokers and all the other places from which advice can be obtained.

Some banks and building societies operate as tied advisers under the terms of the Financial Services and Markets Act 2000, whereas others provide independent financial advice (for definitions of these categories of advice, see below). Some may even have separate subsidiary organizations operating in each of the two different categories. The FSA has recently put forward plans which could lead to the end of the present system which differentiates between tied and independent advisers in favour of 'multi-tied' advisers.

Tied intermediaries

Under the current polarization rules, which were first introduced by the Financial Services Act 1986 and continue to operate for the time being under the FSMA 2000, everyone who gives investment advice must be either tied or independent. They must also – as soon as they introduce themselves to a new customer – make it perfectly clear which category they are in and what each category means.

Tied intermediaries are restricted to advising on products from the range of one company – or one marketing group of related companies (for instance a life insurance company and its pensions and unit trust subsidiaries). Since March 2001, however, there has been an interim change to the rules, which permits tied agents whose company does not offer stakeholder pensions to recommend the stakeholder product of another organization.

Tied advisers can be individuals employed by the product provider – eg direct sales staff – or they may be individuals or organizations working as insurance brokers or advisers.

The rules of best advice require that tied advisers may only recommend a product to a client if the company to which they are tied offers a product that meets that client's needs. If no such product exists in the company's range, it is not permissible to offer the nearest alternative. Instead, the client should be recommended to seek independent advice.

As an example, consider a customer who is proposing to take out a life assurance-based product. The situation in many of the banks and larger building societies is that branch-based financial advisers are normally authorized to advise only on the products of one life office (ie they are tied advisers). In some, but not all, cases, the host life company is a subsidiary within the same group (for instance Halifax Life). If the life office does not have an appropriate product, the client will be recommended to seek independent financial advice, which may be available through a separate arm of the organization.

Independent financial advisers

Independent financial advisers (IFAs) are not tied to any life office, unit trust company or other product provider. They are therefore able to review the whole financial services marketplace to select the most suitable product for their customer (in fact they are required to do so by the regulations established under the Financial Services Act 1986 and which continue to operate under the FSMA 2000).

Organizations offering independent financial advice range in size from self-employed sole traders to large multinational corporations. To comply with all the regulations can be a time-consuming and expensive business for the smaller organizations, so many have joined a network such as DBS. By joining together with other IFAs in a network that provides centralized training, compliance and research facilities (for a fee based usually on a percentage of their earnings), they are able to satisfy the regulatory requirements without having to divert too much of their time and energy from the process of meeting clients and providing financial advice.

Other sources of financial advice

Professionals in many walks of life find that advice on financial products is an integral – if incidental – part of the service they give to their clients. Prior to December 2001, under the terms of the Financial Services Act 1986, if they gave any investment advice they had to be authorized. This was normally achieved through certification by their recognized professional body – for example by the Law Society for solicitors.

Under the Financial Services and Markets Act 2000, such professionals are exempt from authorization, provided the investment advice they give is only incidental to their main business.

Brief notes are included below on some of the individuals and organizations whose work may include the giving of incidental financial advice.

Insurance brokers

Many insurance brokers deal only in general insurance, and therefore do not have to be authorized to give investment advice under the Financial Services and Markets Act 2000. However, if they also transact life assurance and pensions business, authorization is likely to be required. Many brokers are members of the General Insurance Standards Council (GISC), a non-statutory body set up to regulate the sales, advisory and service standards of the general insurance industry. Members are expected to follow the standards of good practice set out by the GISC.

Accountants

For many self-employed people and small business owners, their accountant is their main regular point of contact regarding financial matters. It is, therefore, not surprising that accountants are often asked for advice, particularly on pensions, but also on other insurance and investment matters. If they give such advice, they must consider whether their advice is merely incidental to their normal work. If it is more than that, and in particular if they receive commission from product providers for products which they recommend to customers, they will need to be authorized by the Financial Services Authority.

Solicitors

Investment advice is incidental to a number of aspects of solicitors' work. For example:

- Preparation of a client's will may lead to discussion of inheritance tax liabilities and of the ways in which life assurance could be used to mitigate the effects of the tax.

- Dealing with the distribution of a deceased client's estate could lead to beneficiaries' enquiring about how best to invest their legacies.

- Acting for a client who is purchasing a house may involve a solicitor in the business of obtaining or repaying a mortgage.

Provided that their involvement in investment advice is genuinely incidental, they should be exempt from authorization.

Estate agents

Although it is not essential to use the services of an estate agent in order to sell a property, the majority of people do so. Every sale provides the estate agent with contacts that could lead to the sale of financial services products of various kinds.

While estate agents are of course working for the vendor, it is the contact with prospective purchasers in particular that can open up avenues for financial advice and sales. For example, since they normally work on a percentage commission basis, estate agents' fees depend on a sale being made: they therefore have more than a passing interest in the ability of the purchaser to obtain a mortgage. For this reason, many estate agents are actively involved in assisting purchasers to obtain a mortgage. If they wish to be able to advise on the different types of mortgage, they will need to comply with the Mortgage Code. If they wish to give advice on possible repayment vehicles such as ISAs and personal pensions, they need to be authorized under the terms of the Financial Services and Markets Act 2000.

Recognition of the opportunity to cross-sell financial products led, in the late 1980s, to a significant number of financial institutions following the example set by Lloyds Bank a few years before, and moving into the estate agency market, often through the purchase of existing agencies. It proved to be a painful experience for many organizations, with cross-selling proving to be much more difficult to achieve than had been anticipated. The situation was compounded by a downturn in the housing market which seriously undermined the basic profitability of estate agency. Many institutions reviewed their estate agency operations, among them Prudential, which concluded that the level of investment necessary to put its estate agency network back on its feet would not be an effective use of resources, and withdrew from the market by selling the chain at a considerable loss.

Direct operations

A major development in the late 1990s has seen the emergence of a number of direct organizations offering banking, insurance and investment products through telephone call centres. The best known are perhaps First Direct banking, Direct Line which has expanded from insurance to other areas, and Richard Branson's Virgin organization which deals in banking, insurance and investment.

Running call-centre operations in the life assurance and investment fields is less straightforward, for the simple reason that the Financial Services Authority regulations demand an in-depth fact-finding process before advice can be given. For this reason, call centres tend to offer a straightforward product on an execution-only basis. This means that full information is provided about the product but no advice is given as to its suitability to the individual client.

Stockbroking and share dealing

Most investors deal in shares through agency brokers, whose offices can be found in all cities and many towns throughout the UK. Their role is described in Chapter 2. Bank customers often ask their bank to arrange share deals on their behalf.

Agency brokers and the banks' own share-dealing departments are also able to give advice to clients on the selection of shares and the timing of purchases and sales. The giving of this advice is governed by the Financial Services and Markets Act 2000 and advisers must be authorized by Financial Services Authority.

4.15 Key Issues Affecting the Market

The financial services market is very large and extremely complex. Its size, characteristics and direction depend on the subtle interaction of variety of factors. Some of those factors are:

Government policy

The extent to which individuals become involved in the purchase of financial services products depends very largely on how much disposable income (and capital) they have. Governments may, for a variety of economic and political reasons, seek to control the amount of money in supply by the manipulation, for instance, of interest rates or taxation. A discussion of monetary and fiscal policy is included in Chapter 1.

Privatization: one element of government policy that had an impact on the investment habits of the British public was the privatization of utilities that were previously in public ownership, such as British Telecom. This was a prominent policy of the Conservative government in the 1980s and early 1990s, but has not been a significant issue for some years now. There were several reasons for its implementation, some ideological and some financial: privatization raised a lot of revenue which permitted certain tax and spending plans to be implemented.

One of its aims was to encourage the development of a share-owning democracy, and there is no doubt that many people became shareholders who had not previously considered that form of investment.

Taxation

As mentioned earlier, governments use taxation not only for the basic process of raising revenue, but also as a means of controlling the money supply. Manipulation of the taxation regime can have an impact on the financial services marketplace in two ways:

- Increased general taxation reduces the amount of money available for investment or to fund loan repayments.

- Tightening of the taxation regime for particular products makes them less attractive to investors. An example of this is the government's decision in 1998 to remove the right of pension fund managers to reclaim tax deducted from dividends received. The effect of this step is that pension funds are now taxed on a large proportion of their income, whereas previously they were effectively tax-free. Although this move was clearly made in order to bring in more tax revenue, it seems to be in conflict with the government's need to persuade individuals to contribute more toward their own pension provision. A similar change was planned for PEPs and stocks and shares ISAs with effect from 6 April 2001; after that date fund managers were not be able to reclaim tax deducted from dividends.

It is worth mentioning that, with many of the more popular investment schemes, such as unit trusts and investment trusts, there are two possible levels at which taxation can occur: the fund managers can be taxed, and the investor can be taxed. It is essential to view both aspects when assessing the tax position of an investment.

Before considering the three main UK taxes that affect the personal sector, a final thought about taxation principles in general. Taxes can be either:

- **Progressive:** The burden of taxation weighs more heavily on higher income earners or on the more wealthy. Income tax is a progressive tax, because higher tax rates apply successively to higher bands of income and higher earners therefore pay a greater proportion of their earnings in tax.

- **Regressive:** In this case the tax bears more heavily on people with lower incomes. Indirect taxes (ie taxes on expenditure rather than income) are generally regressive. Value added tax (VAT) is an example: if two people buy the same item and pay the same VAT, the tax is a higher proportion of the income of a low earner than of a high earner.

4.16 Personal Tax

Domicile and residence

Whether or not a person is liable to pay income tax, capital gains tax and inheritance tax will depend on the taxpayer's residence or domicile according to UK law.

Residence affects mainly income tax and also capital gains tax. Any person who is present in the UK for at least 183 days in a given tax year is regarded as a UK resident for tax purposes. A person who is not a UK resident in a particular tax year may however be defined as ordinarily resident if they normally live in the UK.

A person who is resident and ordinarily resident in the UK should be subject to UK income tax on his or her worldwide earned and unearned income, whether or not such income is brought into the UK. Similarly capital gains tax is charged on the realization of gains anywhere in the world. However the UK has double taxation agreements with many other countries, the purpose of which is to ensure that individuals are not in fact taxed twice on the same income or gains.

Domicile is best described as the country which an individual treats as his or her home, even if he or she were to live for a time in another country. Everyone acquires a domicile of origin at birth. This is the domicile of their father on the date of their birth (or the domicile of the mother if the father is not known).

A person can change to a different domicile (known as domicile of choice) by going to live in a different country, intending to stay there permanently and showing that intent by generally 'putting down roots' in the new country and severing connections with the former country. There is no specific process for this.

Domicile mainly affects liability to inheritance tax. If a person is domiciled in the UK, inheritance tax is chargeable on assets anywhere in the world, whereas for persons not domiciled in the UK, tax is due only on assets in the UK. However, persons who are not UK domiciled but have lived in the UK for at least 17 of the previous 20 years are deemed to be UK domiciled for inheritance tax purposes.

Income tax

Income tax is one of the main sources of government revenue. Liability for income tax is based income received in a tax year or fiscal year which, in the UK, runs from 6 April in one calendar year to 5 April in the following year. Tax is due from individuals on their income from employment (including benefits in kind such as company cars) and also on interest, dividends and other income they receive from investment.

Not all the income that an individual receives is taxable. For instance, certain types of income – such as the interest on cash ISAs – are exempt from tax. In addition, all UK residents, including children from the day of their birth, have a personal allowance, in other words an amount of income that can be received each year before income tax begins to be charged. In the 2001/2002 tax year, this allowance is £4,535, rising to £5,990 for people aged 65 and over, and to £6,260 at age 75.

Prior to April 2000, married couples were entitled to receive an additional allowance, but this has now been withdrawn, except that it continues to be available to couples where at least one spouse was 65 or over on 6th April 2000.

In addition to these allowances, taxpayers are permitted to make certain deductions from their gross income before their tax liability is calculated. These include:

● Pensions contributions (within specified limits);

● Allowable expenses, such as costs incurred wholly in carrying out one's employment.

When all the relevant deductions have been made from a person's gross income, what remains is his or her taxable income. This is the amount to which the appropriate tax rate or rates is applied in order to calculate the tax due.

Income tax rates, and the bands of income to which they apply, are reviewed by the government each year. Any changes are announced in the Budget – normally in March – and included in the subsequent Finance Act. In the 2001/2002 tax year, the lowest rate of tax (applying to taxable income up to £1,880) is 10%; the basic rate (on taxable earned income from £1,881 to £29,400) is 22%, and the higher rate (on taxable income above £29,400) is 40%.

A different basic rate (20%) is applied to income from investments, for instance the interest on bank and building society deposit accounts.

For most forms of investment income, tax is normally deducted at source. This applies, for example, to interest on bank and building society deposit accounts and to ordinary shares. In the case of deposit accounts, non-taxpayers can choose to receive their interest without deduction of tax by signing an appropriate declaration.

The method of collection of income tax from employment depends on the nature of a person's work:

- Employees pay income tax on the pay-as-you-earn (PAYE) system, under which the amount of tax due is calculated by their employers (using tables supplied by the Inland Revenue), deducted from their wages or salary, and passed on by their employers to the Inland Revenue.

- Self-employed persons (including partners in a business partnership) pay income tax directly to the Inland Revenue on the basis of a declaration of net profits calculated from their accounts. Under the current self-assessment rules, taxpayers are expected to calculate their own liability and submit their figures to the tax authorities for approval (although tax-payers who submit their returns promptly can ask the Inland Revenue to do the calculation for them). Many self-employed people engage an accountant to prepare their accounts for them and to deal with the Inland Revenue on their behalf.

In the past, husbands and wives were treated as a single unit for income tax purposes, with the wife's income being treated as if it belonged to the husband! Amazingly, this anachronism survived until 1990, when the introduction of independent taxation resulted in income tax rules being applied separately to all individuals.

National Insurance

National Insurance contributions are a form of taxation in everything but name. They are in effect a tax on earned income, and are payable in different ways according to whether the earner is employed or self-employed.

They are classified as follows:

- **Class 1:** These are paid by employees on earnings between certain levels known as the primary threshold and the upper earnings limit. They are also paid by employers on employees' earnings above a lower limit called the secondary threshold – but with no upper limit. Reduced contributions apply if employees are contracted out of the state earnings-related pension scheme (SERPS).

- **Class 2:** These are flat-rate contributions paid by the self-employed if their annual profits exceed a specified lower threshold (£3,955 in 2001/02). They are quoted as a weekly amount (£2 per week in 2001/02), but are normally paid monthly by direct debit. Many self-employed people also pay Class 4 contributions.

- **Class 3:** These are voluntary contributions that can be paid by people who would not otherwise be entitled to the full basic pension or sickness benefits. This can occur because a person has, for instance, taken a career break or spent some time working overseas. They are flat rate contributions (of £6.75 per week in 2000/01).

- **Class 4:** These are additional contributions payable by self-employed persons on their annual profits between specified minimum and maximum levels. They are paid to the Inland Revenue in half-yearly instalments along with income tax. The rate for 2001/02 is 7% of profits between £4,535 and £29,900.

Capital gains tax

Capital gains tax (CGT) is payable on the net gain made on the disposal of certain physical assets and the realization of many financial assets, including shares and unit trusts.

There are some circumstances under which CGT is not due – in particular it is not payable when property changes hands as the result of a death.

Similarly there are certain assets which are exempt from CGT, for instance a person's main (or only) private residence, and personal tangible movable possessions ('goods and chattels') valued at less than £6,000. A number of investment products also excluded, including gilt-edged stocks, National Savings products and ISAs.

Tax is payable on net gains made in the tax year, after deducting any allowable capital losses which were made in the same year or carried forward from previous years. Each individual also has an annual CGT allowance (£7,500 in 2001/2002); rather like the personal income tax allowances, this is the level of gains which can be made in the tax year before CGT starts to be payable.

The calculation of the amount of a taxable gain is governed by a number of rules which make it more complex than merely a simple subtraction of purchase price from sale price; for example:

- Costs of purchase can be added to the purchase price, and selling costs can be deducted from the sale price.

- The cost of improvements to an asset can be treated as part of its purchase price (but costs of maintenance and repair cannot).

- Capital gains made prior to 31 March 1982 are not taxed, so for an asset acquired before that date, its value on that date can be substituted for the actual purchase price.

● The purchase price (or value at 31 March 1982, as appropriate) can also be increased in line with the increase in the retail price index (RPI) between the acquisition date (or March 1982) and April 1998. This benefit, known as indexation, is allowed because the government seeks to tax only those gains which are above and beyond the increase in an asset's value due to inflation.

When the amount of the gain has been established, and combined with other gains and losses made by the individual in the same tax year, the net gain is taxed as if it were an addition to the individual's income for that tax year, using the current income tax rates. For personal assets that have been held longer than two years, the amount of capital gains tax is then scaled down on a sliding scale which reaches a minimum of 60% for assets held for 10 years or longer. A different sliding scale applies for business assets.

One constant source of complaint about the capital gains tax regime is that CGT is due on the whole gain in the year in which the gain is realized, even where that gain has actually been made over a longer period. This means that only one annual exemption can be set against what may be many years' worth of gain. In the past, some holders of shares and unit trusts sought to minimize the effect of this by selling their holding each year and repurchasing it the following day, thus realizing a smaller gain which could be covered by that year's exemption. This was known as bed and breakfasting, but the government effectively outlawed the process by a new rule introduced in the 1998 Budget: any shares and unit trusts that are sold and repurchased within a 30-day period will now be treated, for CGT purposes, as if those two related transactions had not taken place.

Retirement relief: At present, CGT retirement relief is available when people over 50 (or those retiring due to ill-health) sell all or part of their business. However, it was announced in the 1998 Budget that retirement relief would be phased out over five years, disappearing altogether with effect from April 2003.

Inheritance tax

This tax, as its name suggests, is levied mainly on the estates of deceased persons. The tax is charged at 40% of the amount by which the value of the estate exceeds the nil-rate band, which is £242,000 in 2001/2002. In order to prevent avoidance of tax by 'death-bed' gifts or transfers, the figure on which tax is based includes not only the amount of the estate on death but also the value of any money or assets that have been given away in the seven years prior to death.

Inheritance tax (IHT) is also payable in certain circumstances when assets are transferred from a person's estate during their lifetime (usually in the form of gifts). Most gifts made during a person's lifetime are potentially exempt transfers (PETs) and are not subject to tax at the time of the transfer. If the donor survives for seven years after making the gift, these transactions become fully exempt and no tax is payable. If the donor dies within seven years of making the gift, the tax becomes due (although the amount is scaled down by tapering relief over the final four years of the seven).

Some lifetime gifts – notably those to companies, other organizations, and certain trusts – are not PETs but chargeable lifetime transfers, on which tax at a reduced rate of 20% is immediately due. As with PETs, the full tax is due if the donor dies within seven years (subject to the same tapering relief), and any excess over the 20% already paid then becomes payable.

There are a number of important exemptions from inheritance tax:

- Transfers between spouses both during their lifetime and on death.

- Small gifts of up to £250 (cash or value) per recipient in each tax year.

- Donations to charity, to political parties, and to the nation.

- Wedding gifts up to £1,000 (increased to £5,000 for gifts from parents, or £2,500 from grandparents).

- Gifts that are made on a regular basis out of income, and which do not affect the donor's standard of living.

- An annual exemption of up to £3,000 per tax year for gifts not covered by other exemptions. If not used, all or part of this £3,000 can be carried forward for one year but no further.

4.17 Value Added Tax

Value added tax (VAT) is an indirect tax levied on the sale of most goods and the supply of most services in the UK. The current rate (2001/2002) is 17.5%.

Some goods and services are exempt from VAT, including certain financial transactions such as loans and insurance. The supply of financial advice is not exempt, and advisers who charge a fee for their service are subject to VAT in the same way as solicitors or accountants.

The supply of health and education services is exempt, and a number of related goods and services are currently zero-rated. This is not technically the same as being exempt: zero-rated goods and services are theoretically subject to VAT but the rate of tax applied is currently 0% (though this could be changed). Zero-rated items include food, books, children's clothes, domestic water supply and medicines. Domestic heating is charged at a reduced rate, currently 5%.

Businesses, including the self-employed, are required to register for VAT if their annual turnover (not profit) is above a certain figure (£54,000 in 2001/02). Firms with turnover below this figure can choose to register for VAT if they wish, but are not obliged to. An advantage of registering is that VAT paid out on business expenses can be reclaimed; two disadvantages are (i) the fact that the firm's goods or service are more expensive to customers (by the amount of the VAT which the firm must charge), and (ii) the additional administration involved in collecting, accounting for and paying VAT.

5

TRENDS AND MAJOR ISSUES IN THE FINANCIAL SERVICES INDUSTRY

5.1 Introduction

The Financial Services industry is constantly changing. The social, cultural and legislative background against which it operates is evolving more quickly than at any time in the past and the industry is responding by developing its products, services and marketing strategies and techniques.

This section of the book provides a brief introduction to some of the strategic issues likely to face the industry in the coming years. These issues have the potential to alter considerably the nature and structure of financial services markets and thus to affect the day-to-day roles of companies and individuals throughout the industry.

Because of the rapidly evolving nature of many of the issues, this section can give only a brief overview of these topics, some of which have also been referred to elsewhere in the book. For those readers who are using this book as an aid to their preparation for the Financial Services Environment examination (an element of the Diploma in Financial Services Management), an essential part of their study is to read widely in the quality financial press and in key periodicals such as *Financial World* and the *Economist*, because candidates for this examination will be expected to display familiarity with relevant current developments.

5.2 Europe and the Euro

The impact of European monetary policy

The euro is now a fact of economic life. It was introduced in January 1999 and in January 2002 it became the legal tender currency of the 12 countries which have adopted it. Out of the 15 members of the European Union, only the UK, Sweden and Denmark remain outside the euro-zone. The UK government has shown a willingness to commit the country to prepare for entry to the euro subject to a referendum and to the economy's fulfilling five economic tests which relate to the following:

- sustainable convergence between the UK economy and the euro area

- the flexibility of the UK economy to adapt to shocks

- the impact on long-term investment decisions in the UK

- the impact on the UK financial services industry

- the long-term impact on jobs

The advantages to the UK of joining the euro are:

- the nominal exchange rate certainty which business will enjoy together with greater price transparency, more efficient allocation of resources and potentially a more dynamic economy

- the development of deep and liquid euro markets which will increase competition and reduce spreads between borrowing and lending rates

The main disadvantages are:

- the loss of UK sovereignty over monetary policy, which would be carried out by the Eurosystem and not the Bank of England

- a 'one size fits all' monetary policy whereby interest rates would be set to suit the euro-zone as a whole and would not necessarily fit the needs of the UK economy. This explains why one of the Chancellor's five economic tests is economic convergence between the UK and euro area.

We saw in Chapter 1 that UK monetary policy is directed by the Monetary Policy Committee of the Bank of England and that this body is committed to achieving the government's direct inflation target of 2.5%. There are no official intermediate targets, although the growth rates of the monetary aggregates M0 and M4 are monitored. The instrument which the MPC uses to keep inflation within its set boundaries is the rate of interest in the short-term repo market, and changes in this rate filter through to all other interest rates in the economy and thence to aggregate demand, expenditure and employment.

Monetary policy in the euro-zone is carried out by the Eurosystem, which consists of the European Central Bank (ECB) and the national central banks of those countries which have joined the euro. The main tasks of the Eurosystem are as follows:

- to define and implement the monetary policy of the euro area

- to conduct foreign exchange operations

- to hold and manage the official foreign reserves of the member states

- to promote the smooth operation of payment systems

- to contribute to the smooth conduct of prudential supervision of credit institutions and the stability of the financial system.

The Eurosystem has set itself both an intermediate and a direct target. The intermediate target is that M3 (its main monetary aggregate) should grow at around 4.5% and the direct target is for inflation (as measured by the Harmonized Index of Consumer Prices) to be below 2%.

If the UK joins the euro, the Bank of England will lose control of monetary policy and this will be given to the ECB. The UK monetary authorities will not have the same control as it now has over either the targets set nor over the instruments used to achieve them However the Bank of England would represent the UK in the European System of Central Banks and would thus have some influence over monetary policy, although only as one member among 13 or more.

In practice there is not much difference between the overall targets and aims of monetary policy between the UK and the euro-zone. Both aim at long-term price stability and both believe that the way to achieve this is to use interest rates and to keep a tight control over public spending.

However there could be problems for the UK if its economy is not in step with those of the other members as the interest rate set on the euro might not be suitable. For example, if inflation in the UK were running at a higher rate than in the euro-zone the UK would need a higher interest rate to combat this but might have to accept a lower rate designed to expand the economies of the other countries. Over the last year or two, the UK has been operating closer to full capacity than have other European economies, giving rise to the fear that inflation could begin to rise; however the recession which has originated in the USA, and which has been exacerbated by the events and consequences of 11 September, has kept the inflation rate down. At the time of writing the UK base rate is 4% and the euro-zone equivalent is 3.5%.

5.3 Changes in Regulation

The most significant change in the regulation of financial services in the UK during 2001 was undoubtedly the advent of the new regulatory regime under the terms of the Financial Services and Markets Act 2000, the main elements of which came into force on 1 December 2001. As described in Chapter 3, the scope of the Financial Services Authority (FSA) was widened to include regulation of virtually the whole of the financial services industry, either with effect from December 2001 or within a relatively short time afterwards.

The Authority's goals have been summarized – in its own words – as being 'to maintain efficient, orderly and clean financial markets, and help retail consumers achieve a fair deal'.

The FSA has made it clear that its approach will be radically different from that of earlier regulators. In particular, it will :

- employ a 'risk-based' approach;

- aim to act in a proactive rather than a reactive way.

It also recognizes that regulation has to be built on realistic aims, and has stated that it will not aim to prevent all failure. It stresses not only the responsibilities of firms' own managements in this regard, but also the need for consumers to take some responsibility for their own decisions. This appears to be a tacit admission that there is a danger in the 21st century of consumerism going too far and eventually acting to the detriment both of providers and of consumers themselves.

The FSA claims that its new approach will 'integrate and simplify' the different approaches employed by its predecessors. These are early days, and it remains to be seen whether regulation of the different sectors of the industry can actually be achieved under an integrated system. Many practitioners and commentators would, however, almost certainly feel that simplicity has not been – and is unlikely to be – achieved.

The integrated approach is based on systems and controls that reflect the risk factors involved rather than the business sector from which the firm comes – reflecting the fact that many firms now operate across a wide range of product areas. Draft integrated prudential standards were published in June 2001, which, while not yet reflecting an international review of standards currently in progress, are intended to provide a platform on which a single set of integrated standards can be implemented when agreed. It is hoped to implement an Integrated Prudential Sourcebook by 2004, if possible at the same time as other new international standards such as the revised Basel Capital Accord come fully into effect.

The FSA has listed the main risks that financial services consumers face as:

- **Prudential risk** – eg the risk of a firm collapsing because of incompetent management.

- **Bad faith risk** – the risk of loss due to fraud, misrepresentation, mis-selling or non-disclosure.

- **Complexity/unsuitability risk** – the risk of a customer not understanding a product or not realizing it is not suitable for his or her needs.

- **Performance risk** – the risk that investments fail to deliver hoped-for returns.

The FSA aims to reduce prudential and bad faith risks, and possibly some aspects of complexity/unsuitability risk, but is not responsible for protecting consumers from performance risk – although it will aim to educate consumers about opportunities, risks and potential rewards.

The FSA's risk-based approach seeks to identify risks which may prevent it from achieving its objectives, to assess those risks, and to prioritize them. The risks may arise from a number of different areas, for instance firm-specific risks, product-specific risks, and macro-economic risks.

Assessment of risks is a complex process, but the following illustration may help to clarify the FSA's approach (which is set out in more detail in their booklet *A new regulator for the new millennium*). Consider a firm-specific risk, for instance the risk of a particular firm collapsing. The overall level of risk is defined by the FSA as being a combination of probability factors and impact factors. This reflects the fact that the seriousness of a problem depends on both the chance of it happening and the effects of it happening.

● Probability factors relate to the likelihood of a problem occurring and might be categorized under various headings, eg :

  – Business risk – such as the firm's business strategy, its capital adequacy, its accounts.

  – Control risk – such as the quality of its management, internal systems and controls.

  – Consumer relationship risk – such as marketing and advice practices.

● Impact factors relate to the effect on the economy, the industry or the customer if a particular event occurred. This might include :

  – The likely effect of the collapse of the firm on the whole industry, or even on the economy.

  – The size of its customer base and the nature of the customer relationship (eg investors, borrowers).

  – The availability of compensation for loss.

This risk assessment process will be applied to all firms and will determine how closely supervised each firm will be.

5.4 Demographic and Social Trends

Demography is the study of populations. It can refer to many different characteristics of populations, but the main factor affecting financial services concerns changes in the relative proportions of different age groups in the population and how these can affect the demand for financial services.

With the rapid advance of medical science in the 20th century, people are, on average, living much longer than was the case 100 or even 50 years ago. The inevitable result is that the proportion of the population who are retired is increasing all the time, with the relative size of the working population decreasing.

This can have a dramatic effect on the nation's finances. For instance, more money is needed to pay the state retirement pensions. More funds are also needed for health care, the cost of which tends to be concentrated at older ages. All of this must be paid for by taxation, the burden of which falls mainly on the now smaller proportion of the population who are working.

One consequence of these demographic changes has been an attempt by government to persuade people to make their own provision for retirement, and for health care and care in old age. Evidence of this can be seen, for instance, in the national insurance rebates offered to people who opt out of the state earnings-related pension scheme (SERPS) in favour of taking out their own personal pension plan, and the essentially low-cost nature of stakeholder pensions.

Social, economic and industrial factors have combined to exaggerate the influence of the demographic factors mentioned above. In times of recession, for instance, the so-called 'dependent population' becomes even larger as greater unemployment has the effect of reducing even further the proportion of the population who contribute to the tax revenue (as well as increasing the amount paid out in social security benefits).

Similarly, the trend towards earlier retirement not only increases the retired population but at the same time decreases the working population, thus widening the gap between revenue and outgoings.

Pension provision

One of the great difficulties faced by governments in recent years has been to convince the population of the UK, brought up for the most part in the era of the 'welfare state', that changes in the demographic structure and social environment in the UK make it increasingly difficult for the state to provide social security benefits – and particularly pensions – which will be sufficient for their lifestyles but which will represent a realistic and acceptable cost to the taxpayer.

The level of the basic state pension – set at about one quarter of the national average earnings level – is clearly inadequate for anything more than subsistence living. Successive schemes to boost the pensions of those who are employees (first the graduated pension scheme and then the state earnings related pension scheme, SERPS) were doomed to failure, as confirmed by the decision to close down SERPS from April 2002. At its maximum possible level, SERPS increased a person's state pension only to about one half of national average earnings – and it was not in any case available to people who were self-employed, nor of course to people who had no earned income.

And yet many people are continuing to reach retirement age with little or no pension provision to look forward to apart from the basic state pension. This is particularly – though by no means exclusively – true of people at the lower end of the earnings scale. They are more often than not financially unsophisticated and probably unaware of products such as personal pensions or free standing additional contributions (FSAVCs) which could be used to boost their pension. Even when aware of them they may have more pressing demands on their income; and if they do know of the products they may have been put off by talk of high charges or product mis-selling.

This led to the introduction, from 6 April 2001, of the stakeholder pension (of which product details are given in Chapter 4). This new scheme was supposedly targeted at people in the income range £9,000 to £20,000 – believed to include the greatest proportion of people who are failing to make adequate provision for their retirement. The product was designed with a number of features intended to attract the savings of this particular group, for example :

● The maximum permitted charges are lower than those typically applied to personal pensions and FSAVCs;

● The minimum contribution cannot be set at more than £20;

● Contributions can be started and stopped;

● There must be a default investment fund so that customers do not have to make an investment decision if they do not wish to;

● There must also be at least one very low risk fund (such as a cash fund).

Despite this, there is evidence (much of it anecdotal at present) to suggest that there has been very little take-up of stakeholder pensions among the main target group, with most of the sales being to people who would have been making pension provision anyway through other schemes and have chosen stakeholder pensions because of the lower costs. Some people feel that one of the reasons for the low demand for these pensions is that the maximum charge providers can incorporate is 1% of the fund. Not only does this low figure discourage providers from doing the necessary marketing, but – perhaps more significantly – it effectively prevents them from paying realistic commission to independent financial advisers who might sell stakeholder pensions.

A further aspect of the government's plan to encourage private pension provision was targeted at those employers who do not provide a pension scheme for their employees. Subject to certain exemptions, employers with five or more employees but no occupational scheme are now obliged to provide a stakeholder pension scheme for their employees, including the facility to deduct contributions from wages/salary. Sadly, this move has, so far, also proved to be largely unsuccessful in persuading more people to contribute to their own pension provision. This is perhaps not surprising in view of the fact that – while employers are obliged to provide the scheme – employees are not obliged to join it (and even if they do, employers are not obliged to contribute anything).

Protection for pension scheme members

Protecting investors against financial crime has been an important objective of financial legislation and regulation for many years, although it became more focused with the Financial Services Act 1986 and even more so subsequently with the FSMA 2000. One of the FSA's statutory objectives is the reduction of financial crime.

It is at least tacitly acknowledged that one of the most vulnerable groups of investors are the members of pension schemes of various kinds. This is because :

- relatively large amounts of money are involved for each investor (often more than any other transactions except perhaps their mortgage); and

- their standard of living during their latter – and most vulnerable – years is at stake.

The danger facing pensioners was sharply and painfully highlighted in the UK by the Maxwell affair, in which pensioners' funds were appropriated and used for other purposes within the business. This led to a strengthening of regulation through the Pensions Act 1995 (see Chapter 3), but recent events in the USA have shown that pension scheme members – and regulators – need to remain vigilant.

The events surrounding the collapse of the Houston-based energy trader Enron Corporation (which has European subsidiaries, including some in the North East of England) are becoming a major issue, both economically and politically. One of the important effects of the failure is on the pension savings of many of the corporation's employees. The situation is complex, but to summarize it briefly :

- Many Enron employees (like 42 million other American workers) have pension savings plans known as 401(k) accounts.

- Employees' and employers' contributions to these accounts can be invested in shares of the company (the employer), with little or no restriction on what proportion is invested in the company. Many Enron employees had Enron shares in their accounts.

- It is alleged that the Enron management did not tell their workers that the corporation was in difficulties and the share price was therefore likely to fall.

- It is also alleged that at the same time, members of the Enron management were selling their own personal holdings of Enron shares. In the UK, such allegations might fall under the insider trading or market abuse rules.

- In any case, most Enron employees were prevented – by a currently legal clause in their savings contract – from selling Enron stocks contributed by the corporation to their 401(k) accounts before age 50. They could not therefore have protected their savings by switching out of the stock even if they had been aware of the situation.

The case is of course the subject of much litigation and government investigation, and the final outcome will not be known for a long time. Its direct impact in the UK is fairly limited – although one senior public figure, who was on the board of an Enron subsidiary in the UK, has resigned from his position. Nevertheless it illustrates what can happen, and the FSA will undoubtedly wish to know what can be learned from it as they attempt to move from a reactive to a proactive regulatory environment.

The nature of work

A trend that has emerged in recent years and which looks likely to remain for the foreseeable future is that people can no longer expect to have a 'job for life'. Unemployment has happened in all sectors including those that were always considered to provide 'safe' jobs eg banking. People are made redundant and have to look for jobs in other companies and other sectors and even switch to becoming self-employed. On top of this, modern job culture values someone who has worked for several employers more than someone who has been in the same job for 20 years because it is felt that the former has gained more experience and is more likely to be a dynamic person. This situation is changing people's demand for financial services and they need:

● a pension that they can transfer from one employer to another

● a pension that is flexible enough to allow them to vary their payments according to their varying monthly income

● self-employed people need income protection, permanent health insurance and critical illness insurance to cover them if they are unable to work

● flexible savings schemes where they can vary contributions and have instant access

● flexible mortgages where they can make over-payments or under-payments according to their incomes or where they can take payment holidays without being subject to a penalty or gaining an adverse report on their credit records.

Financial inclusion

There are still an estimated 3 million adults in the UK who do not have a bank account. These people are unable to take advantage of the many financial services offered by banks and building societies and are increasingly being seen as disadvantaged for this reason. Some people do not have a tradition of keeping their money in a bank account but these are likely to be drawn into the network eventually as an increasing number of employers pay wages and salaries directly into bank accounts and are forsaking cash pay packets for security and administrative reasons.

However, there is another group of people who have been turned down for an account by banks because of their bad credit record, in particular people who have had a County Court Judgement made against them. The government would like to include even these people in the banking system and feels that the post office network could well be used as a sort of 'universal bank' which could offer basic banking services to everybody, whatever their background. A specific advantage of this is that the government could then pay pensions and social security benefits straight into people's bank accounts using BACS and costs would be reduced. This proposal would also benefit the nation's small post offices, many of which are under threat, and could throw them a lifeline to keep their business going. (See later section on Post Office banking).

Financial inclusion is a topic which is being much debated today. It concerns not only those people who do not have bank accounts but also those who do not have access to savings, loans, pensions and insurance policies.

5.5 Low Inflation

Rates of inflation have been falling throughout the industrialized world for the past 20 to 25 years, and this is particularly true of the UK, where inflation in 2000 was lower than in all other EU countries. Low inflation is generally considered to be good for the economy, and most governments make low inflation a key target in setting economic policy. It is a sign of price stability and it means that people are more certain of what prices will be in the future. Life is easier for consumers, savers and borrowers.

Low inflation does, however, normally go hand-in-hand with low interest rates and low investment returns generally. This can cause problems in a number of areas of financial service provision, and two of these in particular have recently arisen in the UK. This led the FSA to institute a broad review of the effect of low inflation on financial services and products, and to publish a paper on the subject.

The two areas of concern for the UK regulators have been

- the maturity values of investment vehicles used to repay interest-only mortgages (in particular endowment policies);

- levels of annuity rates – with particular reference to the purchase of pensions by people who had been saving for retirement through money-purchase and similar schemes.

These are particularly significant because they relate to mortgages and pensions, the two largest financial commitments made by most individuals and families.

Endowment policy returns

For people with interest-only mortgages, any decrease in the rate of interest charged is very welcome, as it reduces their regular monthly outgoings and takes some pressure off their budgeting. It seems on the surface, then, that low interest rates are an unreservedly good thing for mortgage borrowers. Sadly, however, the situation is not as simple as that.

The problem is that, while low interest rates reduce the costs of servicing the borrowing, they tend at the same time to increase the costs of repaying the borrowing. For borrowers with a repayment mortgage, that fact is allowed for in changes to the repayment amount (which includes both interest and capital repayment) each time interest rates change, so that the capital should be fully repaid by the end of the term.

This is not the case with interest-only mortgages, especially those that are being repaid by vehicles such as endowments which have fixed premium payments. In periods where interest rates / inflation are lower, the returns on the policies will be lower, resulting in reduced maturity values. In the worst cases, this can mean that the policy may not provide sufficient funds to repay the mortgage at the end of the term.

What this means in practical terms is that the apparent extra cash-flow which results from lower interest payments is not necessarily available for immediate spending – because it may be needed to establish an additional savings vehicle to fund any shortfall which results from the lower yield on the endowment policy.

A compulsory review by endowment providers of policies known to be being used for mortgage repayment was instituted some years ago by the Personal Investment Authority (PIA), and is continuing under the Financial Services Authority (FSA). This makes customers aware of possible problems with projected values on their policies and enables them, if they wish, to make increase payments or change their repayment method.

In line with their aim to be more proactive in the future, the FSA hopes that the paper on the effects of low inflation will increase awareness of the dangers among both borrowers and product providers.

Annuity rates and the Equitable Life

Another effect of low interest rates is that they result in low annuity rates. An annuity is a series of payments (normally monthly) from a life assurance company to an individual known as the annuitant in exchange for a lump sum investment. Although there are other types, the most common type of annuity is payable for the remainder of the annuitant's lifetime.

The amount of annuity payable per £1,000 or per £10,000 of investment (the annuity rate) depends on two main factors:

● At what rate of interest can the lump sum be invested by the insurance company? The annuity rate is fixed by the interest rate on the day of investment, and lower interest rates mean lower annuity rates. With interest rates currently at their lowest for many years, annuity rates have been decreasing and are also at the lowest for a long time.

● How long will the annuitant live (based on appropriate mortality tables)? The most obvious comment to make here is that annuity rates depend on age and are higher for older people. In addition to this, however, people are on average living longer, and this means that annuity rates across the board are inevitably lower to compensate for that fact.

The combination of these two effects means that annuity rates are quite considerably lower than they were, say, twenty to thirty years ago.

Equitable Life, in common with some other insurance companies, had issued policies which contained guaranteed annuity rates (GARs). In other words, policyholders could, when their policies matured, convert the policy proceeds from a lump sum to a monthly pension at a specified minimum annuity rate, depending on age. These guaranteed annuities were set at what were felt at the time to be cautiously low rates, but circumstances (ie low interest rates) have overtaken them and made them unduly generous.

Unlike other companies, however, Equitable Life had not built up any specific reserves to cover the cost of the guaranteed annuities. The FSA was already, from 1998 onwards, conducting a review of the GAR issue, and Equitable Life had explained to the regulator that it did not hold specific reserves for its GAR policies because it was its practice to pay lower terminal bonus rates on policies where the GAR option was being exercised by the policyholder, thus balancing the cost of higher annuity rates.

In 1999, the Equitable's right to pay differential terminal bonuses was challenged in a court case. The Court ruled in Equitable's favour, and held that it could pay different bonus rates according to whether or not GAR policyholders chose to take up the guarantee. Equitable's relief, however, was short-lived, as the Court of Appeal reversed the decision, although their ruling did initially seem to suggest that a different rate of bonus could be declared for all GAR policies, which would have offered Equitable a way out of the problem.

The case then went to the House of Lords, where it was ruled that Equitable could not, after all, 'ring-fence' the GAR policies and pay them a different bonus. The effect of this was to necessitate the setting aside of more funds as reserves, and while this did not actually make Equitable insolvent, it left it in a weak and vulnerable position and effectively meant it needed to seek a buyer for its business.

When no buyer initially came forward, the management of Equitable decided to close to new business. Eventually a sale was agreed with Halifax Group plc; the sale covered all aspects of Equitable's business except its With Profits fund, which – in a now stronger position following the sale – remains within an independent mutual organization.

At a meeting in January 2002, the members of Equitable Life voted overwhelmingly to accept lower payments in order to ensure the continuing stability of the company, but it seems likely that some members will choose to challenge this in the courts on an individual basis. Since the company's credibility has been damaged, it also faces the possibility of many people withdrawing their funds, albeit at a reduced pay-out.

The FSA has responded by initiating a number of projects designed to improve insurance regulation for the future.

Consumers' reactions to low inflation

The general public tends to suffer from 'money illusion', ie it tends to think of interest rates in their nominal sense and not to adjust in its mind for inflation. Since it is perceptions that make people act, we need to consider the possible effects of the above reactions to low interest rates. Both savers and borrowers are affected:

- Savers feel that the low interest rates currently being paid on savings are a poor return for their money. They may therefore react to lower inflation by putting their money into riskier assets in order to seek higher returns and demand for high-yield bonds has certainly increased in recent years. If a greater number of people on average incomes lose their money because of opting for riskier investments, they may not be able to afford to retire and social problems could result.

- Borrowers (particularly those repaying mortgage loans) feel that they are gaining from the lower monthly repayments which have resulted from interest rate falls. This may persuade them either to prefer to repay their mortgage over a shorter period of time or to take out a larger mortgage since they feel they can more easily afford the monthly repayments. However there is a misperception here as, although less cash flows out in interest payments at the start of the mortgage term, a higher proportion of cash-flow will be necessary to repay the capital later. The capital sum borrowed is not being 'eaten up' by inflation. Again problems may be stored up for the future as people take on debt they cannot in practice afford, especially if interest rates rise again. In the meantime, an increased demand for houses will push up house prices and threaten price stability.

5.6 Technology

The rapid development of information technology is probably the single most significant factor driving change in the financial services industry. All other elements of change in the industry are made possible by, and are wholly dependent on, the rapid advances in computer technology which are now part of our everyday life.

Today's financial services industry is based on the ability to store vast amounts of data electronically, to process it at speeds which are apparently instantaneous and to communication information electronically to virtually anywhere in the world. This is particularly true in the world of banking where it is now possible to transact volumes of business that would be quite impossible – or prohibitively expensive – using manual systems. This enables institutions to achieve economies of scale, although the installation costs can be very high.

Initially computers were used merely as accounting machines, keeping records, calculating interest payments or charges and producing statements. As technology improved, the functions carried out have increased dramatically, for instance magnetic or optical character reading speeded up cheque clearing. A major step forward was the development of real-time systems which enabled the checking of customers' accounts in seconds, closely followed by the ability to access accounts through ATMs and later by telephone, on-line and point-of-sale services.

The use of computer systems is not restricted to account handling. It has, for instance, greatly simplified and speeded up the processing of loan applications through credit scoring techniques. Although it is thought by some to be rather impersonal, credit scoring quickly eliminates cases which are clearly outside the lender's acceptable range and enables decisions to be quickly made at lower levels of the organization than would have otherwise have been possible. Assessment of credit status is also automated and direct links to electoral rolls and other relevant databases help to reduce the risk of fraud.

Technology has also had a significant impact in the marketing field, where it has many applications including:

● the use of graphics in the design and production of publicity material.

● production and presentation of quotations and illustrations. This can now be done by salespersons and advisers in the field by the use of notebook (portable) computers, either using pre-loaded programs or on-line via modem and telephone line to the company's central computer system.

● database management, particularly the development of relational databases which provide instant access to accurate and detailed information on all the organization's customers.

The Internet has become a major location for financial services marketing. All organizations of any size now have their own websites which are used partly for advertising but are increasingly interactive so that prospective customers can ask for information or quotations or even apply for services. The Financial Services Authority's requirement to 'know your customer' may restrict the extent to which investment services can be sold in this way in the UK.

Online banking via the Internet has been available since the late 1990s. This service provides the facilities to check balances, transfer money between accounts and make transfers by direct debit or other electronic means. Customers may need to have a commercial accounting package installed on their computers in order to make use of on-line banking. Some concern has been expressed about the security of on-line banking and there have been cases where customers' account details have been released and allegations of computer hackers breaking into accounts and removing or transferring money.

The existence of advanced computer technology and the ability of people to access their accounts from their own telephones and PCs has had an effect on the distribution channels by which financial services are delivered to the personal sector.

5.7 Distribution Channels

The traditional distribution channel for bank and building society services was of course the High Street branch. It has a number of acknowledged advantages, including face-to-face contact with customers, the opportunity to cross-sell other products and services and the creation of a recognized corporate image. It is, however, an expensive way of providing banking services and two main factors have led to a reduction in the size of branch networks since the 1980s:

● increased competition which has led to a squeeze on profits and meant that more cost-effective procedures have had to be found

● the advance of information and communication technology, which has made available alternative ways of interacting with customers.

Banks still retain a strong high-street presence in cities and larger towns. Branches have, however, been closed in many small towns (where the nature, and sometimes even the location, of the town centre may well have changed over the last 20 years) and virtually all village branches have now disappeared.

The marketing functions of branches have been transferred, to some extent, to direct mail, a process that can yield profitable results if correctly planned and managed, but which tends to suffer from the junk mail image. The high costs and possible low response rate can be contained by wise use of the organization's own existing customer base and other carefully selected databases.

Banking transactions for customers (particularly cash withdrawals) have been significantly taken over by ATMs. These machines are increasingly located in superstores and shopping centres. Facilities for automated deposits are also becoming more common. The technology is expensive to install but in the longer term costs fall due to the ability to deal with large volumes of business. There is no doubt that customers are attracted by these facilities which are conveniently located and remain available 24 hours a day.

Building societies are also still to be found on many High Streets, but they too have begun to rationalize their branch networks. Many societies operate a network of agencies through which customers can transact straightforward deposits and withdrawals – a method that clearly has lower costs of operation than a branch. These agencies are often located at the offices of accountants and solicitors and can therefore provide access to a particular market, ie the agent's existing customers, as well as attracting general customers in a particular locations.

Life assurance companies have been steadily reducing their branch networks for the last 20 years and most now retain offices only in the major cities. They operate mainly through independent financial advisers, or through tied agents or their own direct salesforce.

Direct operations

The first large-scale move into the direct provision of financial products was the establishment of Direct Line insurance in April 1985 which began with initial funding from the Royal Bank of Scotland and is now a wholly-owned subsidiary of that banking group. Direct Line initially offered only general insurance, firstly motor insurance, followed a few years later by home insurance. The aim was to offer very competitive premiums by eliminating both the expense of a branch network and the commission paid to intermediaries. Such was the success of the direct concept that many conventional insurers set up direct organizations; and the word 'Direct' became virtually an essential part of the trading name of such businesses.

From 1993 onwards Direct Line branched out into the broader field of financial services, successively introducing unsecured loans, mortgages, life assurance and savings accounts.

When Midland Bank launched its First Direct operation (a telephone banking service) in the early 1990s, it was a move into relatively uncharted banking territory. The success of the venture, which now has over a million customers, led to many other banks and building societies providing services through methods other than face-to-face counter service.

Typically, direct banking services provide all the basic facilities of conventional banks, ie current accounts, savings accounts, loans, credit and debit cards and more. Transactions are carried out by person-to-person telephone calls, at local rates, to specially trained staff at a central location or by post. There are no branches but deposits can normally be made at branches of related institutions. In some cases, enquiries and transactions can be initiated on-line from a personal computer.

The trend towards direct services and Internet banking is continuing, although there are difficulties in applying the concept to the sales of investment products regulated by the Financial Services and Markets Act 2000. This is because of the 'know your customer' rules which require advisers to become familiar with a client's personal and financial circumstances before advising on or recommending a product – which conflicts with the more simplified approach for which direct companies are striving. For that reason, life assurance and investment products are generally sold on an execution-only basis, which means that full details of the products are supplied but no advice is given as to their suitability to individual clients' circumstances.

Egg, a division of Prudential Banking, is an excellent example of a bank that sells its services only through the Internet. Egg offers bank accounts of various kinds, loans, credit cards, insurance and investment services, including ISAs.

Banking at the Post Office

With the continuing closure of bank branches in villages and smaller towns, there has been concern that many people in rural areas – particularly the elderly and those without transport – may lose their access to the basic facilities of banking.

At the same time, small post offices are set to lose a considerable part of their revenue when the payment of social security benefits over the counter is replaced by payments direct to bank accounts. It was therefore proposed that local post offices could step in and provide some banking services.

It is already possible to carry out certain banking transactions at post offices, although customers are advised to check whether their bank is included in the scheme. Private customers can normally :

- cash cheques, using their chequebook and guarantee card;

- pay in cash, using a paying-in slip from their bank;

- pay in cheques, using a paying in slip and a deposit envelope from their bank.

Timescales for deposits may be slightly longer than when paying in at the bank.

The Post Office also offers a range of business banking services through Girobank, including :

- cash and cheque deposits;

- provision of change, or larger supplies of cash;

- cheque encashment by third parties.

In April 2001 the Post Office announced a £50 million deal with information technology suppliers including IBM and ICL. This will provide state-of-the-art systems to enable the Post Office to offer real-time banking transactions through its network of 18,000 branches. This will effectively give online access, through the Post Office, to the 'back office' of banks, providing a physical network for Internet banks as well as a wider network of local branches for conventional retail banks.

From autumn 2002 the Post Office will offer basic banking transactions including cash withdrawals and balance enquiries. It is planned that full banking services will be available from 2003.

5.8 Innovation and New Products

Consumer expectations are changing more and more rapidly and innovation is essential for companies who wish to remain ahead in an increasingly competitive environment. Genuine innovation, however, is rare in the world of financial services products and most new products are simply variations or combinations of existing ones. The innovation is normally to be found in the marketing of the products and in the use of technology to administer them.

Some products, however, can be considered as innovative. For example, the introduction in the 1980s of a protection policy that pays out on the diagnosis of serious illness (critical illness cover) was a genuine innovation designed to meet a newly-recognized need.

Similarly, in the late 1990s, Virgin unveiled an innovative way of bringing together current account, deposit account and mortgage borrowing facilities into a **one-stop account**. Known as Virgin One, it effectively initiated the introduction of flexible mortgages.

In addition to providing customers with complete flexibility as to how much they pay on their mortgage each month, schemes such as Virgin One enable them to combine all their borrowings (which might otherwise be on mortgage, credit cards, personal loans, etc.) into one debt on which the interest rate is a typical mortgage interest rate. The account is based on a loan which is secured by a mortgage on the customer's property, and the customer must agree to have his or her salary or other earnings paid into the account.

There is an upper limit to the total amount of borrowing, and a final date – typically the customer's retirement – by which the borrowing must be repaid. Within those limits, the customer is free to repay more, repay less, or even borrow more, depending on personal needs and circumstances.

It is argued that the account is also tax-efficient because any savings paid into it will benefit customers by reducing their borrowing (and hence the interest they pay) rather than by increasing the amount of (taxable) interest they would receive from a deposit account.

Buy to let mortgages

Despite some dramatic falls from time to time, the overall trend in UK house prices over the last 30 years has been strongly upwards. One unfortunate consequence of this is that young people and other first-time buyers may find it difficult to afford to purchase a property, especially in the South East of England where significant increases have been experienced. In times of economic downturn, this effect is made worse by the uncertain job market, making it difficult for people to commit themselves to a large mortgage.

The situation can be eased if there is a reasonable supply of good quality properties to rent, but traditionally the UK has had a shortage of private rental property – much less than in most other European countries for instance. There are a number of reasons for this, not least of which are :

● Historically, lenders viewed loans to buy property to let as being 'commercial' rather than residential loans – even the property was to be let for residential purposes. This quite simply meant higher rates of interest than for standard mortgage loans on owner-occupied property.

- Rental income was traditionally excluded from a borrower's income when assessing ability to make the mortgage repayments.

'Buy to let' is an initiative designed to stimulate the growth of the private sector of the rental market. The aim is to encourage private investors to borrow at competitive interest rates with a view to investing in rental property which should give them a reasonable expectation of sustained income and capital growth. Lenders involved in this scheme will now take potential rental income into account, and they will charge interest rates in line with those for owner-occupation mortgages.

The scheme is the result of a joint initiative by the Association of Residential Letting Agents (ARLA) and mortgage lenders. Alliance and Leicester, Halifax and NatWest were instrumental in the early stages, though many more banks and building societies now offer buy to let mortgages.

This change in policy results from the knowledge that a buy-to-let scheme will be professionally managed. For many schemes it is a requirement that an agent who is a member of ARLA should be involved in :

- Selecting suitable properties;

- Selecting suitable tenants;

- Arranging appropriate tenancy agreements (normally Assured Shorthold Tenancies);

- Managing the properties.

Where there is no requirement for management by an ARLA member, there is generally some other way of ensuring that the letting is appropriately managed. Skipton Building Society, for instance, will lend only to experienced property investors who already have at least three properties.

Gross rents for buy-to-let properties are typically 150% of the monthly mortgage payments. There are of course other costs, such as agents' commission/fees, insurance and maintenance costs.

Rental income is subject to income tax, but the cost of insurance, agents fees, maintenance, etc, can be offset as a deduction against tax. The initial cost of furniture, fixtures and fittings cannot be deducted, but a wear and tear allowance of 10% per year may be allowed.

INDEX

Index